INJUSTICE

GODS AMONG US: YEAR THREE

VOLUME 1

INJU

GODS AMON

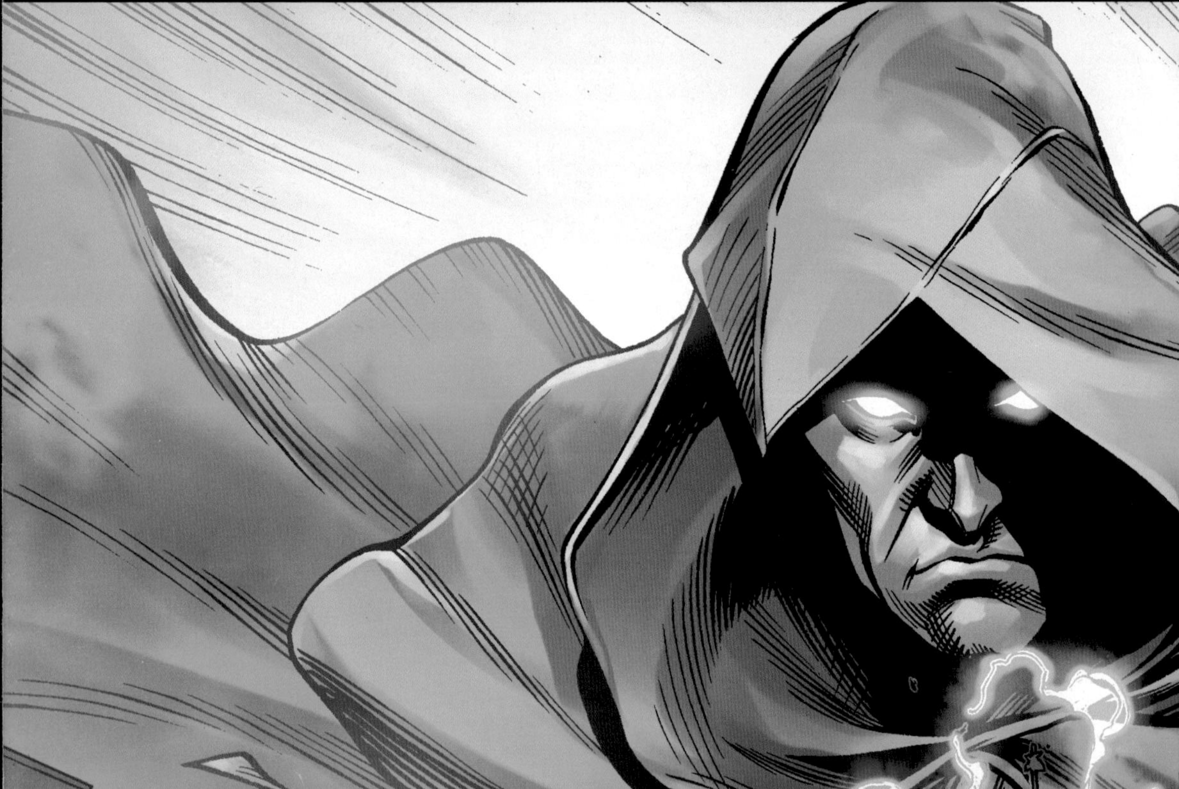

STICE

US: YEAR THREE

VOLUME 1

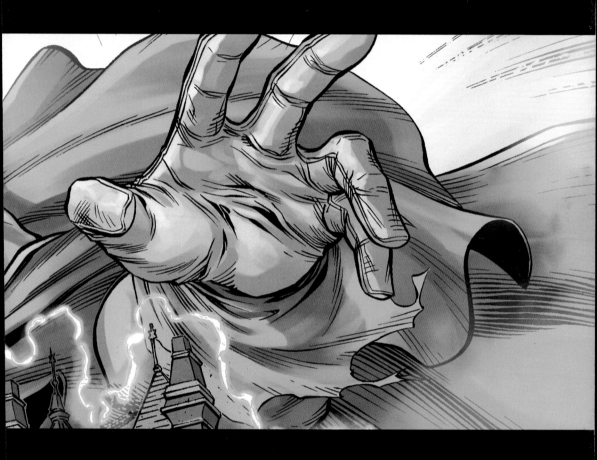

SUPERMAN Created by JERRY SIEGEL and JOE SHUSTER.
By Special Arrangement with the Jerry Siegel Family.

BASED ON THE VIDEOGAME INJUSTICE: GODS AMONG US

Jim Chadwick Editor – Original Series
Aniz Ansari Assistant Editor – Original Series
Jeb Woodard Group Editor – Collected Editions
Paul Santos Editor – Collected Edition
Steve Cook Design Director – Books
Louis Prandi Publication Design

Bob Harras Senior VP – Editor-in-Chief, DC Comics

Diane Nelson President
Dan DiDio and Jim Lee Co-Publishers
Geoff Johns Chief Creative Officer
Amit Desai Senior VP – Marketing & Global Franchise Management
Nairi Gardiner Senior VP – Finance
Sam Ades VP – Digital Marketing
Bobbie Chase VP – Talent Development
Mark Chiarello Senior VP – Art, Design & Collected Editions
John Cunningham VP – Content Strategy
Anne DePies VP – Strategy Planning & Reporting
Don Falletti VP – Manufacturing Operations
Lawrence Ganem VP – Editorial Administration & Talent Relations
Alison Gill Senior VP – Manufacturing & Operations
Hank Kanalz Senior VP – Editorial Strategy & Administration
Jay Kogan VP – Legal Affairs
Derek Maddalena Senior VP – Sales & Business Development
Jack Mahan VP – Business Affairs
Dan Miron VP – Sales Planning & Trade Development
Nick Napolitano VP – Manufacturing Administration
Carol Roeder VP – Marketing
Eddie Scannell VP – Mass Account & Digital Sales
Courtney Simmons Senior VP – Publicity & Communications
Jim (Ski) Sokolowski VP – Comic Book Specialty & Newsstand Sales
Sandy Yi Senior VP – Global Franchise Management

INJUSTICE: GODS AMONG US: YEAR THREE VOLUME 1

Published by DC Comics. Compilation and all new material
Copyright © 2016 DC Comics. All Rights Reserved.

Originally published in single magazine form in INJUSTICE: GODS
AMONG US: YEAR THREE 1-7. Copyright © 2014 DC Comics. All
Rights Reserved. All characters, their distinctive likenesses and related
elements featured in this publication are trademarks of DC Comics.
The stories, characters and incidents featured in this publication are
entirely fictional. DC Comics does not read or accept unsolicited ideas,
stories or artwork.

DC Comics, 2900 West Alameda Avenue, Burbank, CA 91505
Printed by RR Donnelley, Owensville, MO, USA. 1/8/16. First Printing.
ISBN: 978-1-4012-6314-0

Library of Congress Cataloging-in-Publication Data

Taylor, Tom, 1978-
   Injustice : Gods Among Us : Year Three Volume 1 / Tom Taylor, Bruno
Redondo, Mike S. Miller.
       pages cm
   "Based on the videogame Injustice: Gods Among Us"
   ISBN 978-1-4012-6314-0 (paperback)
   1. Graphic novels. I. Redondo, Bruno, 1981- illustrator. II. Miller, Mike S.,
illustrator. III. Title. IV. Title: Gods Among Us Year Three Volume 1.
   PN6727.T293163 2015
   741.5'973—dc23
                                                      2015031529

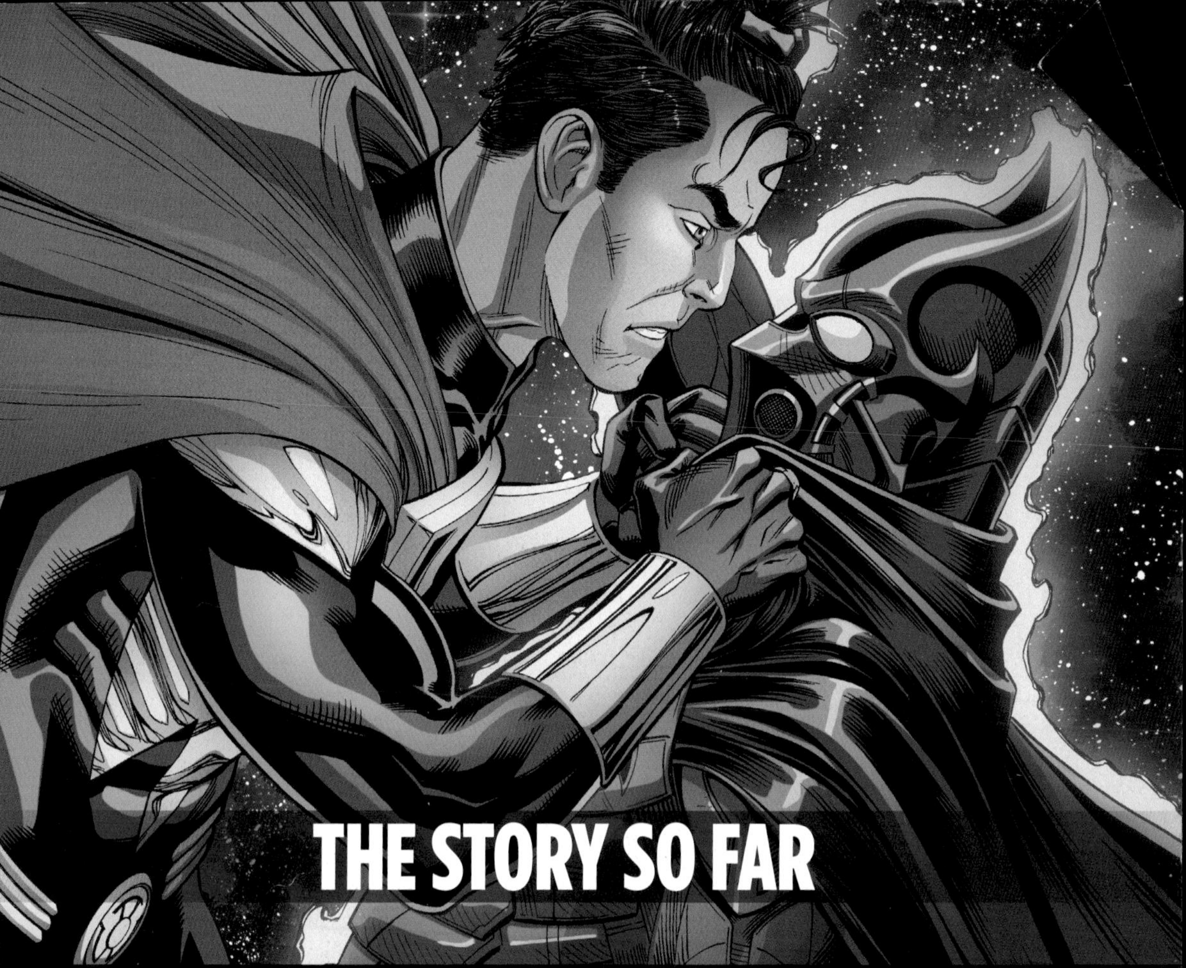

THE STORY SO FAR

When the Joker ditches Gotham and heads for Metropolis, Superman and Lois Lane are the victims of his most sinister plot to date. The aftermath unleashes an atomic explosion that destroys the City of Tomorrow, and with it, Lois Lane and their unborn child. Mad with grief, the Man of Steel does the unthinkable and murders the Joker in cold blood as Batman looks on in horror.

Superman begins a campaign to end violence the world over, involving himself in civil wars and international conflict, but Batman becomes concerned that this level of intervention is a slippery slope towards a police state. The Justice League becomes divided between those who believe in Superman's vision and those who share Batman's concerns, with Superman's team eventually coming under fire from the United States government.

As casualties begin to arise from the conflict, the schism between the two former friends grows even deeper. Batman and his resistance team manage to get their hands on a Kryptonite-powered pill that grants them superpowers, but at the cost of the lives of their teammates Green Arrow and Captain Atom...and of Batman's back being broken.

Faced with a growing resistance, Superman soon finds himself with an unexpected new ally: Sinestro, the former rogue Green Lantern who formed his own fear-powered Sinestro Corps. Sinestro recognizes his own history in Superman's struggle to save his planet from itself, and warns Superman that the Guardians of the Universe will soon send the Green Lantern Corps to intervene, even though Hal Jordan sides with Superman.

As the war between Green Lanterns and Superman's Justice League takes to the skies over Earth, a different war is being waged on the streets, where Superman's super-powered troops have turned Gotham into a totalitarian nightmare. Under the guidance of Jim Gordon, Batman's allies and the remnants of the Gotham City Police Department use the Kryptonite pills to empower themselves to fight back against the troops. But the pills accelerate Gordon's cancer, and he dies on the Watchtower, protecting his daughter Barbara from being traced by Cyborg.

Having earned Superman's trust, Sinestro manipulates Superman and his allies, resulting in the deaths of Earth's other Green Lanterns and in both Superman and Hal Jordan joining the Sinestro Corps. Although Batman's team is able to capture several of Superman's Justice League allies, they suffer a major loss of their own. When Black Canary confronts Superman over the death of her husband Green Arrow, Superman murders her in cold blood...an act broadcast around the world thanks to hidden cameras in her contacts.

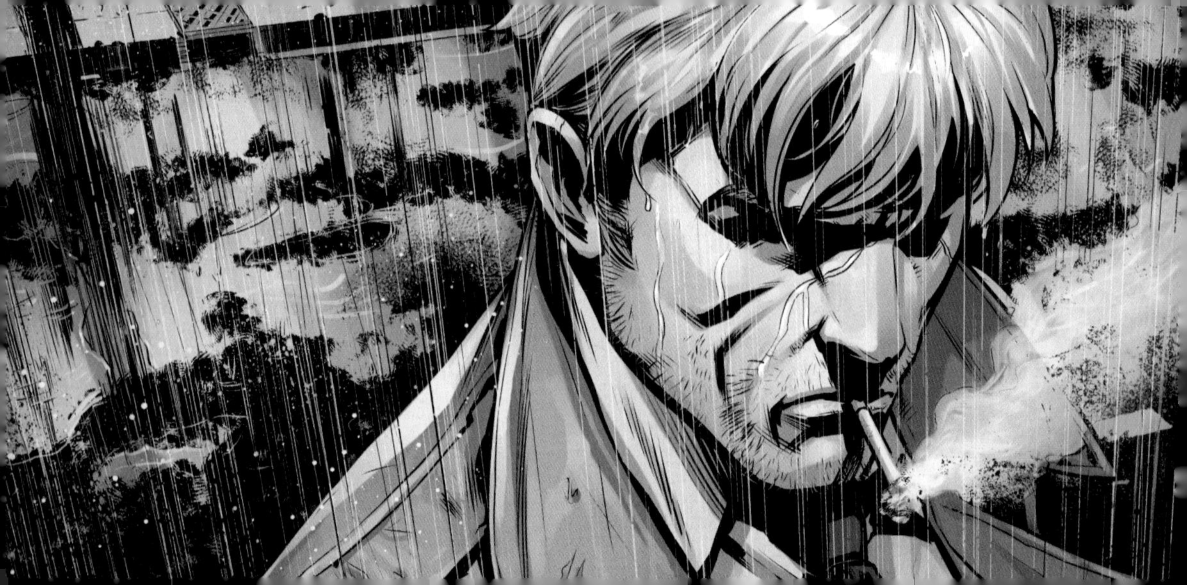

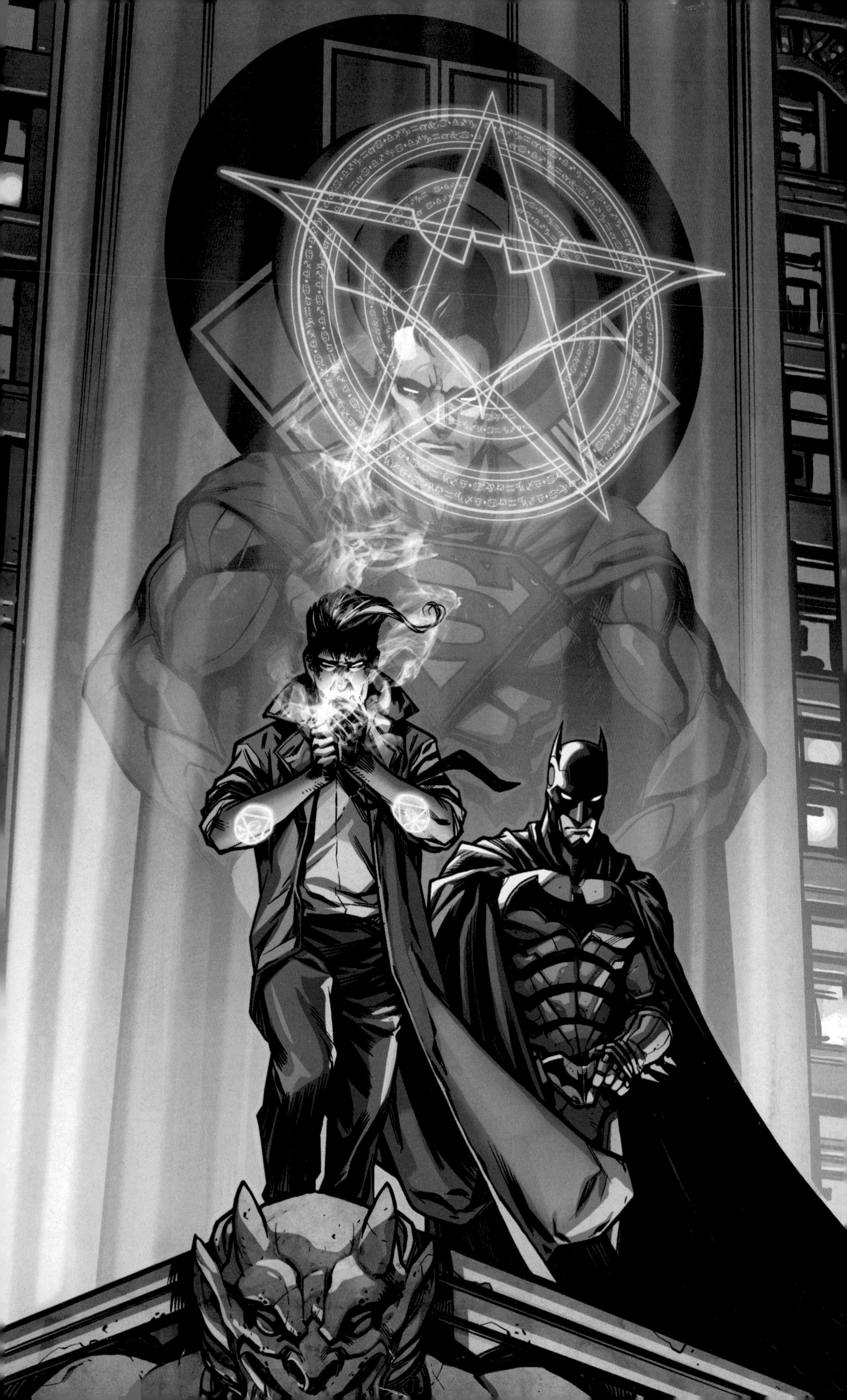

"Rose" **Bruno Redondo & Xermanico** Artists **J. Nanjan** Colorist
"Magic" **Bruno Redondo & Vicente Cifuentes** Artists **Rex Lokus** Colorist
Cover Art by **Neil Googe & Rex Lokus**

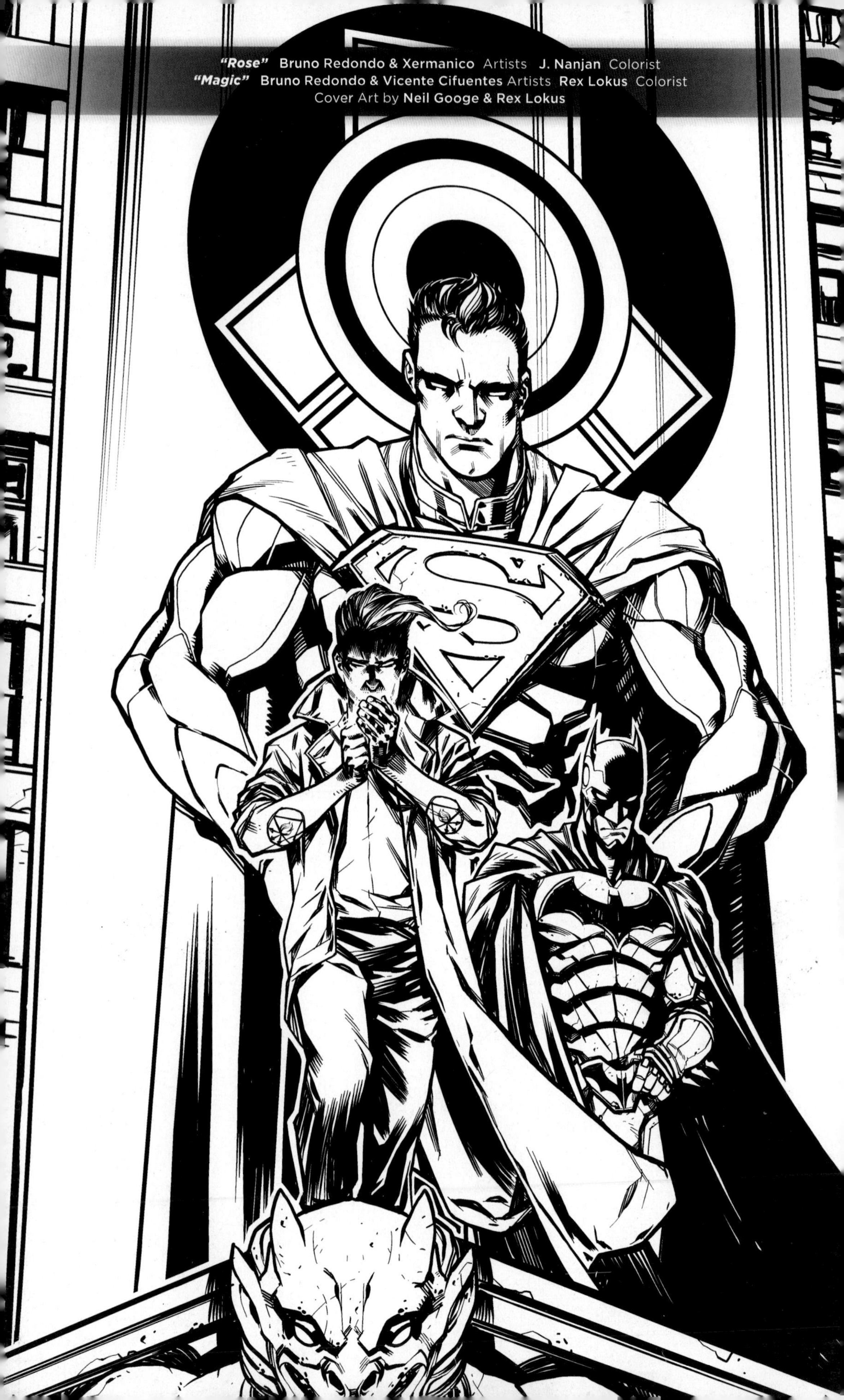

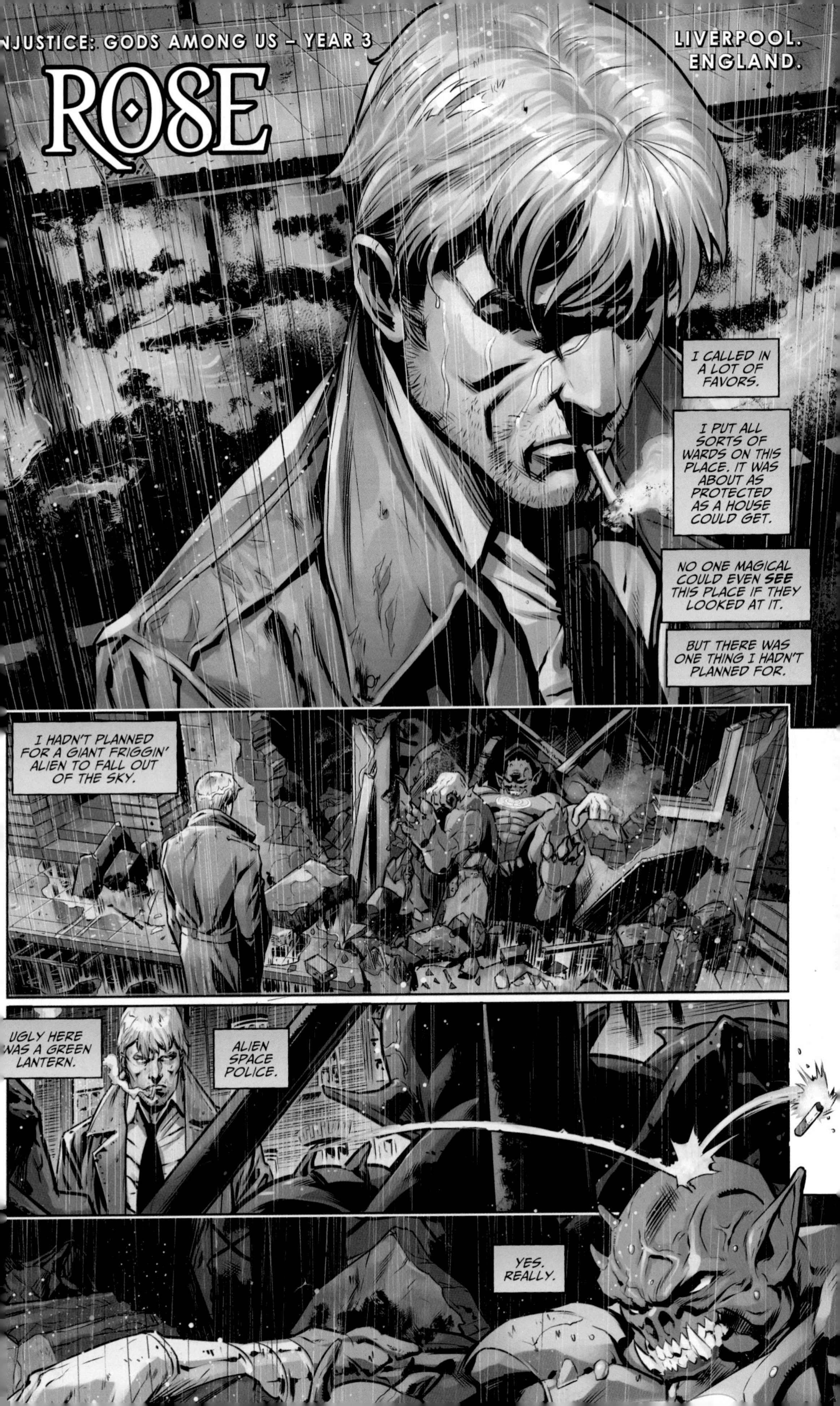

NJUSTICE: GODS AMONG US – YEAR 3
ROSE
LIVERPOOL. ENGLAND.
I CALLED IN A LOT OF FAVORS.
I PUT ALL SORTS OF WARDS ON THIS PLACE. IT WAS ABOUT AS PROTECTED AS A HOUSE COULD GET.
NO ONE MAGICAL COULD EVEN SEE THIS PLACE IF THEY LOOKED AT IT.
BUT THERE WAS ONE THING I HADN'T PLANNED FOR.
I HADN'T PLANNED FOR A GIANT FRIGGIN' ALIEN TO FALL OUT OF THE SKY.
UGLY HERE WAS A GREEN LANTERN.
ALIEN SPACE POLICE.
YES. REALLY.

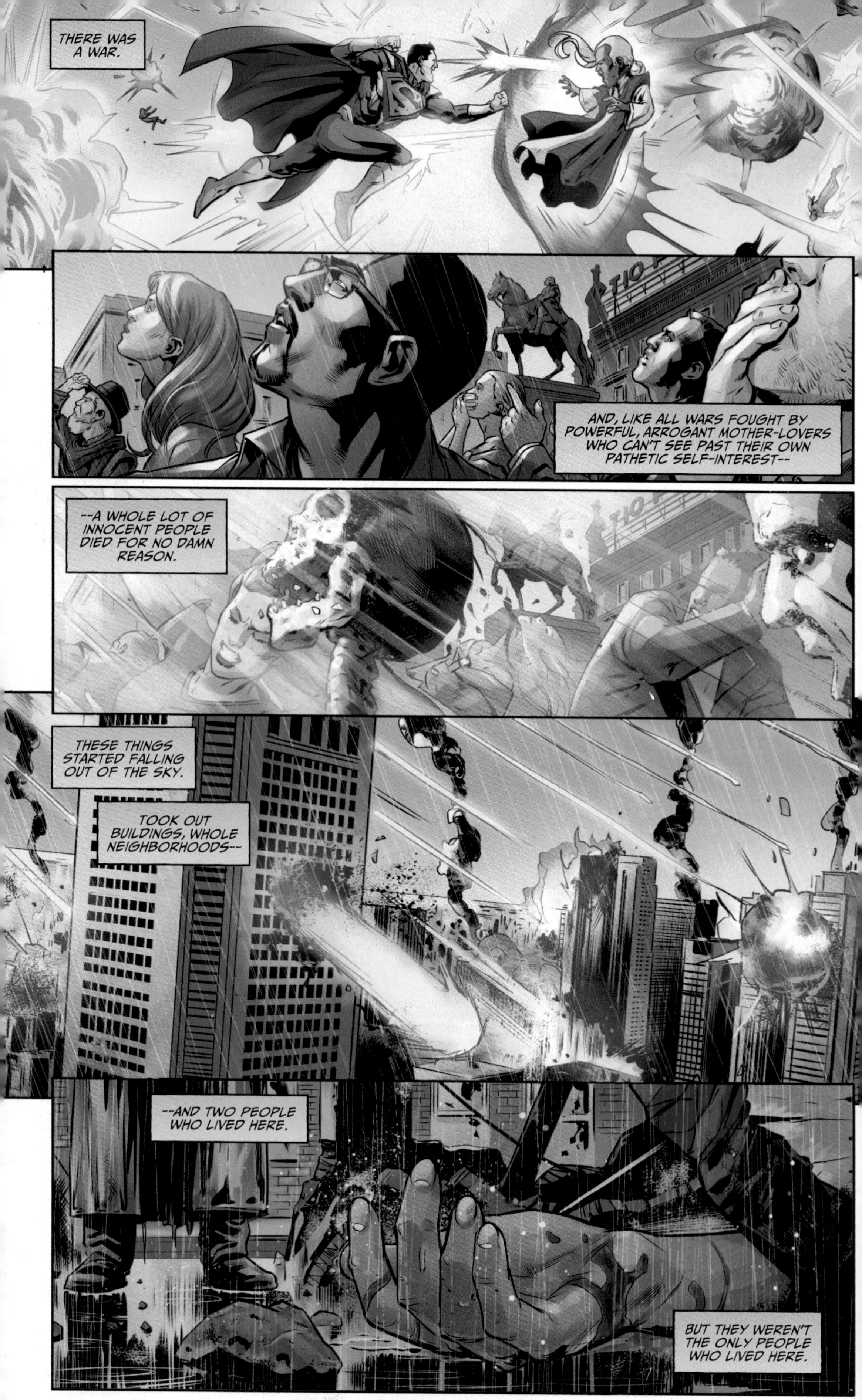
THERE WAS A WAR.
AND, LIKE ALL WARS FOUGHT BY POWERFUL, ARROGANT MOTHER-LOVERS WHO CAN'T SEE PAST THEIR OWN PATHETIC SELF-INTEREST--
--A WHOLE LOT OF INNOCENT PEOPLE DIED FOR NO DAMN REASON.
THESE THINGS STARTED FALLING OUT OF THE SKY.
TOOK OUT BUILDINGS, WHOLE NEIGHBORHOODS--
--AND TWO PEOPLE WHO LIVED HERE.
BUT THEY WEREN'T THE ONLY PEOPLE WHO LIVED HERE.

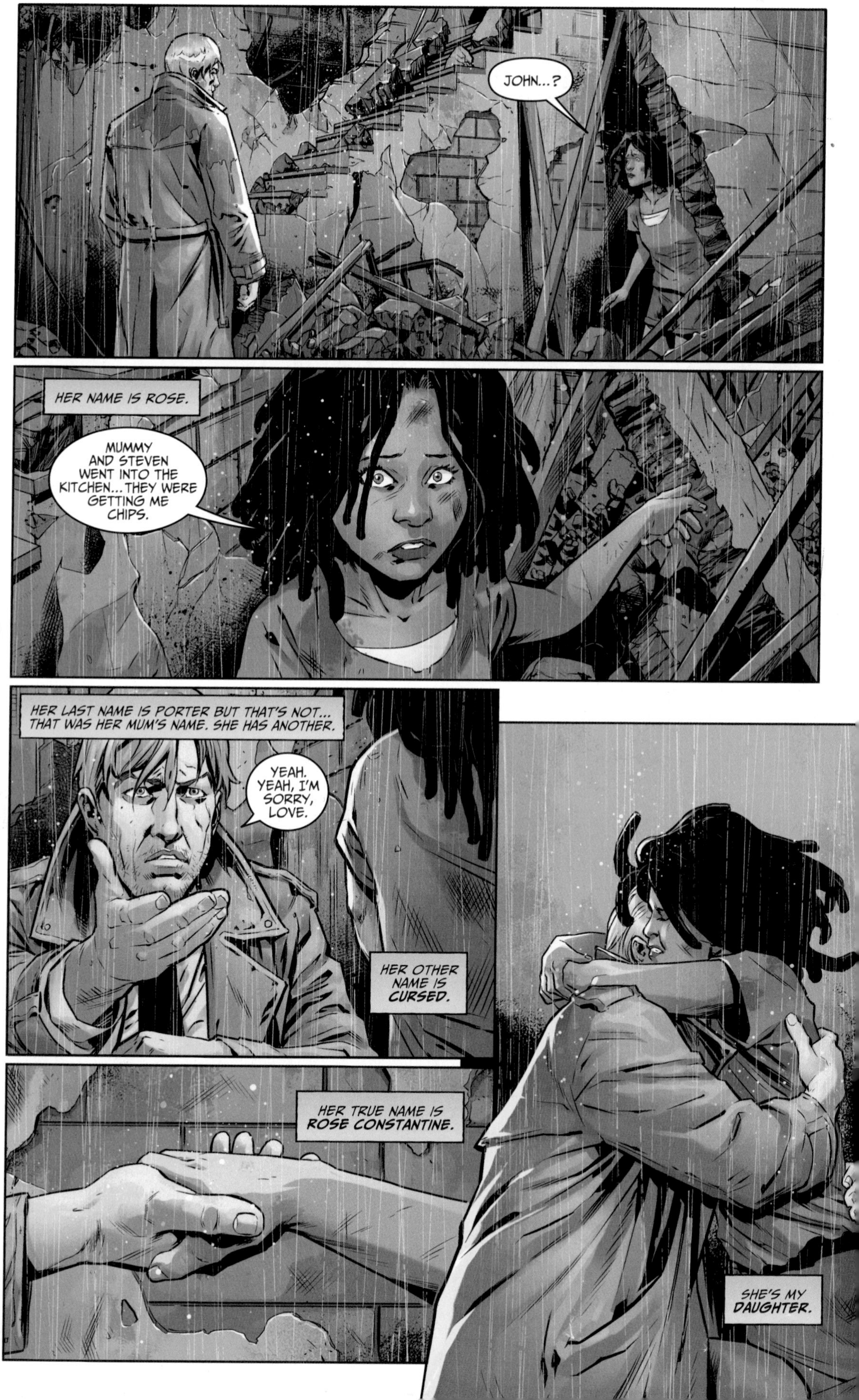

JOHN...?
HER NAME IS ROSE.
MUMMY AND STEVEN WENT INTO THE KITCHEN... THEY WERE GETTING ME CHIPS.
HER LAST NAME IS PORTER BUT THAT'S NOT... THAT WAS HER MUM'S NAME. SHE HAS ANOTHER.
YEAH. YEAH, I'M SORRY, LOVE.
HER OTHER NAME IS CURSED.
HER TRUE NAME IS ROSE CONSTANTINE.
SHE'S MY DAUGHTER.

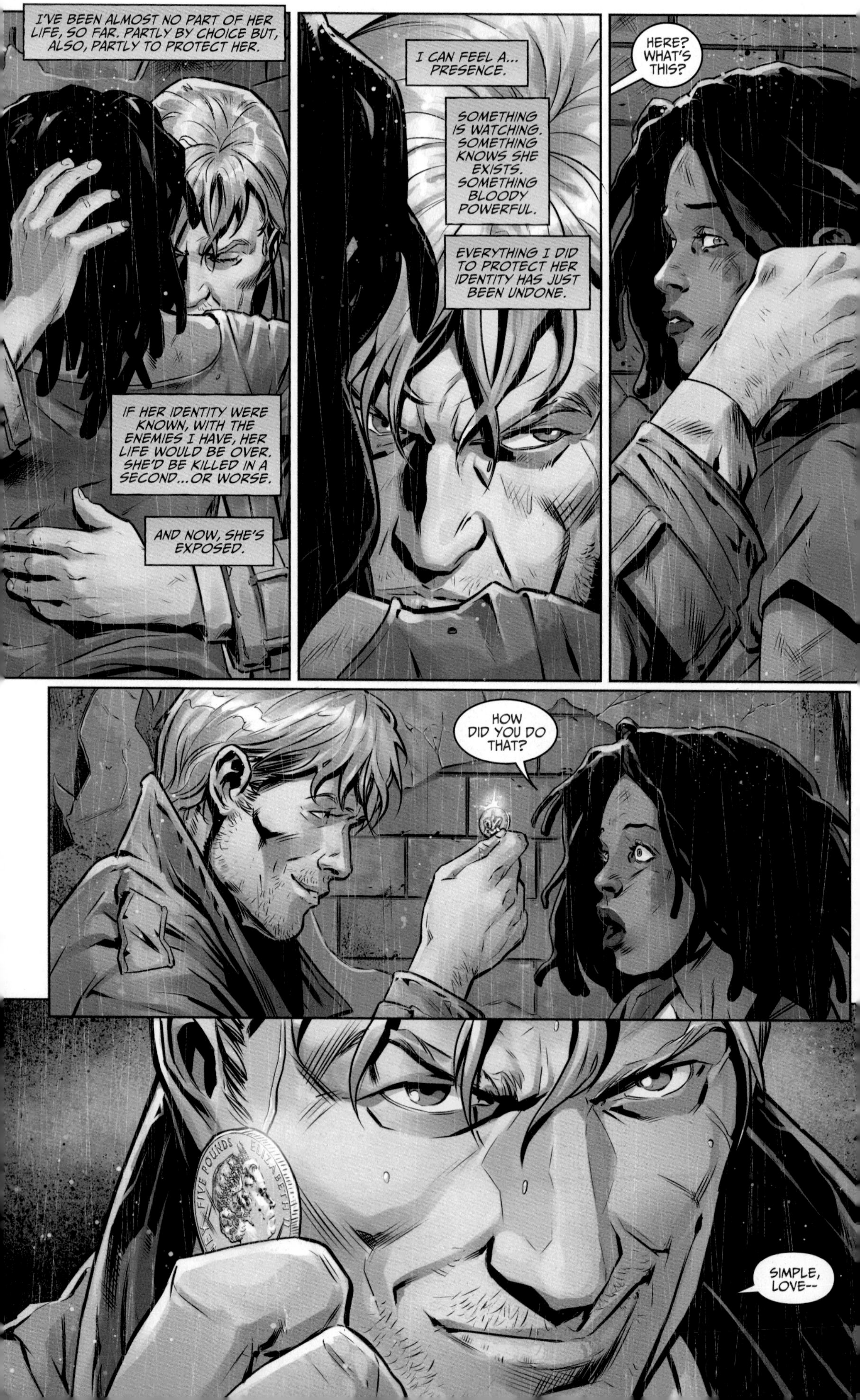

I'VE BEEN ALMOST NO PART OF HER LIFE, SO FAR. PARTLY BY CHOICE BUT, ALSO, PARTLY TO PROTECT HER.
IF HER IDENTITY WERE KNOWN, WITH THE ENEMIES I HAVE, HER LIFE WOULD BE OVER. SHE'D BE KILLED IN A SECOND...OR WORSE.
AND NOW, SHE'S EXPOSED.
I CAN FEEL A... PRESENCE.
SOMETHING IS WATCHING. SOMETHING KNOWS SHE EXISTS. SOMETHING BLOODY POWERFUL.
EVERYTHING I DID TO PROTECT HER IDENTITY HAS JUST BEEN UNDONE.
HERE? WHAT'S THIS?
HOW DID YOU DO THAT?
FIVE POUNDS ELIZABETH II
SIMPLE, LOVE--

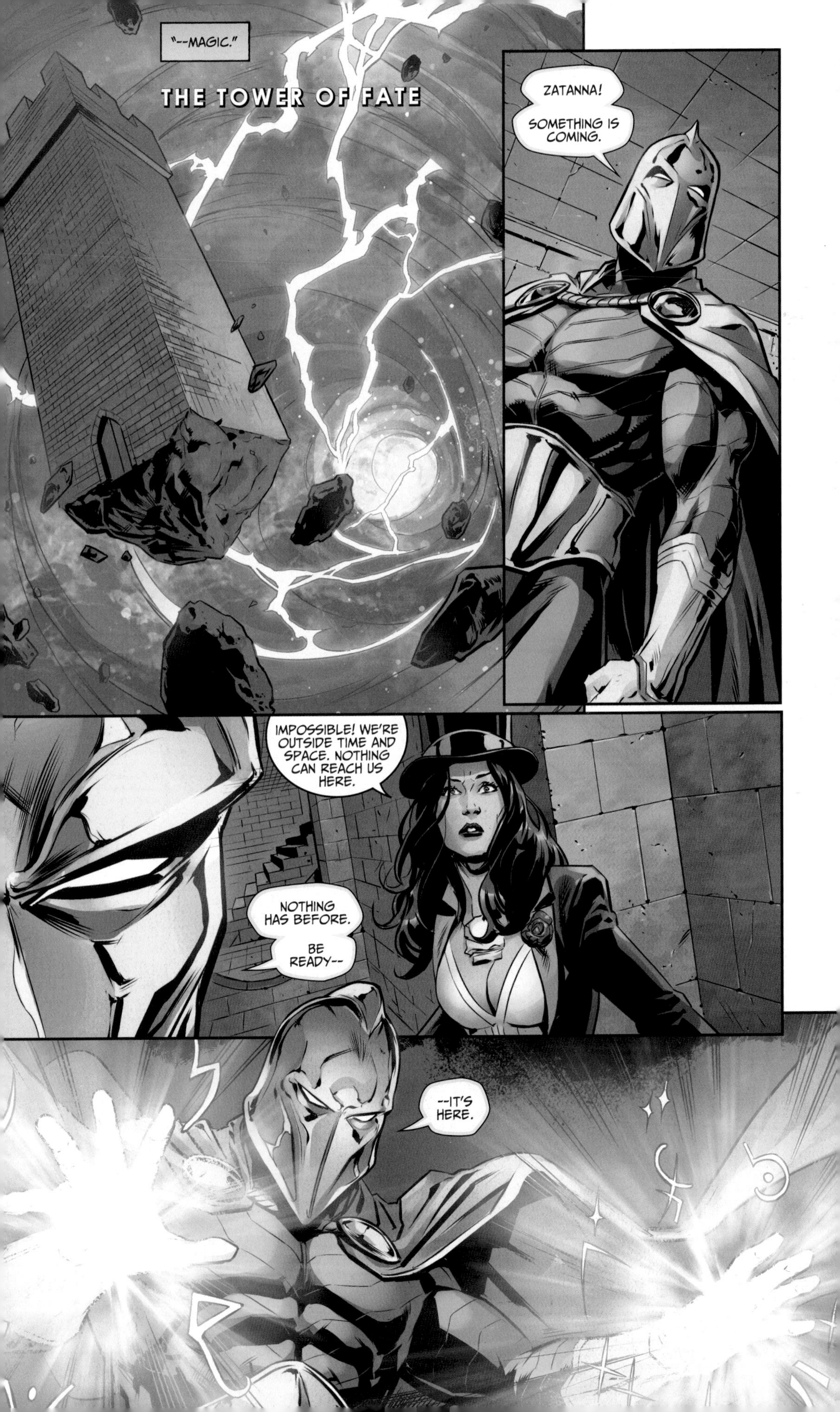
"--MAGIC."
THE TOWER OF FATE
ZATANNA!
SOMETHING IS COMING.
IMPOSSIBLE! WE'RE OUTSIDE TIME AND SPACE. NOTHING CAN REACH US HERE.
NOTHING HAS BEFORE.
BE READY--
--IT'S HERE.

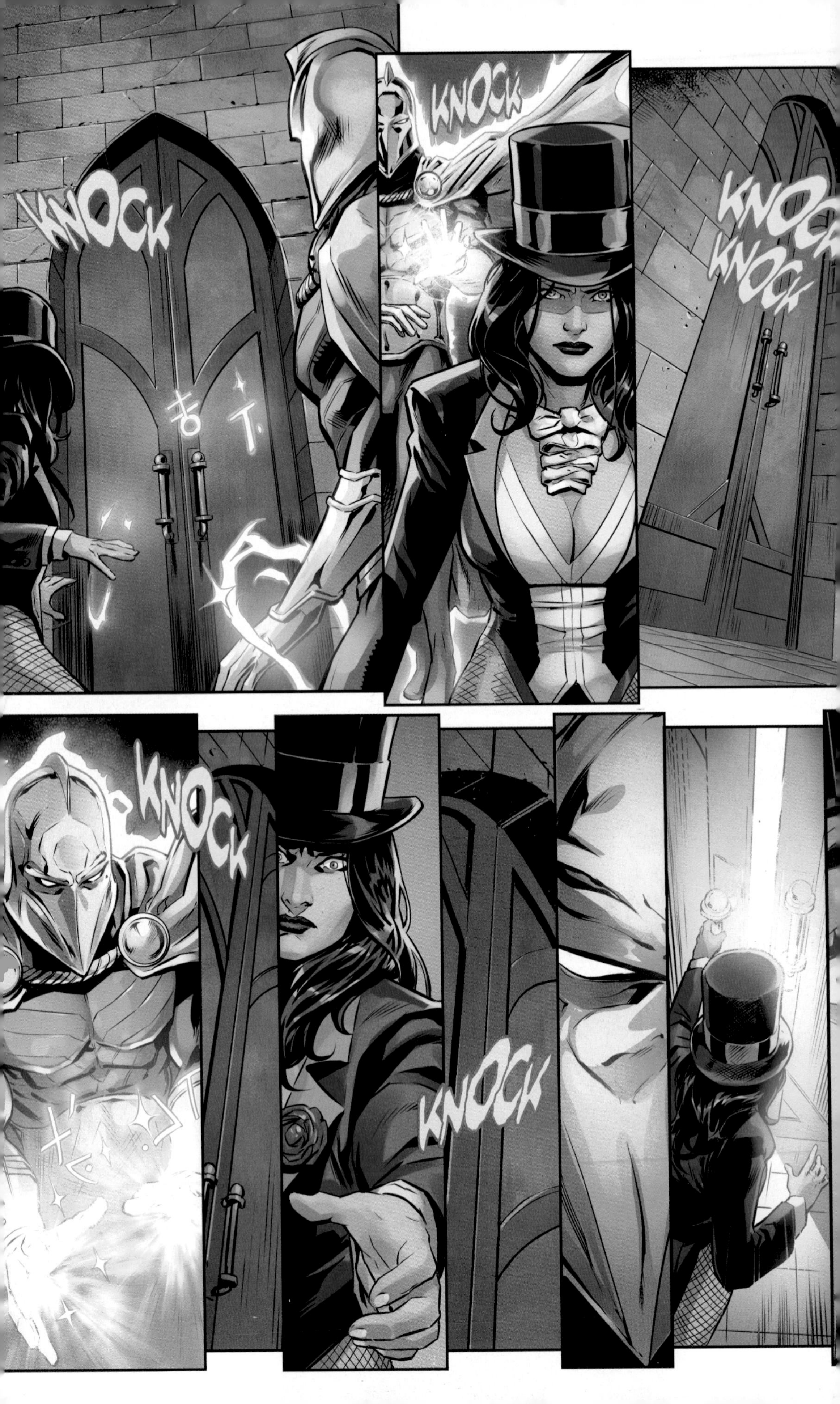
KNOCK
KNOCK
KNOCK
KNOCK
KNOCK
KNOCK

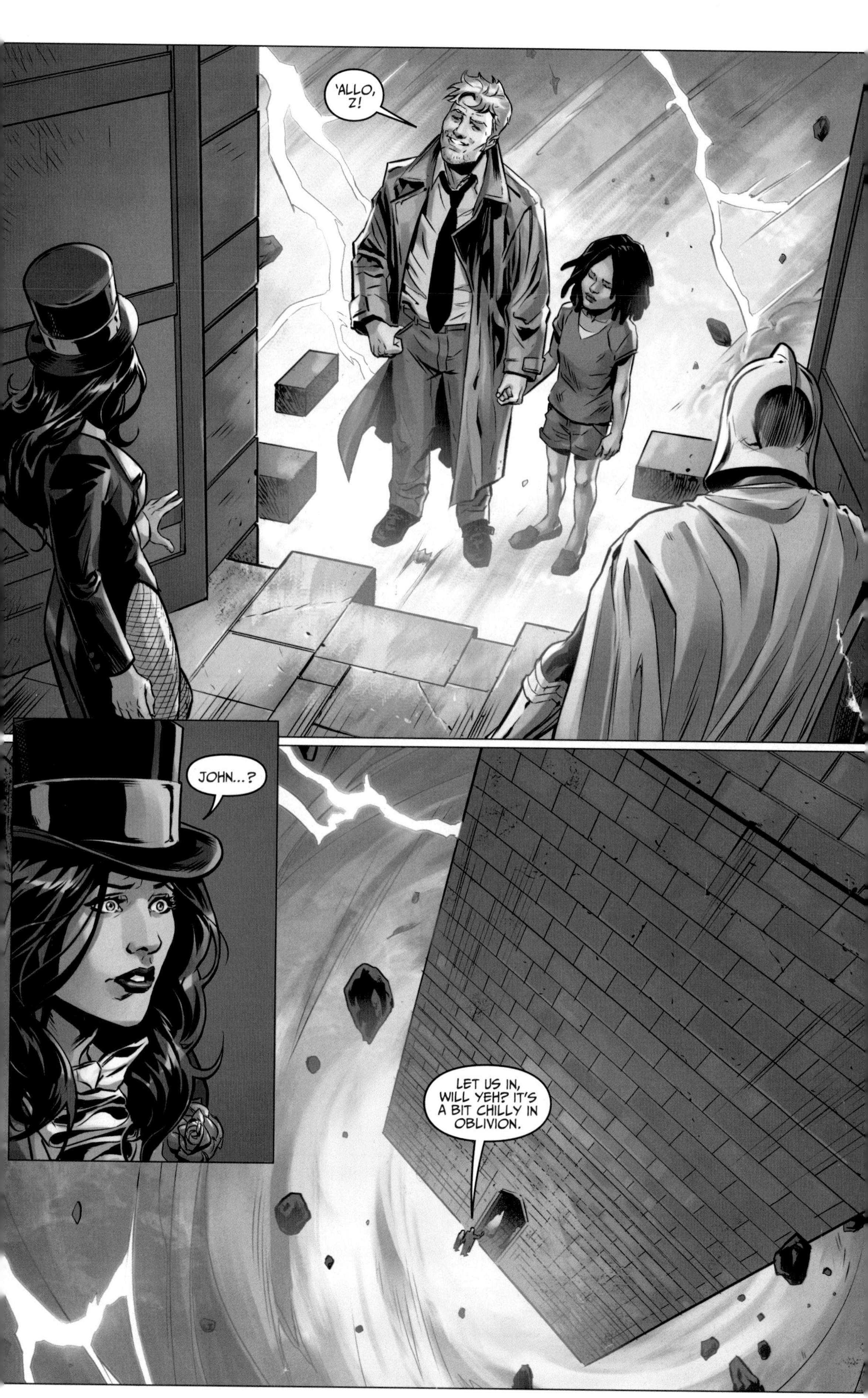
'ALLO, Z!
JOHN...?
LET US IN, WILL YEH? IT'S A BIT CHILLY IN OBLIVION.

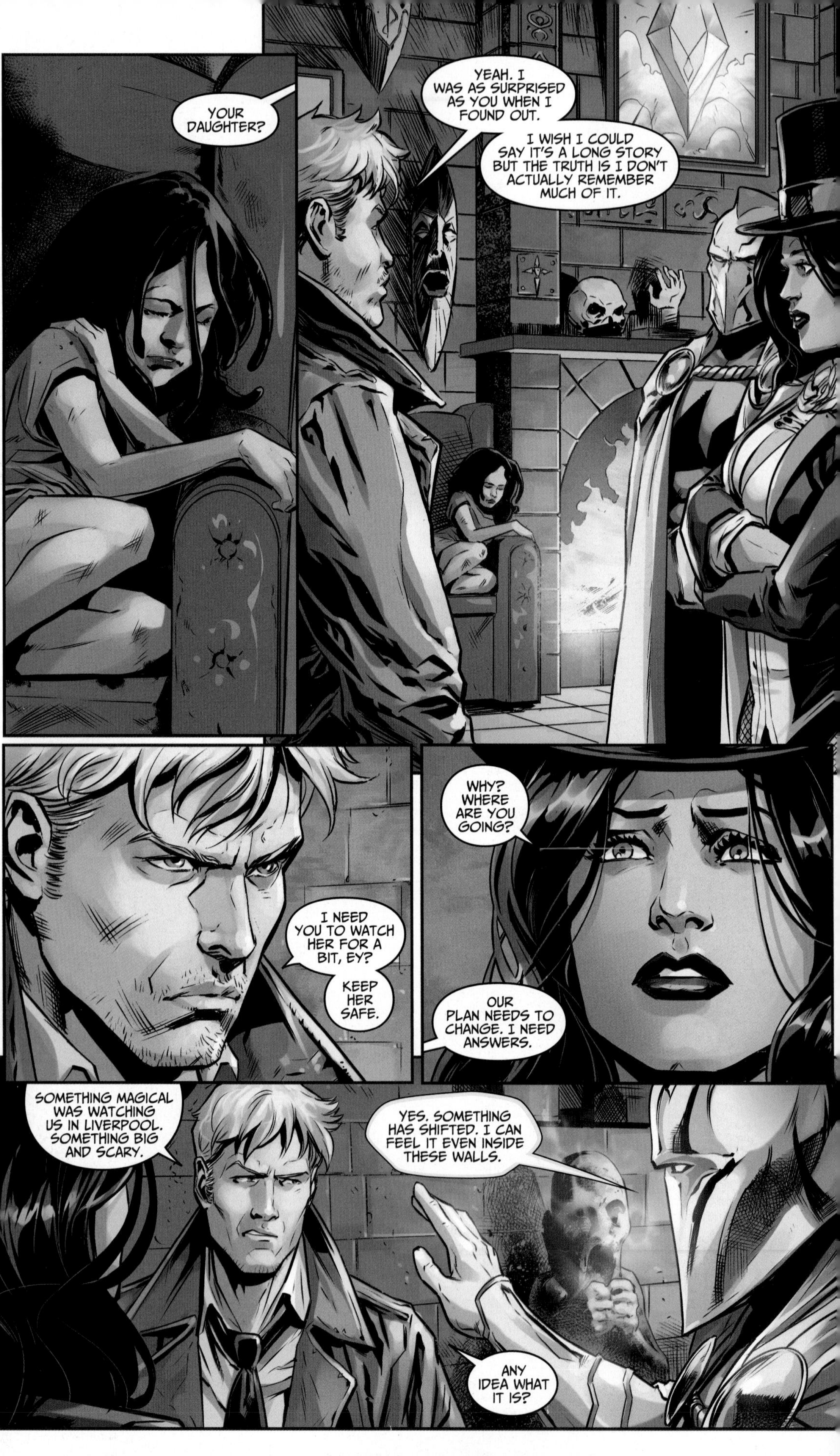
YOUR DAUGHTER?
YEAH. I WAS AS SURPRISED AS YOU WHEN I FOUND OUT.
I WISH I COULD SAY IT'S A LONG STORY BUT THE TRUTH IS I DON'T ACTUALLY REMEMBER MUCH OF IT.
I NEED YOU TO WATCH HER FOR A BIT, EY?
KEEP HER SAFE.
WHY? WHERE ARE YOU GOING?
OUR PLAN NEEDS TO CHANGE. I NEED ANSWERS.
SOMETHING MAGICAL WAS WATCHING US IN LIVERPOOL. SOMETHING BIG AND SCARY.
YES. SOMETHING HAS SHIFTED. I CAN FEEL IT EVEN INSIDE THESE WALLS.
ANY IDEA WHAT IT IS?

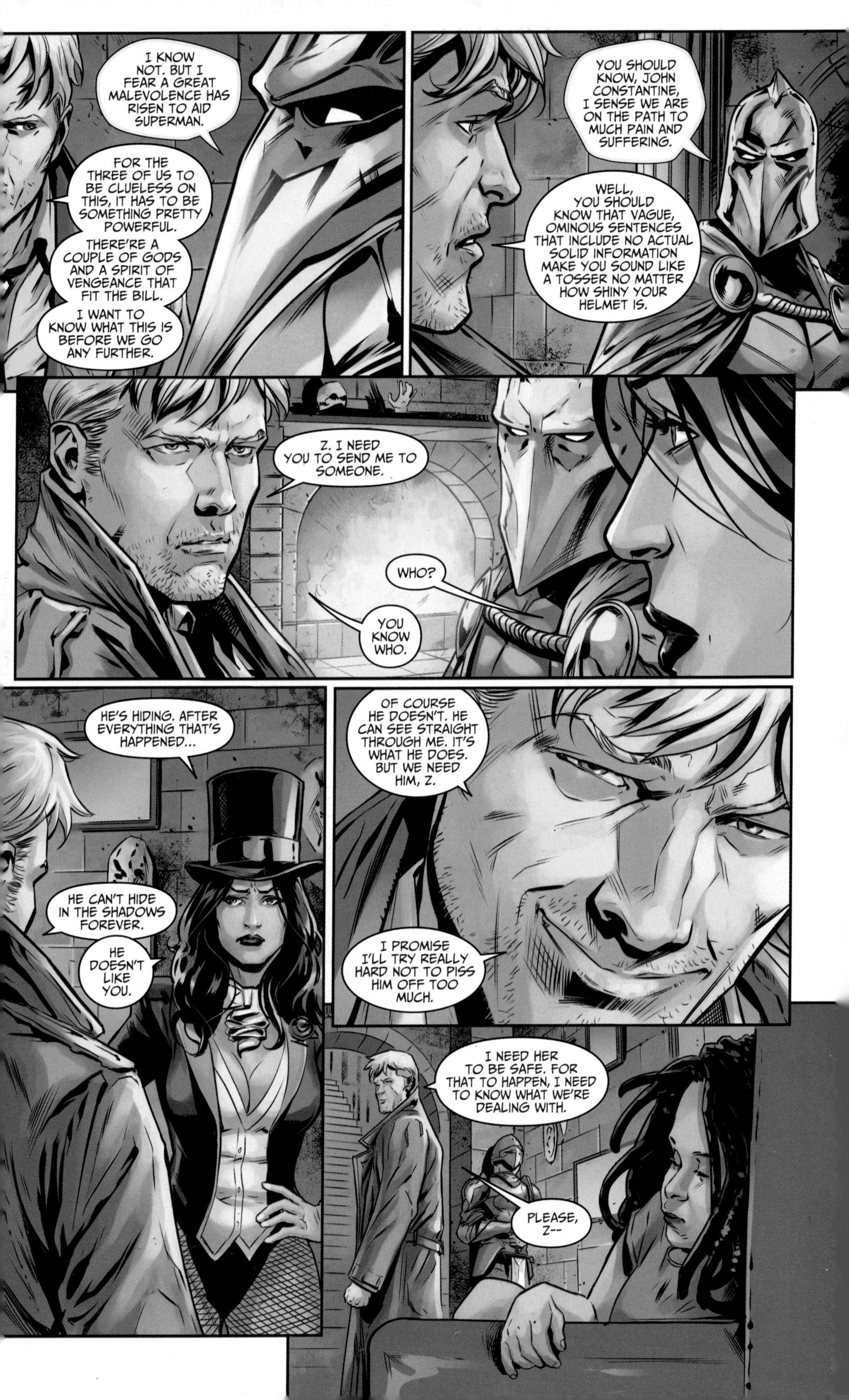
I KNOW NOT. BUT I FEAR A GREAT MALEVOLENCE HAS RISEN TO AID SUPERMAN.
FOR THE THREE OF US TO BE CLUELESS ON THIS, IT HAS TO BE SOMETHING PRETTY POWERFUL.
THERE'RE A COUPLE OF GODS AND A SPIRIT OF VENGEANCE THAT FIT THE BILL.
I WANT TO KNOW WHAT THIS IS BEFORE WE GO ANY FURTHER.
YOU SHOULD KNOW, JOHN CONSTANTINE, I SENSE WE ARE ON THE PATH TO MUCH PAIN AND SUFFERING.
WELL, YOU SHOULD KNOW THAT VAGUE, OMINOUS SENTENCES THAT INCLUDE NO ACTUAL SOLID INFORMATION MAKE YOU SOUND LIKE A TOSSER NO MATTER HOW SHINY YOUR HELMET IS.
Z. I NEED YOU TO SEND ME TO SOMEONE.
WHO?
YOU KNOW WHO.
HE'S HIDING. AFTER EVERYTHING THAT'S HAPPENED...
HE CAN'T HIDE IN THE SHADOWS FOREVER.
HE DOESN'T LIKE YOU.
OF COURSE HE DOESN'T. HE CAN SEE STRAIGHT THROUGH ME. IT'S WHAT HE DOES. BUT WE NEED HIM, Z.
I PROMISE I'LL TRY REALLY HARD NOT TO PISS HIM OFF TOO MUCH.
I NEED HER TO BE SAFE. FOR THAT TO HAPPEN, I NEED TO KNOW WHAT WE'RE DEALING WITH.
PLEASE, Z--

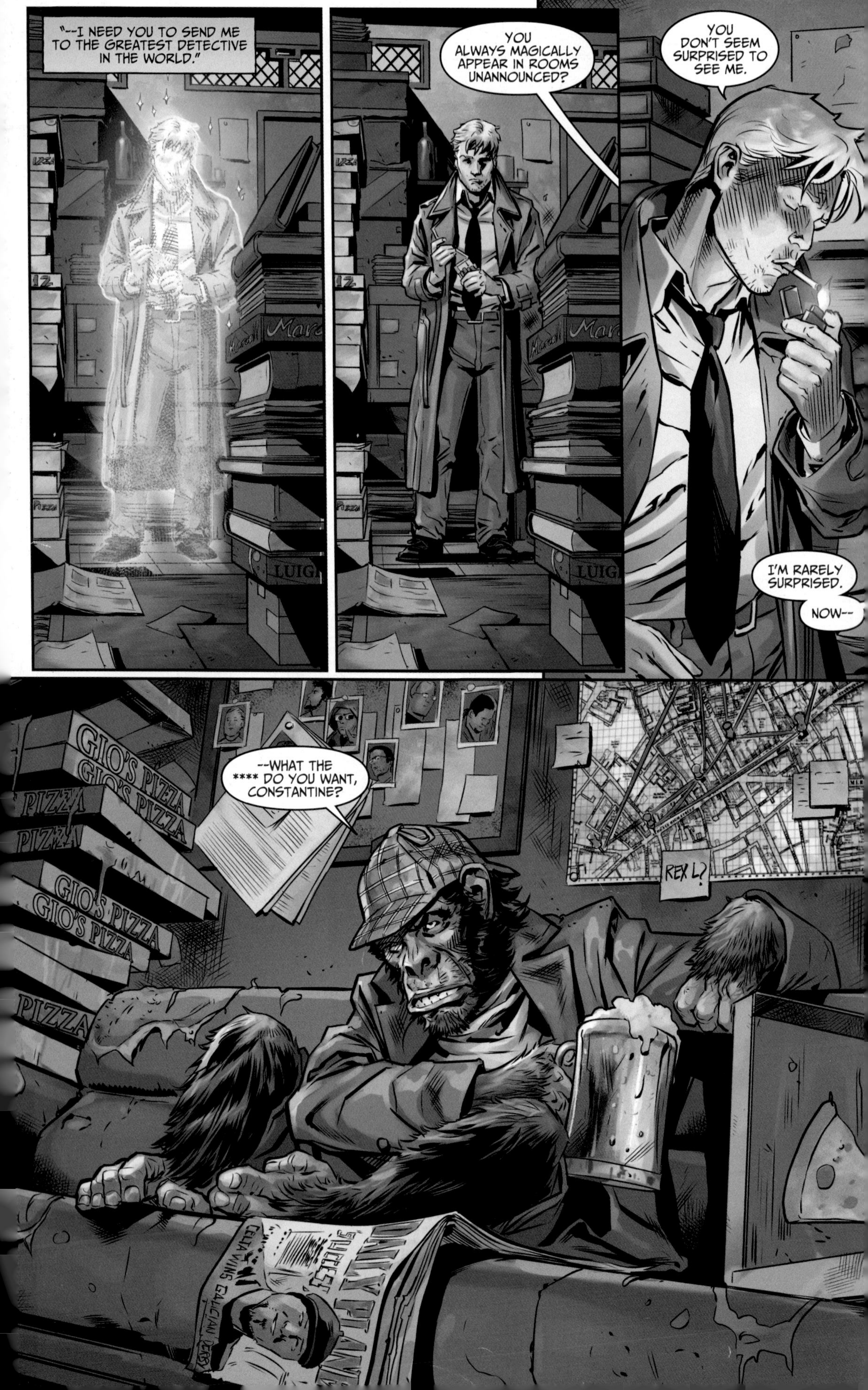
"--I NEED YOU TO SEND ME TO THE GREATEST DETECTIVE IN THE WORLD."
YOU ALWAYS MAGICALLY APPEAR IN ROOMS UNANNOUNCED?
YOU DON'T SEEM SURPRISED TO SEE ME.
I'M RARELY SURPRISED.
NOW--
--WHAT THE **** DO YOU WANT, CONSTANTINE?
GIO'S PIZZA
GIO'S PIZZA
PIZZA
REX L?

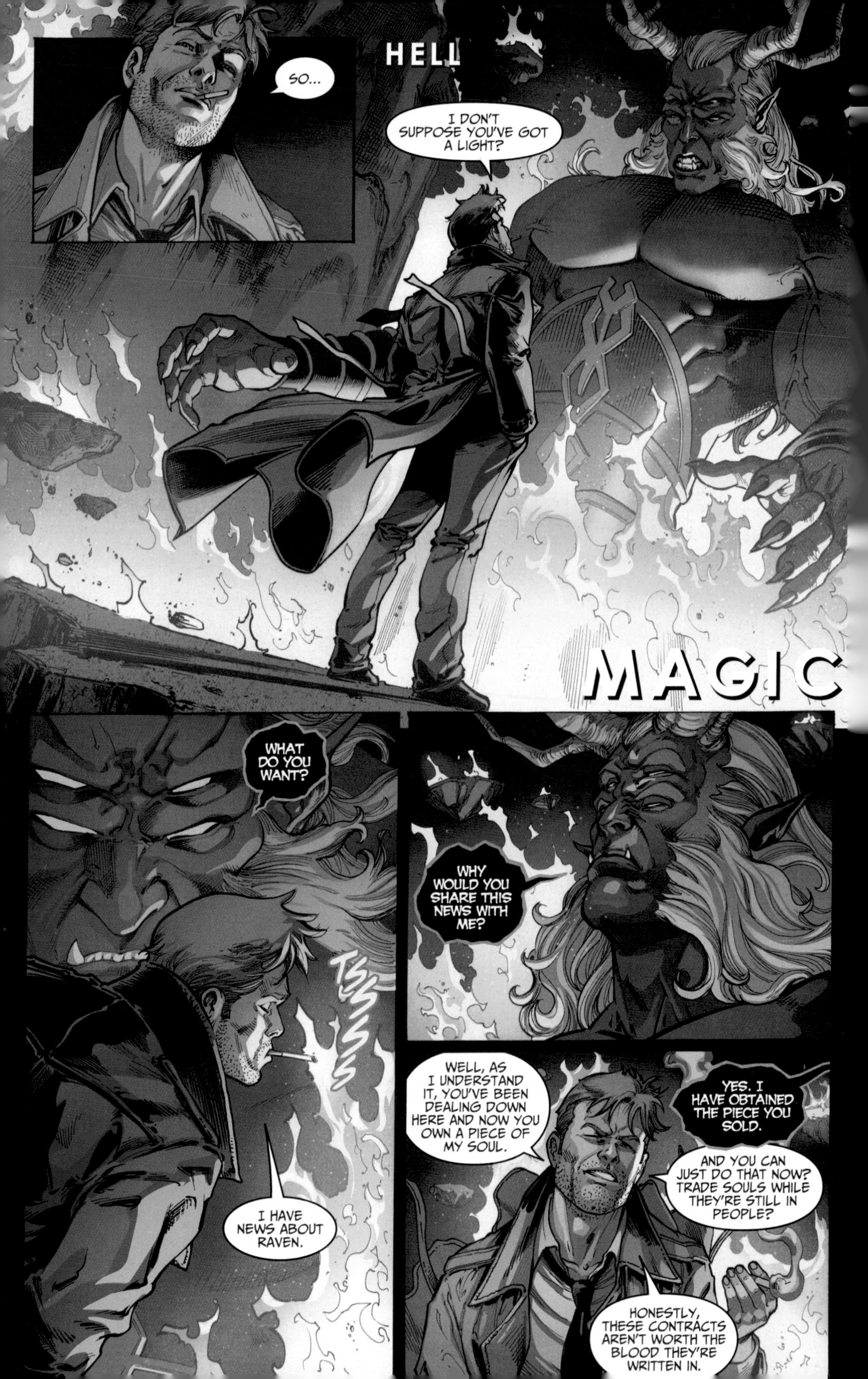
HELL
SO...
I DON'T SUPPOSE YOU'VE GOT A LIGHT?
MAGIC
WHAT DO YOU WANT?
TSSSSS
I HAVE NEWS ABOUT RAVEN.
WHY WOULD YOU SHARE THIS NEWS WITH ME?
WELL, AS I UNDERSTAND IT, YOU'VE BEEN DEALING DOWN HERE AND NOW YOU OWN A PIECE OF MY SOUL.
YES. I HAVE OBTAINED THE PIECE YOU SOLD.
AND YOU CAN JUST DO THAT NOW? TRADE SOULS WHILE THEY'RE STILL IN PEOPLE?
HONESTLY, THESE CONTRACTS AREN'T WORTH THE BLOOD THEY'RE WRITTEN IN.

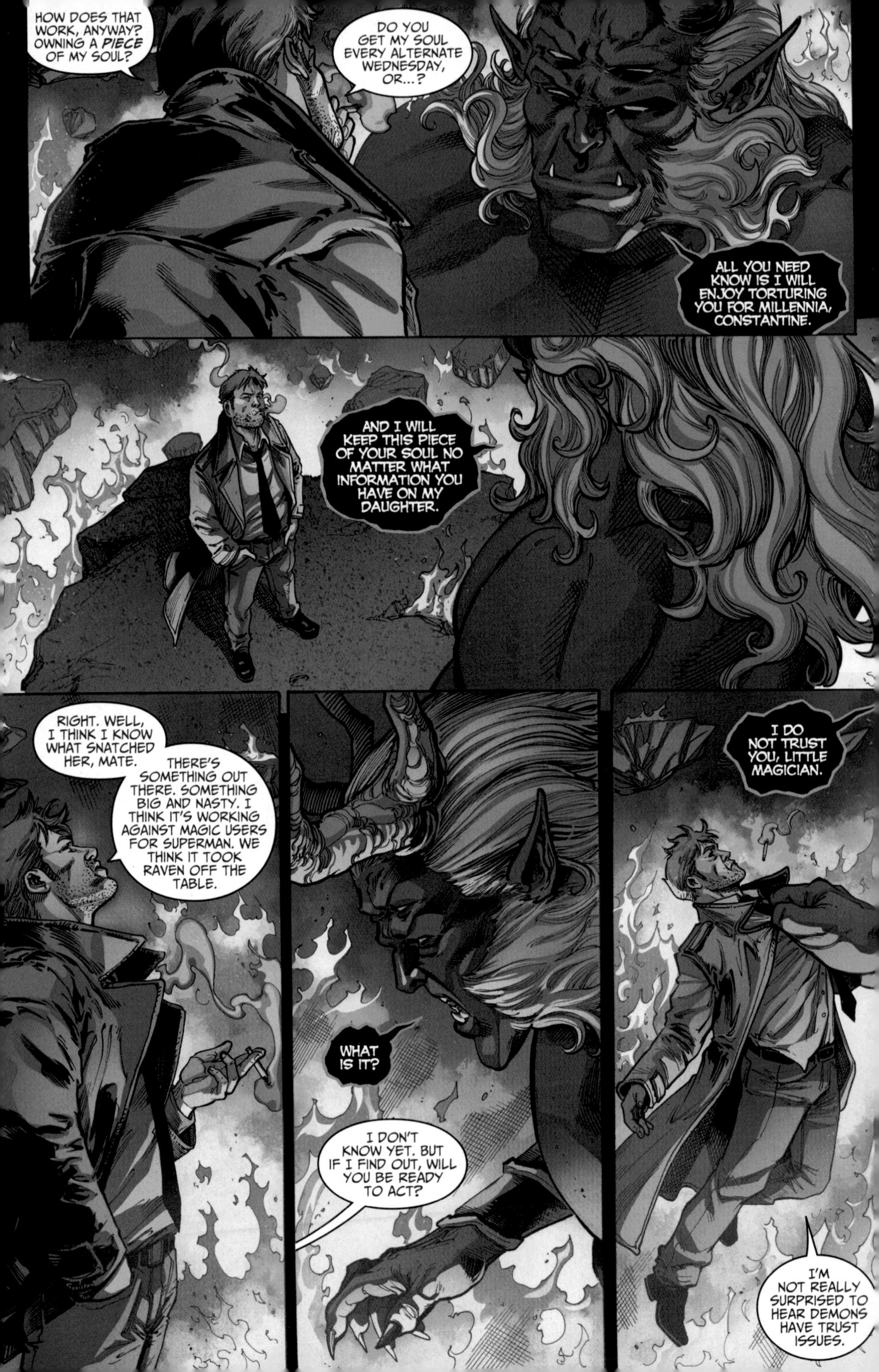
HOW DOES THAT WORK, ANYWAY? OWNING A *PIECE* OF MY SOUL?
DO YOU GET MY SOUL EVERY ALTERNATE WEDNESDAY, OR...?
ALL YOU NEED KNOW IS I WILL ENJOY TORTURING YOU FOR MILLENNIA, CONSTANTINE.
AND I WILL KEEP THIS PIECE OF YOUR SOUL NO MATTER WHAT INFORMATION YOU HAVE ON MY DAUGHTER.
RIGHT. WELL, I THINK I KNOW WHAT SNATCHED HER, MATE.
THERE'S SOMETHING OUT THERE. SOMETHING BIG AND NASTY. I THINK IT'S WORKING AGAINST MAGIC USERS FOR SUPERMAN. WE THINK IT TOOK RAVEN OFF THE TABLE.
WHAT IS IT?
I DON'T KNOW YET. BUT IF I FIND OUT, WILL YOU BE READY TO ACT?
I DO NOT TRUST YOU, LITTLE MAGICIAN.
I'M NOT REALLY SURPRISED TO HEAR DEMONS HAVE TRUST ISSUES.

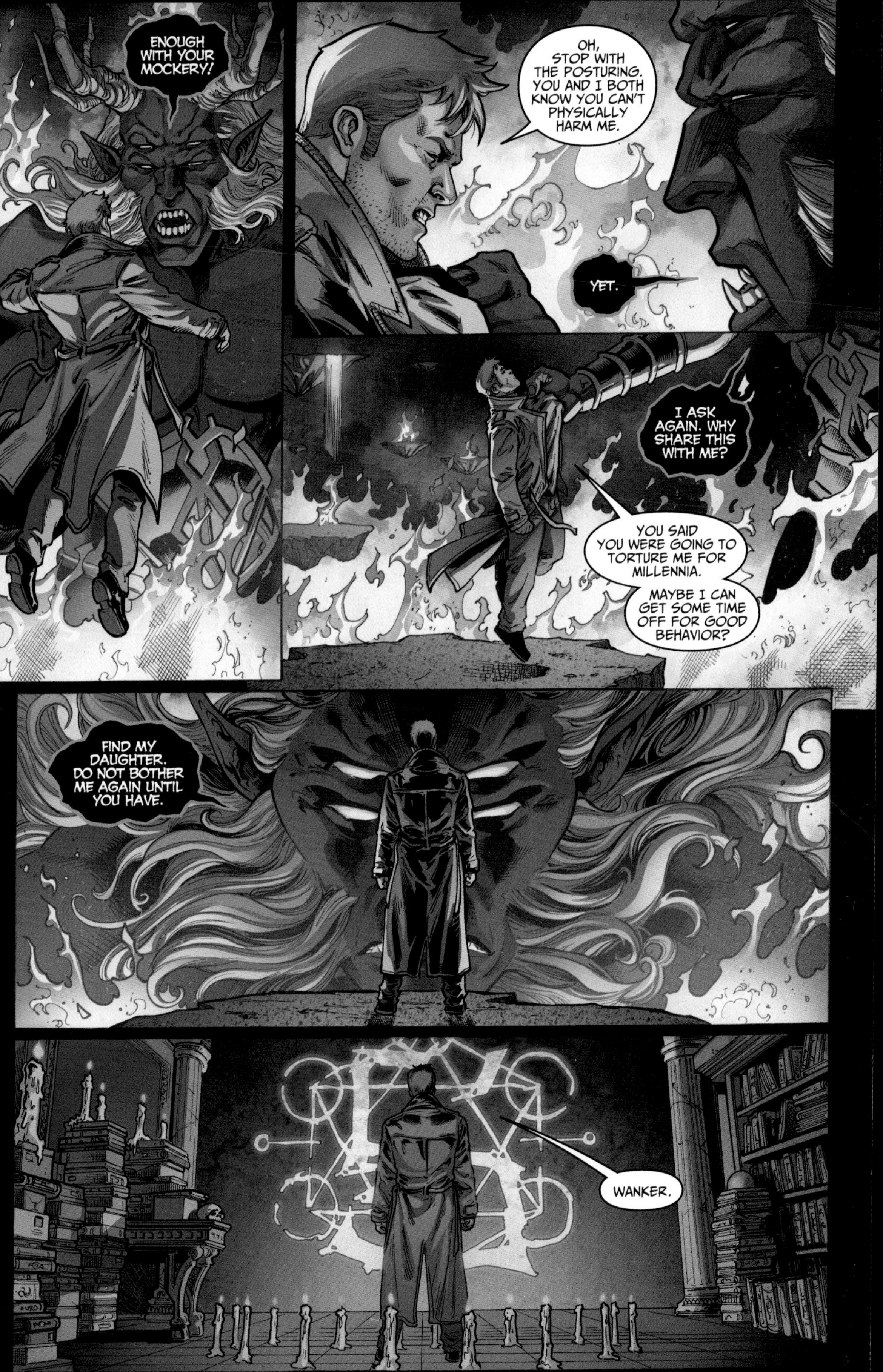
ENOUGH WITH YOUR MOCKERY!
OH, STOP WITH THE POSTURING. YOU AND I BOTH KNOW YOU CAN'T PHYSICALLY HARM ME.
YET.
I ASK AGAIN. WHY SHARE THIS WITH ME?
YOU SAID YOU WERE GOING TO TORTURE ME FOR MILLENNIA.
MAYBE I CAN GET SOME TIME OFF FOR GOOD BEHAVIOR?
FIND MY DAUGHTER. DO NOT BOTHER ME AGAIN UNTIL YOU HAVE.
WANKER.

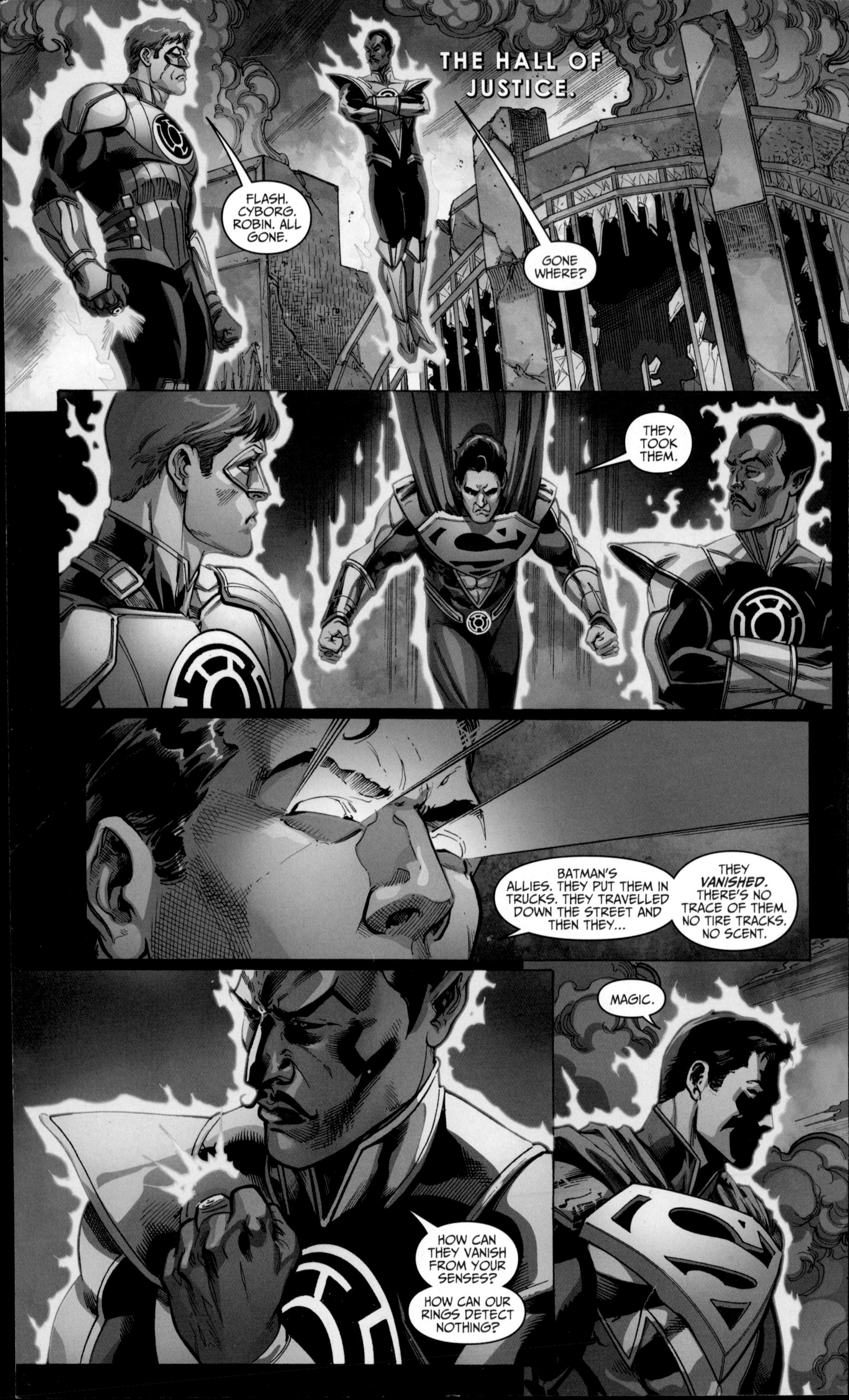
THE HALL OF JUSTICE.
FLASH. CYBORG. ROBIN. ALL GONE.
GONE WHERE?
THEY TOOK THEM.
BATMAN'S ALLIES. THEY PUT THEM IN TRUCKS. THEY TRAVELLED DOWN THE STREET AND THEN THEY...
THEY *VANISHED.* THERE'S NO TRACE OF THEM. NO TIRE TRACKS. NO SCENT.
MAGIC.
HOW CAN THEY VANISH FROM YOUR SENSES?
HOW CAN OUR RINGS DETECT NOTHING?

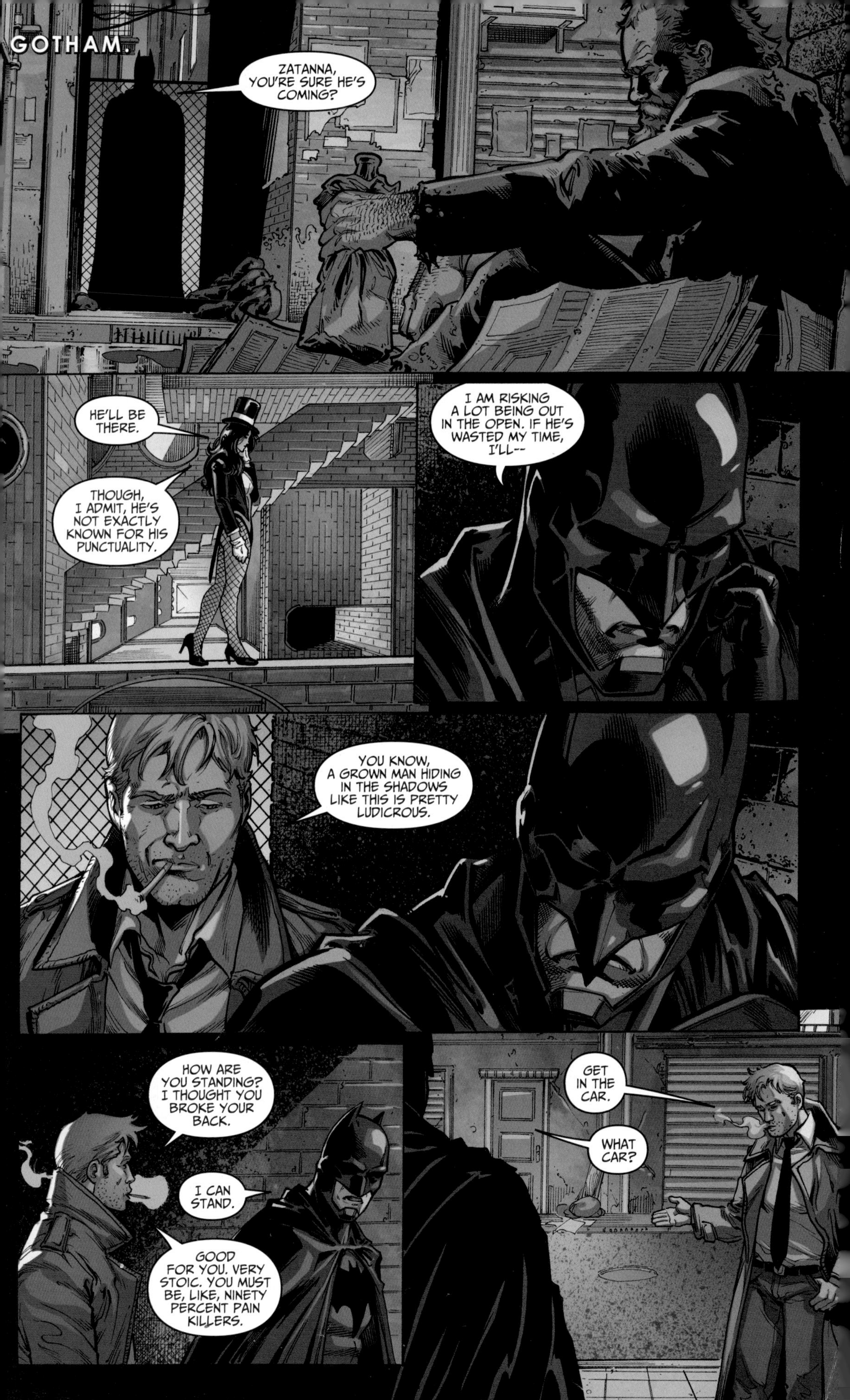
GOTHAM.
ZATANNA, YOU'RE SURE HE'S COMING?
HE'LL BE THERE.
THOUGH, I ADMIT, HE'S NOT EXACTLY KNOWN FOR HIS PUNCTUALITY.
I AM RISKING A LOT BEING OUT IN THE OPEN. IF HE'S WASTED MY TIME, I'LL--
YOU KNOW, A GROWN MAN HIDING IN THE SHADOWS LIKE THIS IS PRETTY LUDICROUS.
HOW ARE YOU STANDING? I THOUGHT YOU BROKE YOUR BACK.
I CAN STAND.
GOOD FOR YOU. VERY STOIC. YOU MUST BE, LIKE, NINETY PERCENT PAIN KILLERS.
GET IN THE CAR.
WHAT CAR?

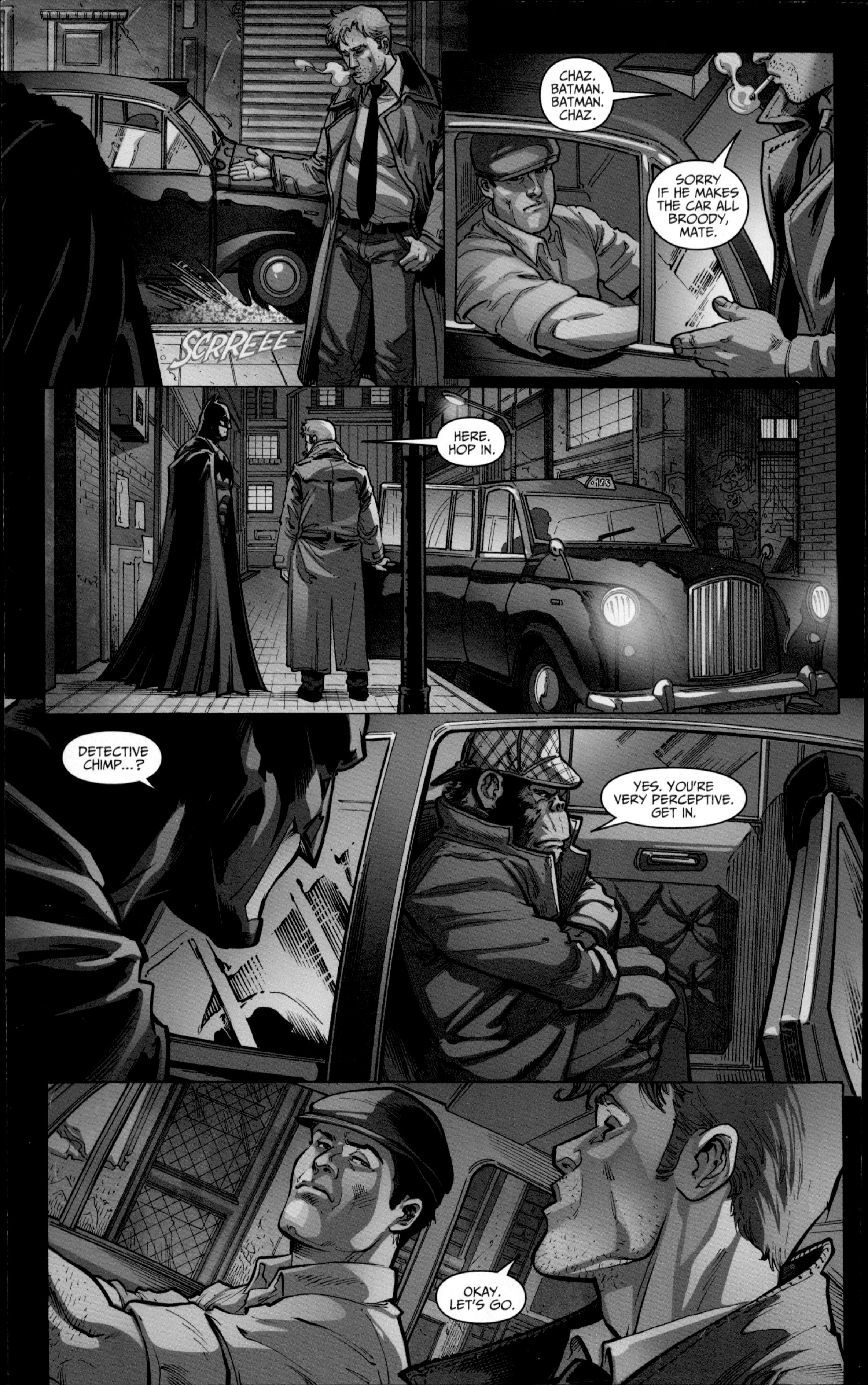
SCRREEE
CHAZ. BATMAN. BATMAN. CHAZ.
SORRY IF HE MAKES THE CAR ALL BROODY, MATE.
HERE. HOP IN.
DETECTIVE CHIMP...?
YES. YOU'RE VERY PERCEPTIVE. GET IN.
OKAY. LET'S GO.

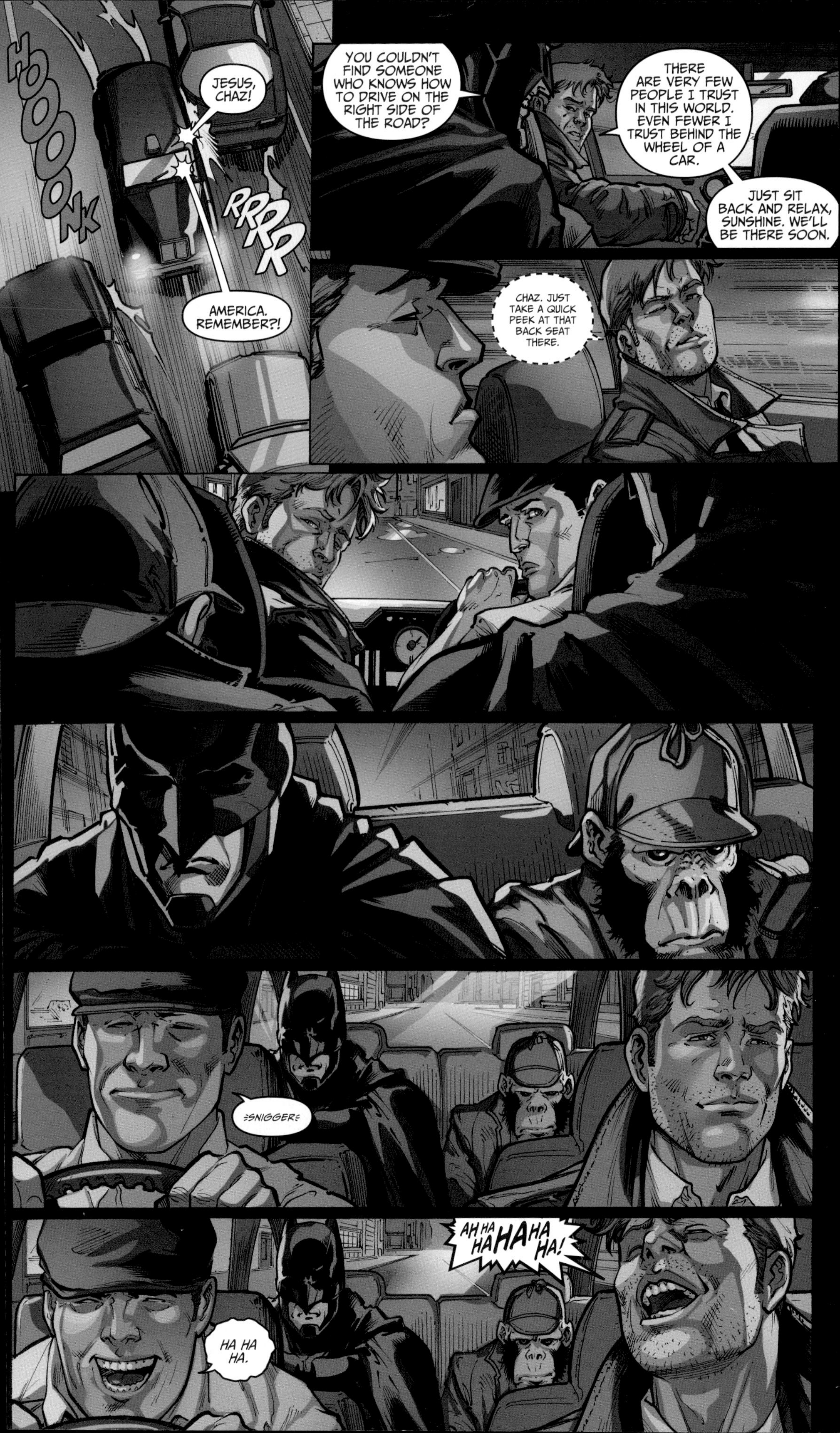
HOOOONK
JESUS, CHAZ!
RRRR
AMERICA. REMEMBER?!
YOU COULDN'T FIND SOMEONE WHO KNOWS HOW TO DRIVE ON THE RIGHT SIDE OF THE ROAD?
THERE ARE VERY FEW PEOPLE I TRUST IN THIS WORLD. EVEN FEWER I TRUST BEHIND THE WHEEL OF A CAR.
JUST SIT BACK AND RELAX, SUNSHINE. WE'LL BE THERE SOON.
CHAZ. JUST TAKE A QUICK PEEK AT THAT BACK SEAT THERE.
SNIGGER
AH HA HA HA HA HA HA!
HA HA HA.

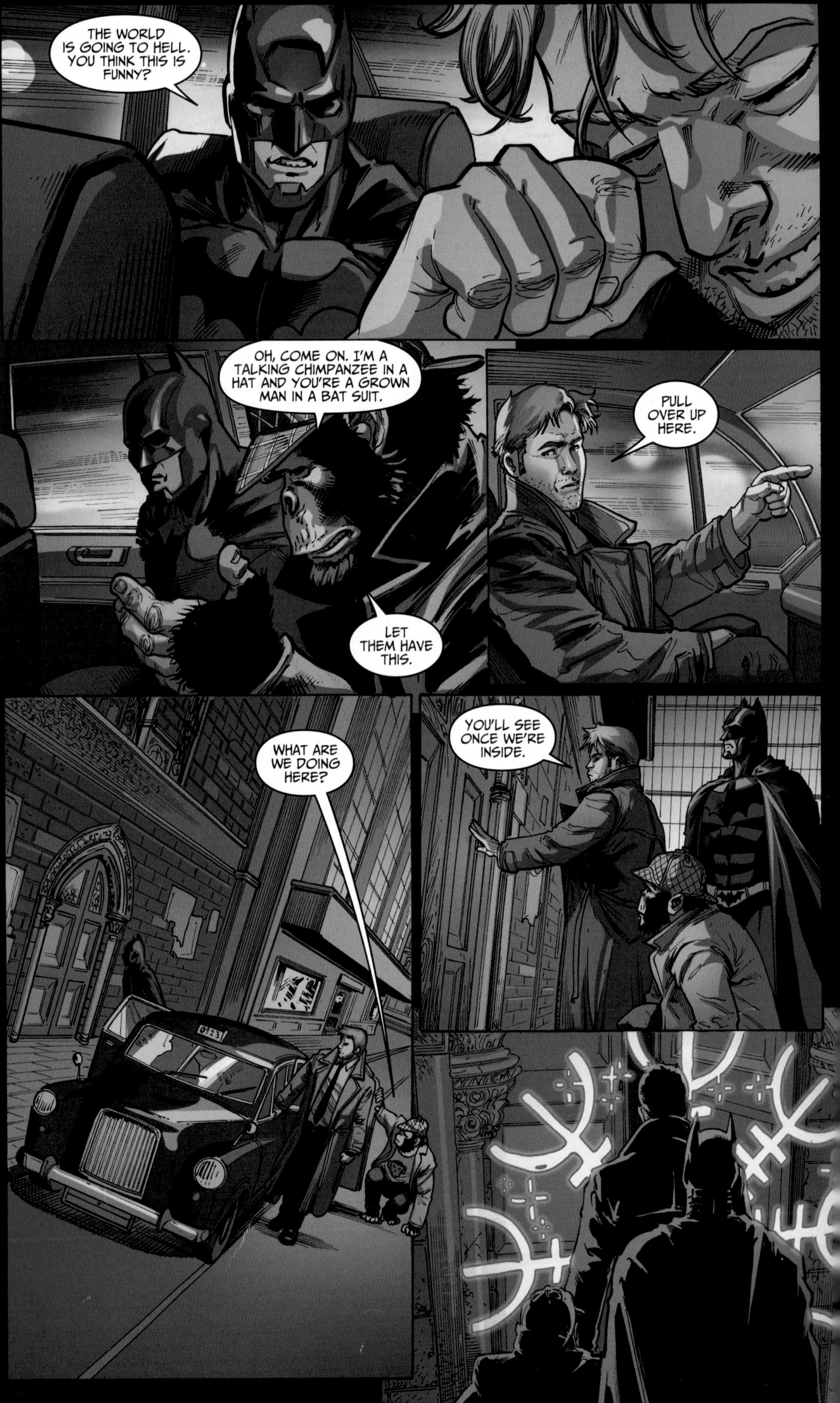
THE WORLD IS GOING TO HELL. YOU THINK THIS IS FUNNY?
OH, COME ON. I'M A TALKING CHIMPANZEE IN A HAT AND YOU'RE A GROWN MAN IN A BAT SUIT.
LET THEM HAVE THIS.
PULL OVER UP HERE.
WHAT ARE WE DOING HERE?
YOU'LL SEE ONCE WE'RE INSIDE.
0123

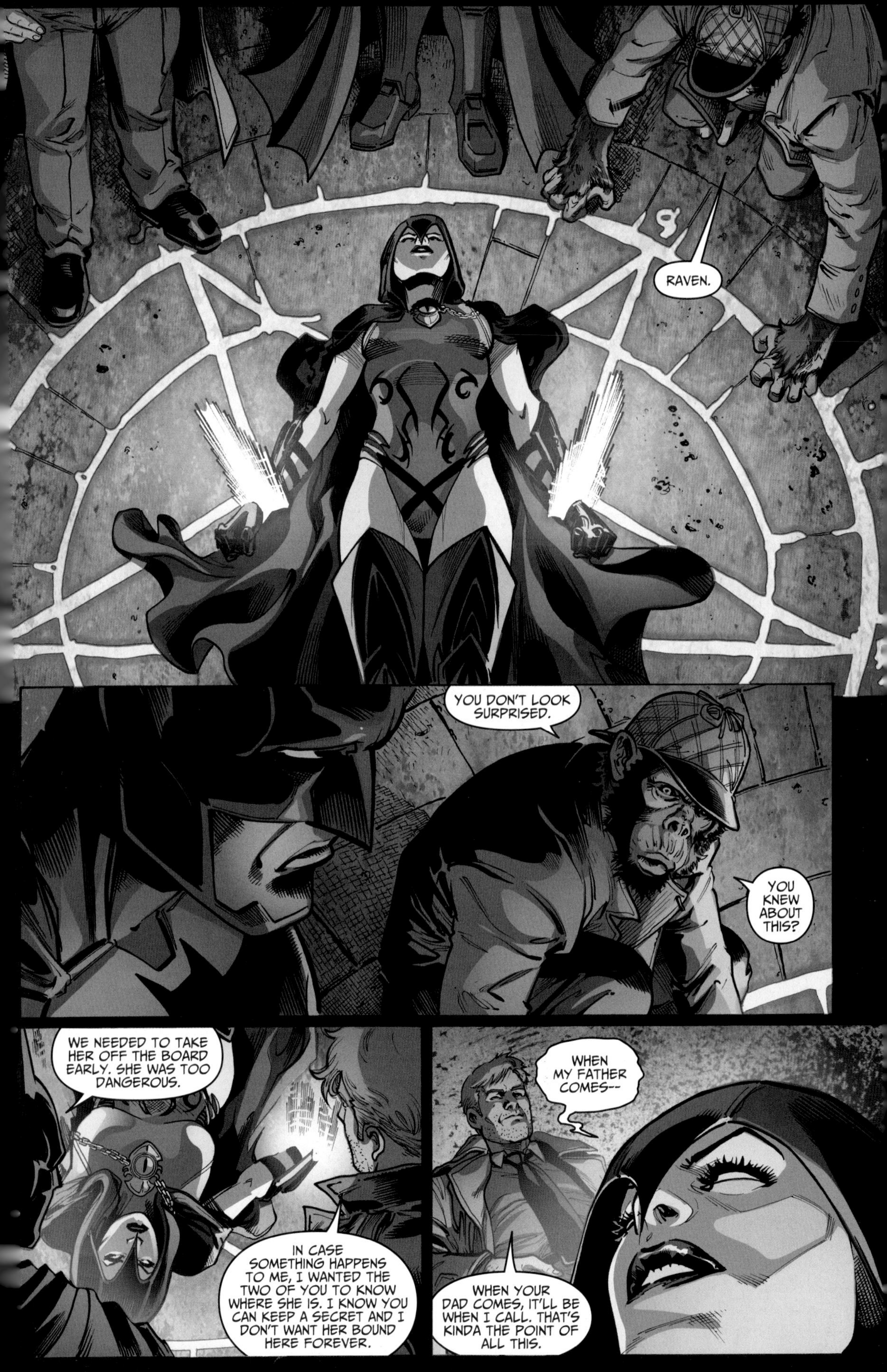
RAVEN.
YOU DON'T LOOK SURPRISED.
YOU KNEW ABOUT THIS?
WE NEEDED TO TAKE HER OFF THE BOARD EARLY. SHE WAS TOO DANGEROUS.
IN CASE SOMETHING HAPPENS TO ME, I WANTED THE TWO OF YOU TO KNOW WHERE SHE IS. I KNOW YOU CAN KEEP A SECRET AND I DON'T WANT HER BOUND HERE FOREVER.
WHEN MY FATHER COMES--
WHEN YOUR DAD COMES, IT'LL BE WHEN I CALL. THAT'S KINDA THE POINT OF ALL THIS.

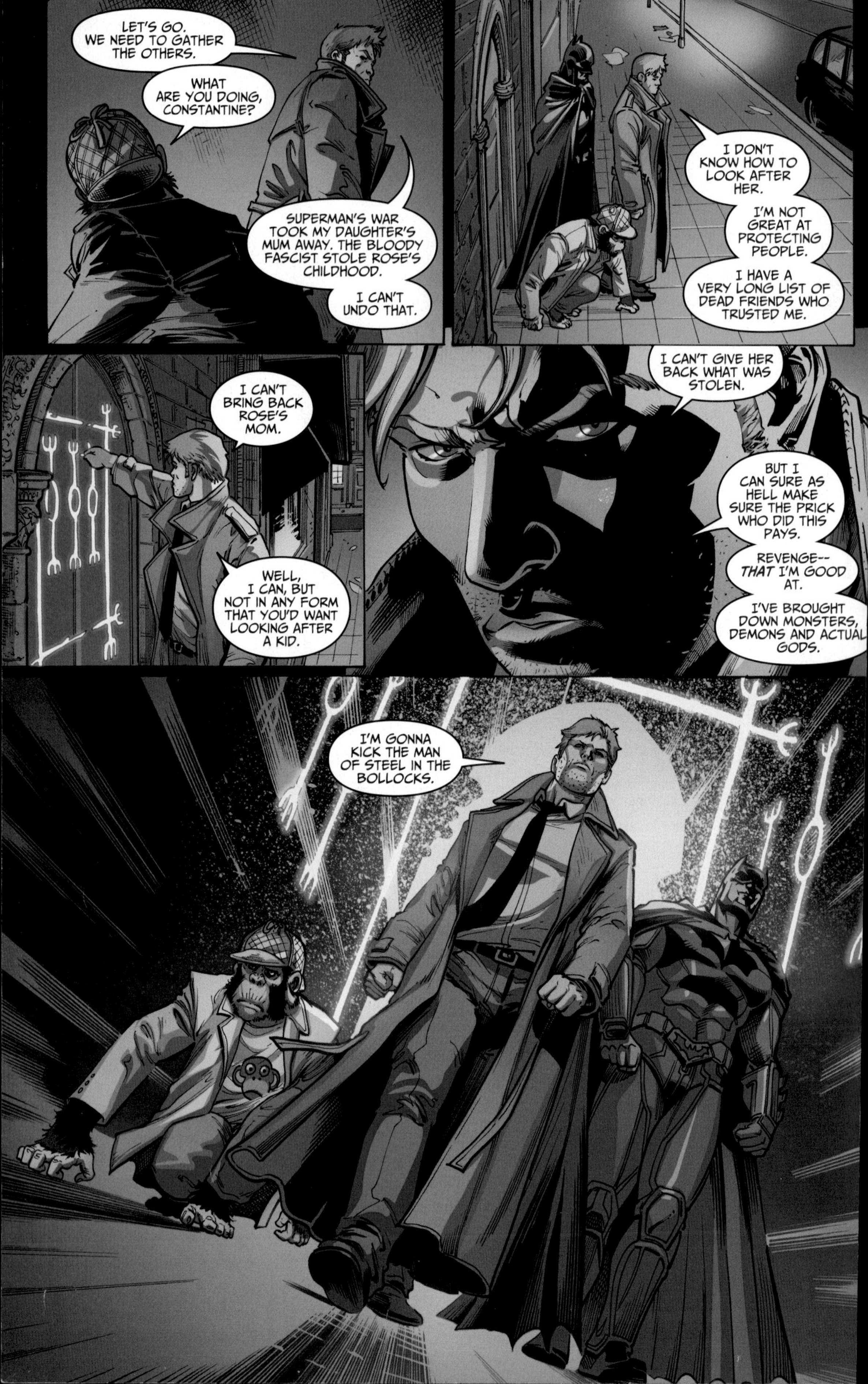
LET'S GO. WE NEED TO GATHER THE OTHERS.
WHAT ARE YOU DOING, CONSTANTINE?
SUPERMAN'S WAR TOOK MY DAUGHTER'S MUM AWAY. THE BLOODY FASCIST STOLE ROSE'S CHILDHOOD.
I CAN'T UNDO THAT.
I DON'T KNOW HOW TO LOOK AFTER HER.
I'M NOT GREAT AT PROTECTING PEOPLE.
I HAVE A VERY LONG LIST OF DEAD FRIENDS WHO TRUSTED ME.
I CAN'T BRING BACK ROSE'S MOM.
WELL, I CAN, BUT NOT IN ANY FORM THAT YOU'D WANT LOOKING AFTER A KID.
I CAN'T GIVE HER BACK WHAT WAS STOLEN.
BUT I CAN SURE AS HELL MAKE SURE THE PRICK WHO DID THIS PAYS.
REVENGE-- THAT I'M GOOD AT.
I'VE BROUGHT DOWN MONSTERS, DEMONS AND ACTUAL GODS.
I'M GONNA KICK THE MAN OF STEEL IN THE BOLLOCKS.

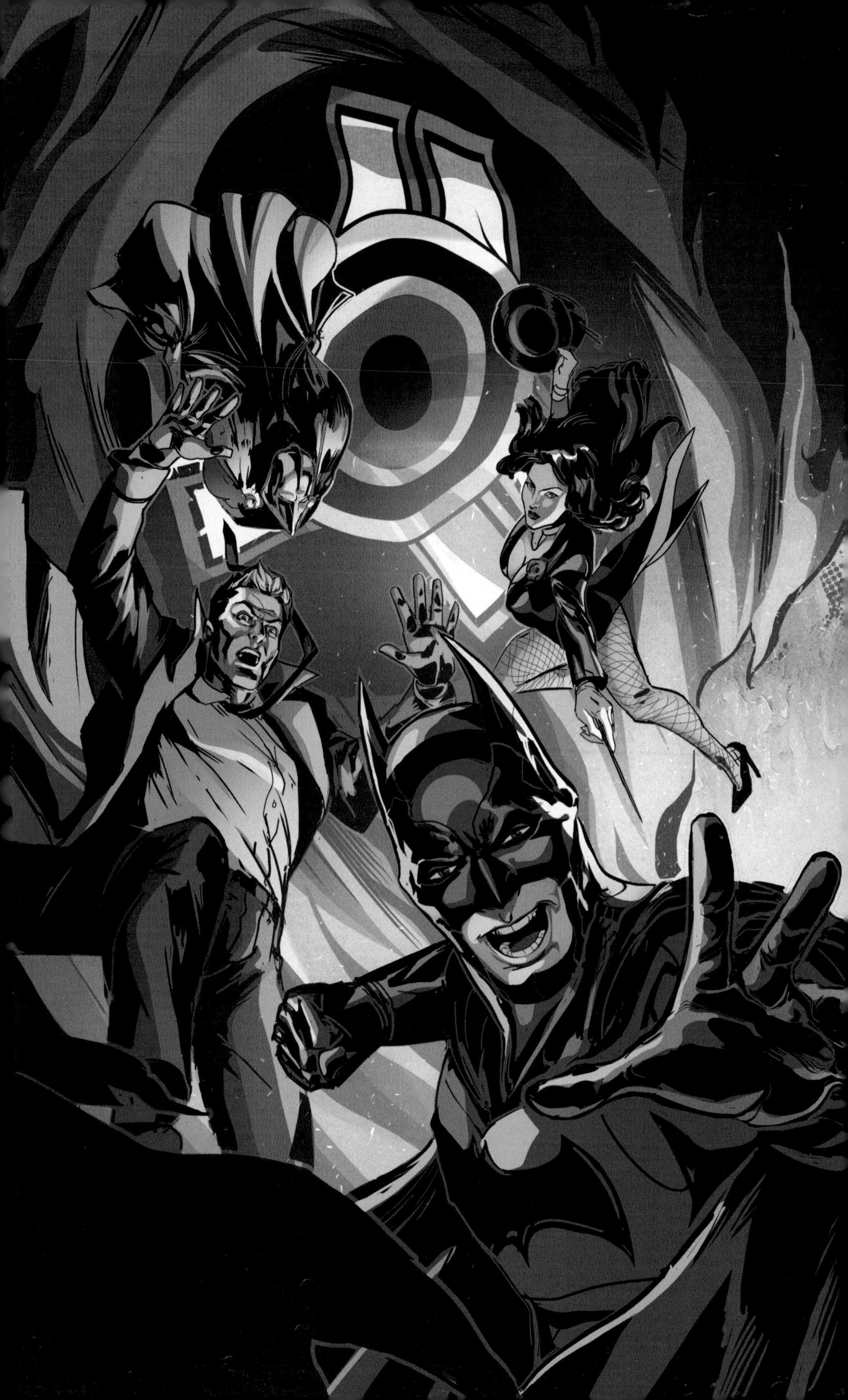

"Gathering Forces" **Mike S. Miller** Artist **J. Nanjan** Colorist
"Spirit of Vengeance" **Bruno Redondo & Xermanico** Artists **Rex Lokus** Colorist
Cover Art by **Trevor McCarthy & Rex Lokus**

GATHERING FORCES

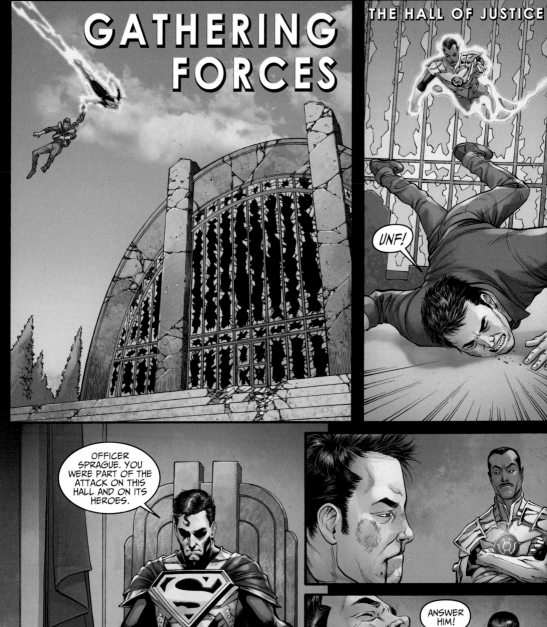

UNF!

OFFICER SPRAGUE. YOU WERE PART OF THE ATTACK ON THIS HALL AND ON ITS HEROES.

ANSWER HIM!

HNNG!

IT'S OKAY, SINESTRO.

LET HIM GO.

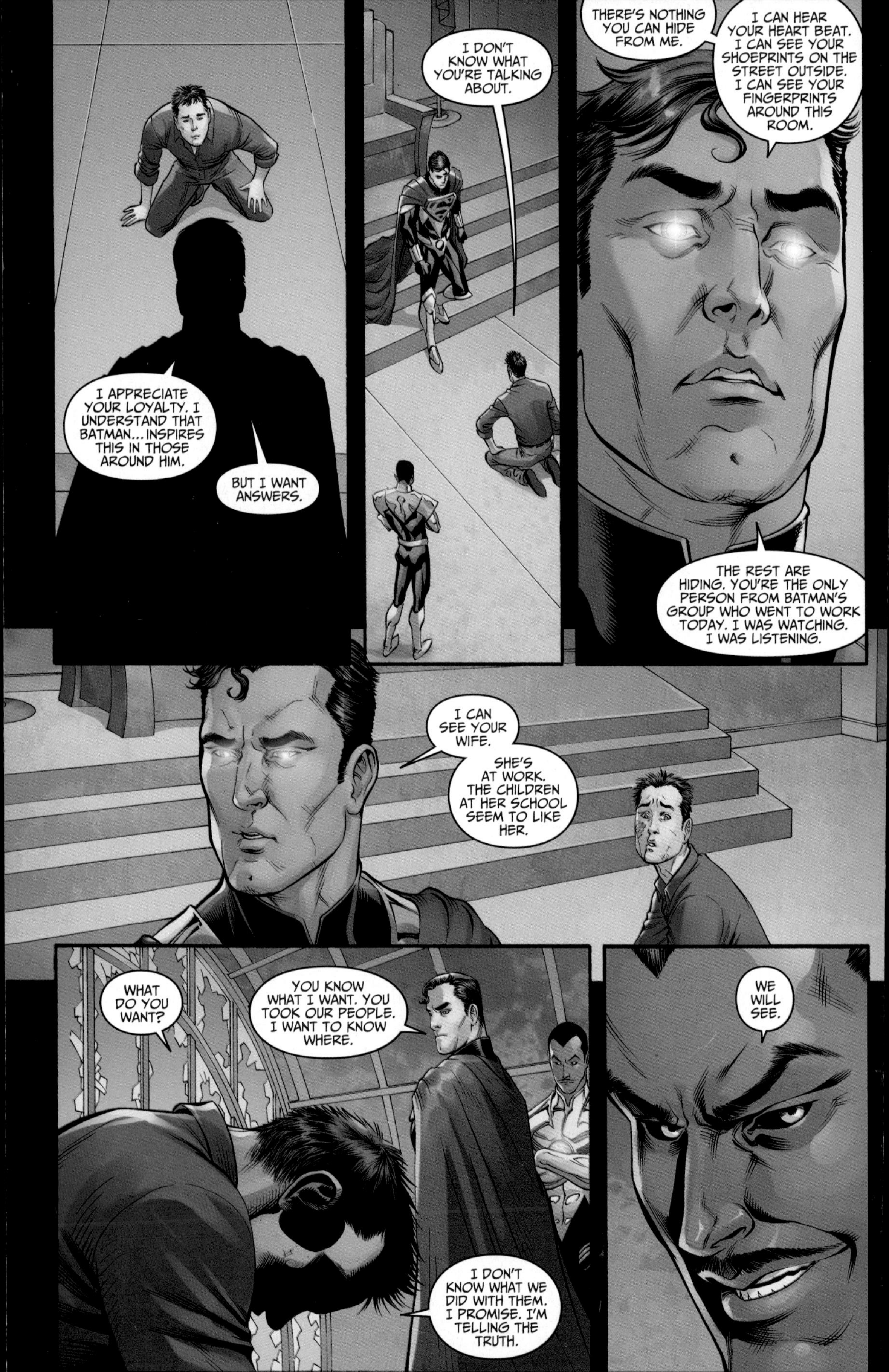
I APPRECIATE YOUR LOYALTY. I UNDERSTAND THAT BATMAN... INSPIRES THIS IN THOSE AROUND HIM.
BUT I WANT ANSWERS.
I DON'T KNOW WHAT YOU'RE TALKING ABOUT.
THERE'S NOTHING YOU CAN HIDE FROM ME.
I CAN HEAR YOUR HEART BEAT. I CAN SEE YOUR SHOEPRINTS ON THE STREET OUTSIDE. I CAN SEE YOUR FINGERPRINTS AROUND THIS ROOM.
THE REST ARE HIDING. YOU'RE THE ONLY PERSON FROM BATMAN'S GROUP WHO WENT TO WORK TODAY. I WAS WATCHING. I WAS LISTENING.
I CAN SEE YOUR WIFE.
SHE'S AT WORK. THE CHILDREN AT HER SCHOOL SEEM TO LIKE HER.
WHAT DO YOU WANT?
YOU KNOW WHAT I WANT. YOU TOOK OUR PEOPLE. I WANT TO KNOW WHERE.
I DON'T KNOW WHAT WE DID WITH THEM. I PROMISE. I'M TELLING THE TRUTH.
WE WILL SEE.

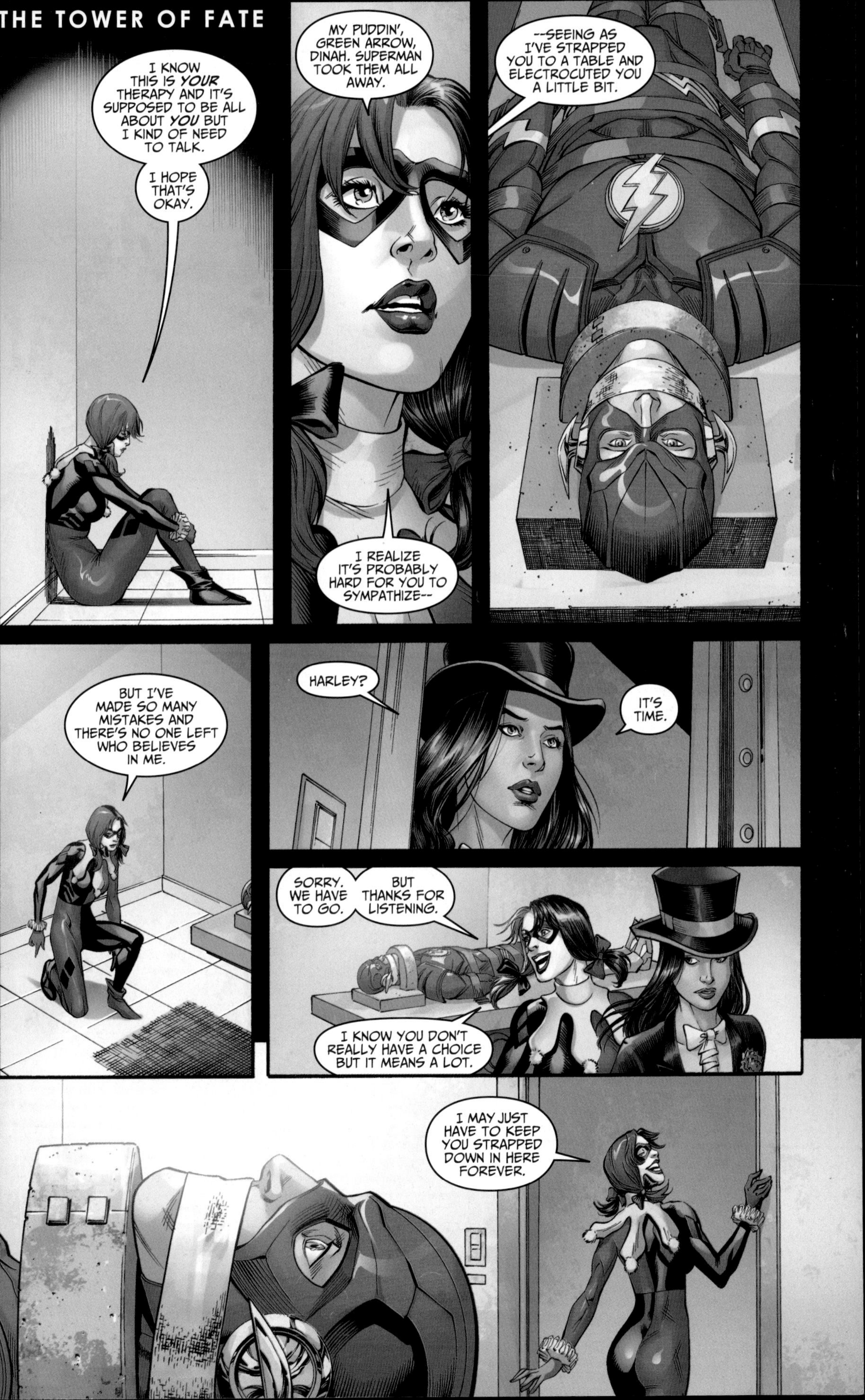
I KNOW THIS IS YOUR THERAPY AND IT'S SUPPOSED TO BE ALL ABOUT YOU BUT I KIND OF NEED TO TALK.
I HOPE THAT'S OKAY.
MY PUDDIN', GREEN ARROW, DINAH. SUPERMAN TOOK THEM ALL AWAY.
I REALIZE IT'S PROBABLY HARD FOR YOU TO SYMPATHIZE--
--SEEING AS I'VE STRAPPED YOU TO A TABLE AND ELECTROCUTED YOU A LITTLE BIT.
BUT I'VE MADE SO MANY MISTAKES AND THERE'S NO ONE LEFT WHO BELIEVES IN ME.
HARLEY?
IT'S TIME.
SORRY. WE HAVE TO GO.
BUT THANKS FOR LISTENING.
I KNOW YOU DON'T REALLY HAVE A CHOICE BUT IT MEANS A LOT.
I MAY JUST HAVE TO KEEP YOU STRAPPED DOWN IN HERE FOREVER.

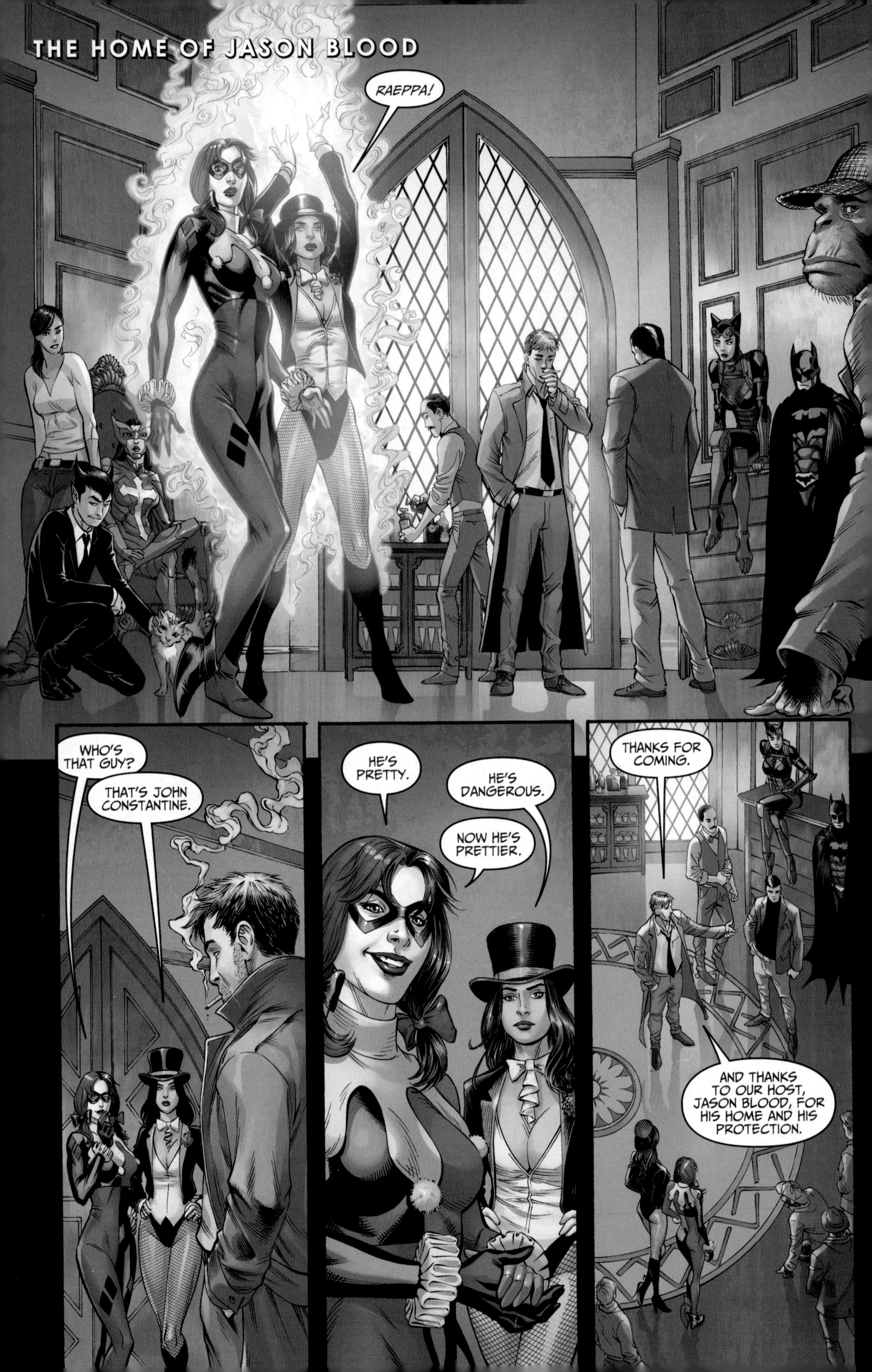
THE HOME OF JASON BLOOD
RAEPPA!
WHO'S THAT GUY?
THAT'S JOHN CONSTANTINE.
HE'S PRETTY.
HE'S DANGEROUS.
NOW HE'S PRETTIER.
THANKS FOR COMING.
AND THANKS TO OUR HOST, JASON BLOOD, FOR HIS HOME AND HIS PROTECTION.

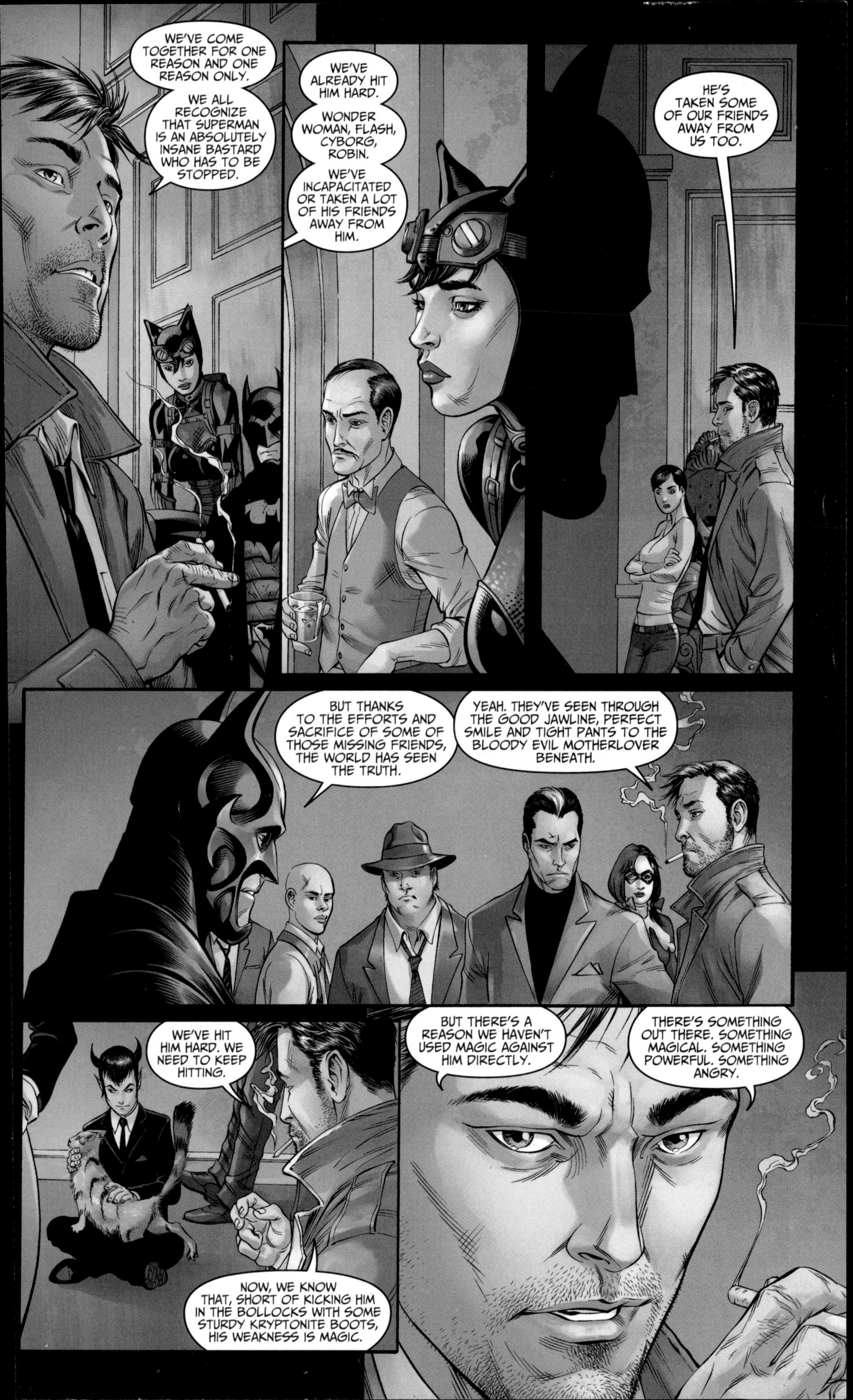

WE'VE COME TOGETHER FOR ONE REASON AND ONE REASON ONLY.
WE ALL RECOGNIZE THAT SUPERMAN IS AN ABSOLUTELY INSANE BASTARD WHO HAS TO BE STOPPED.
WE'VE ALREADY HIT HIM HARD.
WONDER WOMAN, FLASH, CYBORG, ROBIN.
WE'VE INCAPACITATED OR TAKEN A LOT OF HIS FRIENDS AWAY FROM HIM.
HE'S TAKEN SOME OF OUR FRIENDS AWAY FROM US TOO.
BUT THANKS TO THE EFFORTS AND SACRIFICE OF SOME OF THOSE MISSING FRIENDS, THE WORLD HAS SEEN THE TRUTH.
YEAH. THEY'VE SEEN THROUGH THE GOOD JAWLINE, PERFECT SMILE AND TIGHT PANTS TO THE BLOODY EVIL MOTHERLOVER BENEATH.
WE'VE HIT HIM HARD. WE NEED TO KEEP HITTING.
NOW, WE KNOW THAT, SHORT OF KICKING HIM IN THE BOLLOCKS WITH SOME STURDY KRYPTONITE BOOTS, HIS WEAKNESS IS MAGIC.
BUT THERE'S A REASON WE HAVEN'T USED MAGIC AGAINST HIM DIRECTLY.
THERE'S SOMETHING OUT THERE. SOMETHING MAGICAL. SOMETHING POWERFUL. SOMETHING ANGRY.

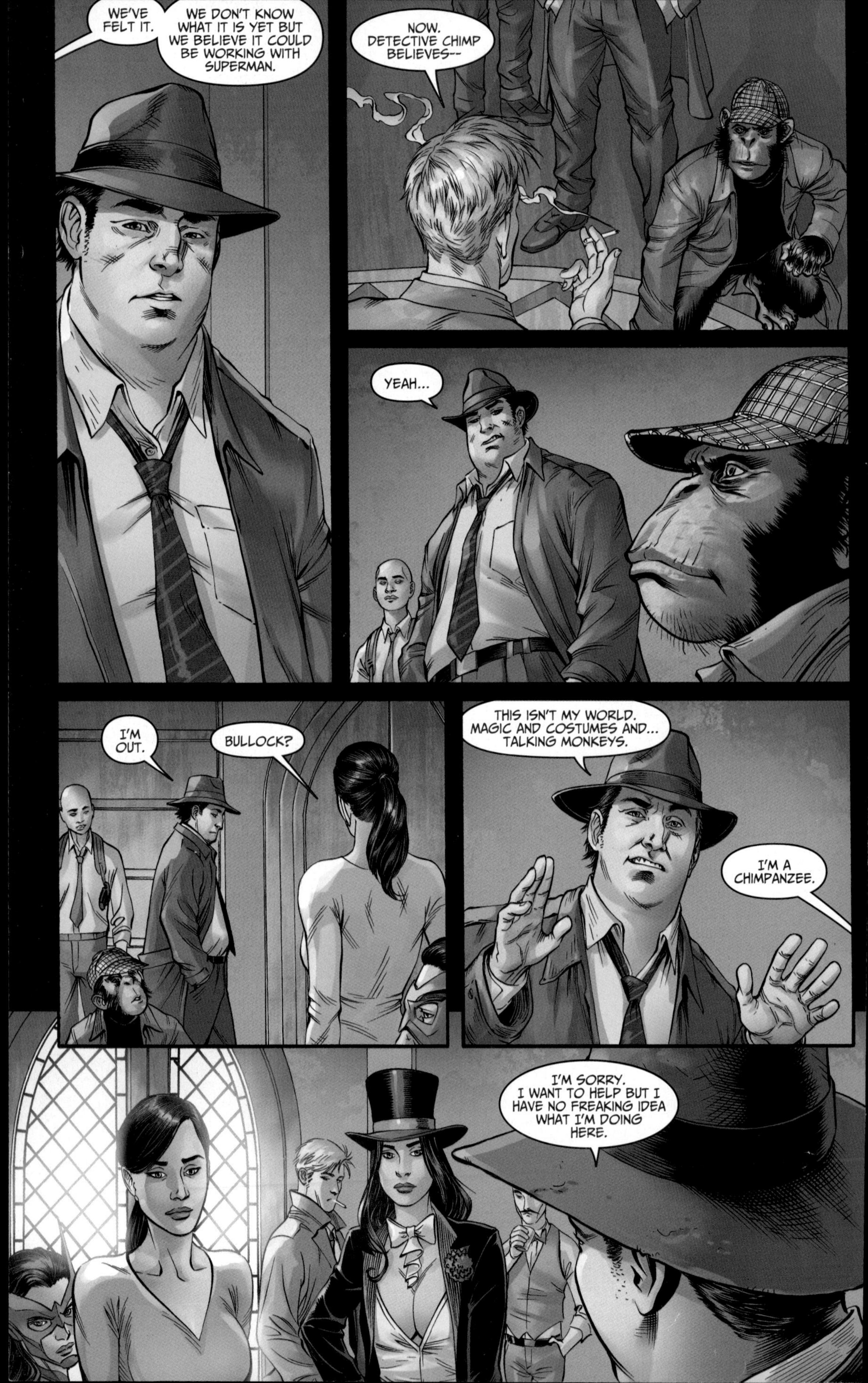
WE'VE FELT IT.
WE DON'T KNOW WHAT IT IS YET BUT WE BELIEVE IT COULD BE WORKING WITH SUPERMAN.
NOW. DETECTIVE CHIMP BELIEVES--
YEAH...
I'M OUT.
BULLOCK?
THIS ISN'T MY WORLD. MAGIC AND COSTUMES AND... TALKING MONKEYS.
I'M A CHIMPANZEE.
I'M SORRY. I WANT TO HELP BUT I HAVE NO FREAKING IDEA WHAT I'M DOING HERE.

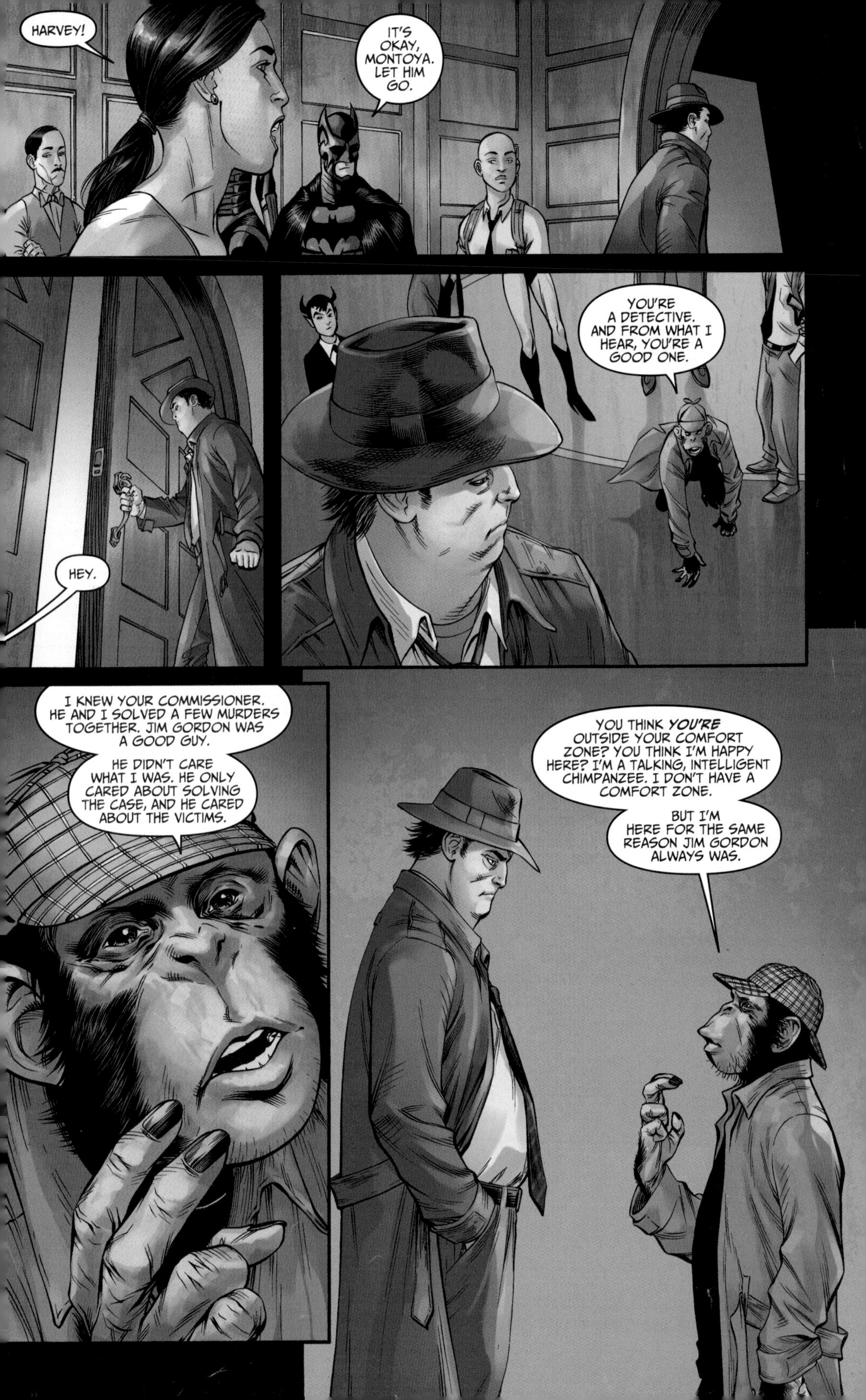

HARVEY!
IT'S OKAY, MONTOYA. LET HIM GO.
HEY.
YOU'RE A DETECTIVE. AND FROM WHAT I HEAR, YOU'RE A GOOD ONE.
I KNEW YOUR COMMISSIONER. HE AND I SOLVED A FEW MURDERS TOGETHER. JIM GORDON WAS A GOOD GUY.
HE DIDN'T CARE WHAT I WAS. HE ONLY CARED ABOUT SOLVING THE CASE, AND HE CARED ABOUT THE VICTIMS.
YOU THINK *YOU'RE* OUTSIDE YOUR COMFORT ZONE? YOU THINK I'M HAPPY HERE? I'M A TALKING, INTELLIGENT CHIMPANZEE. I DON'T HAVE A COMFORT ZONE.
BUT I'M HERE FOR THE SAME REASON JIM GORDON ALWAYS WAS.

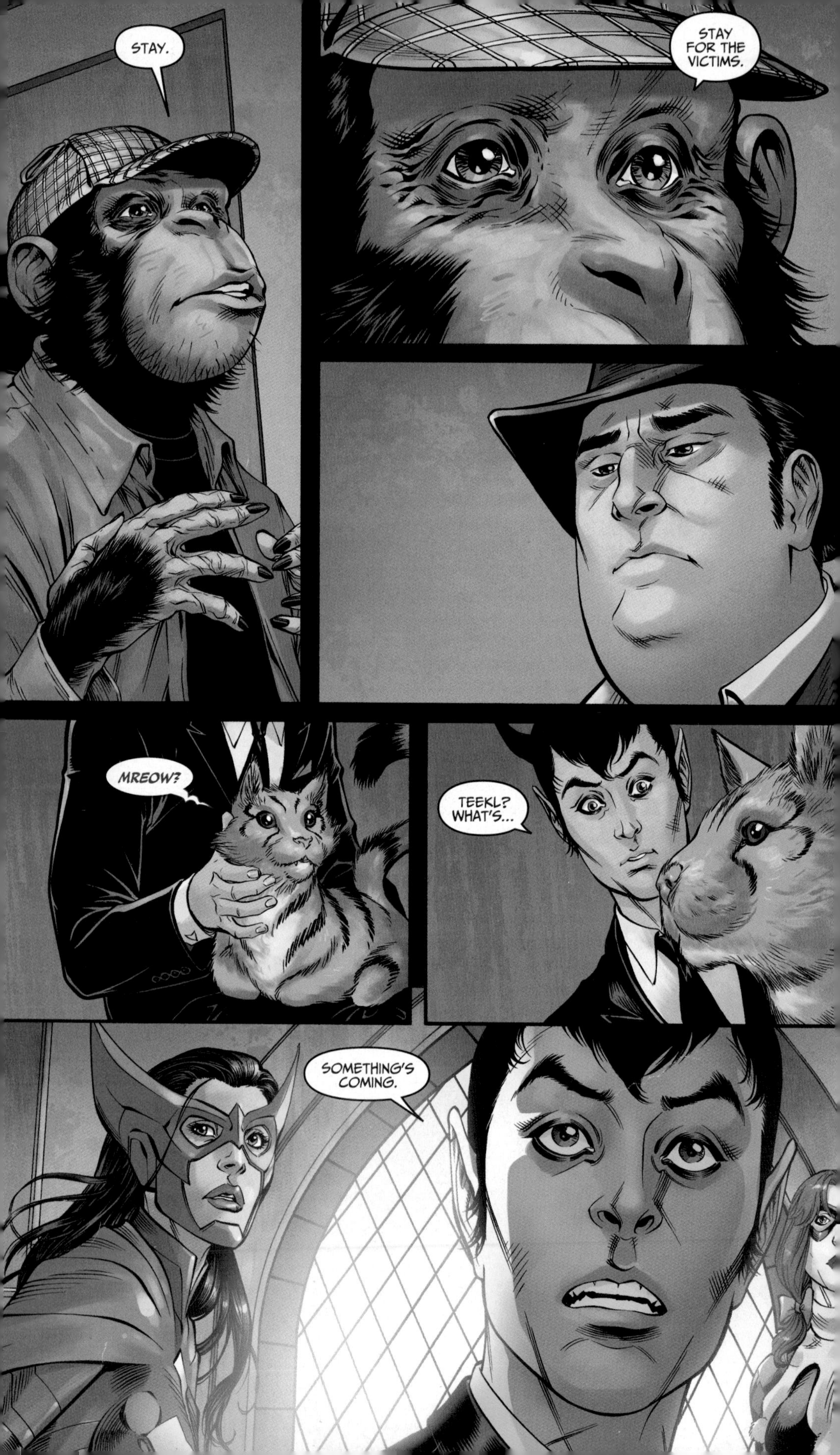
STAY.
STAY FOR THE VICTIMS.
MREOW?
TEEKL? WHAT'S...
SOMETHING'S COMING.

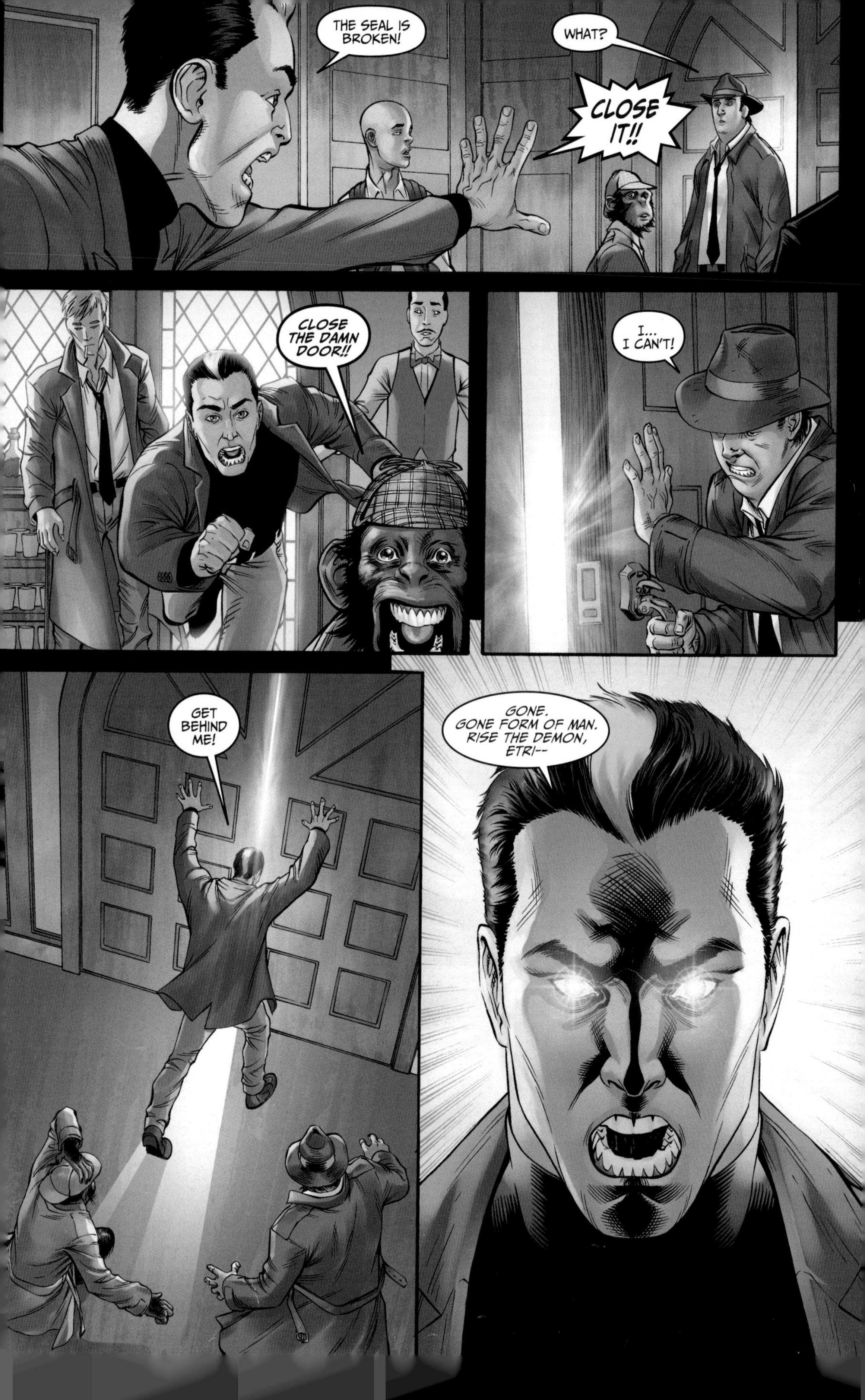
THE SEAL IS BROKEN!
WHAT?
CLOSE IT!!
CLOSE THE DAMN DOOR!!
I... I CAN'T!
GET BEHIND ME!
GONE. GONE FORM OF MAN. RISE THE DEMON, ETRI--

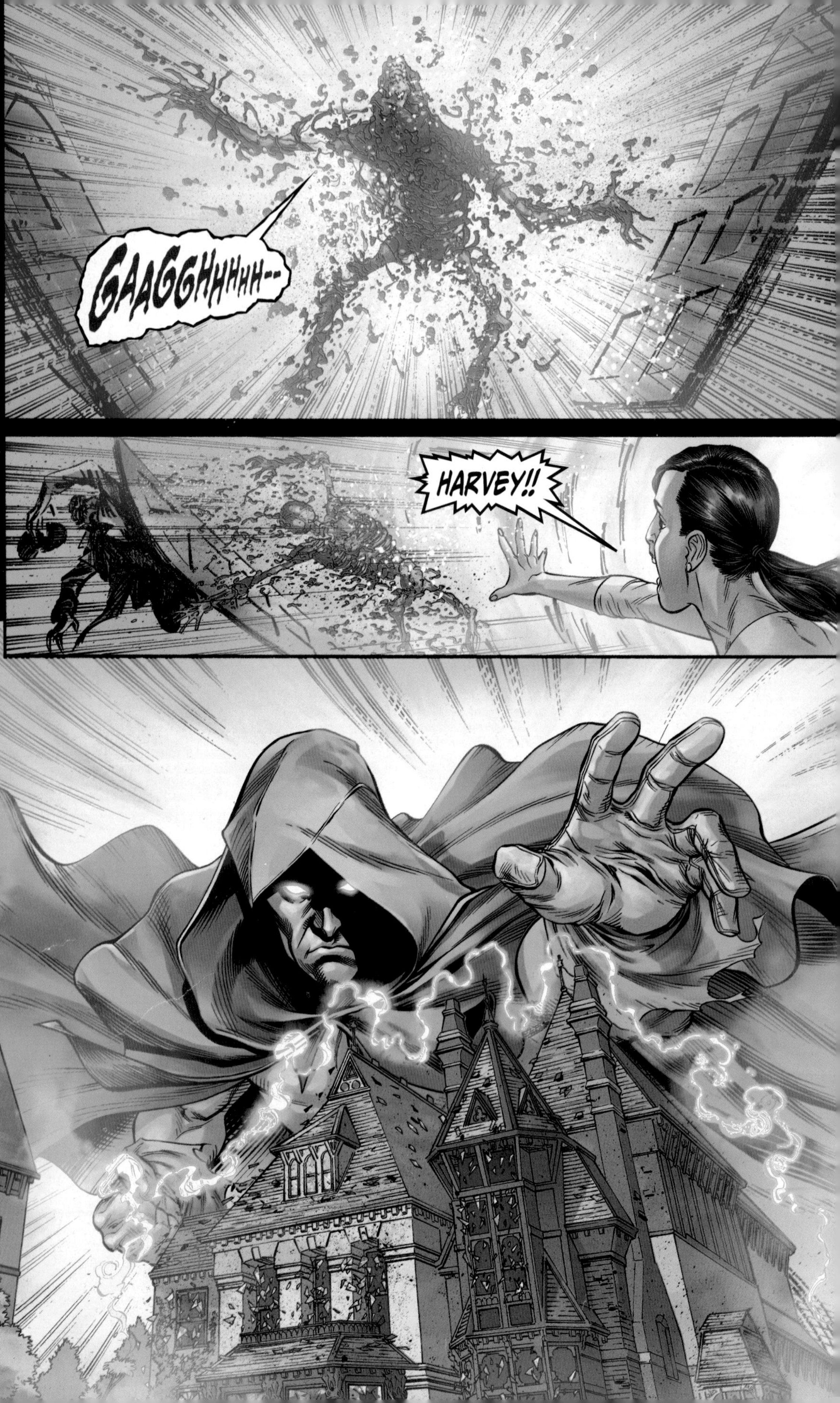
GAAGGHHHH--
HARVEY!!

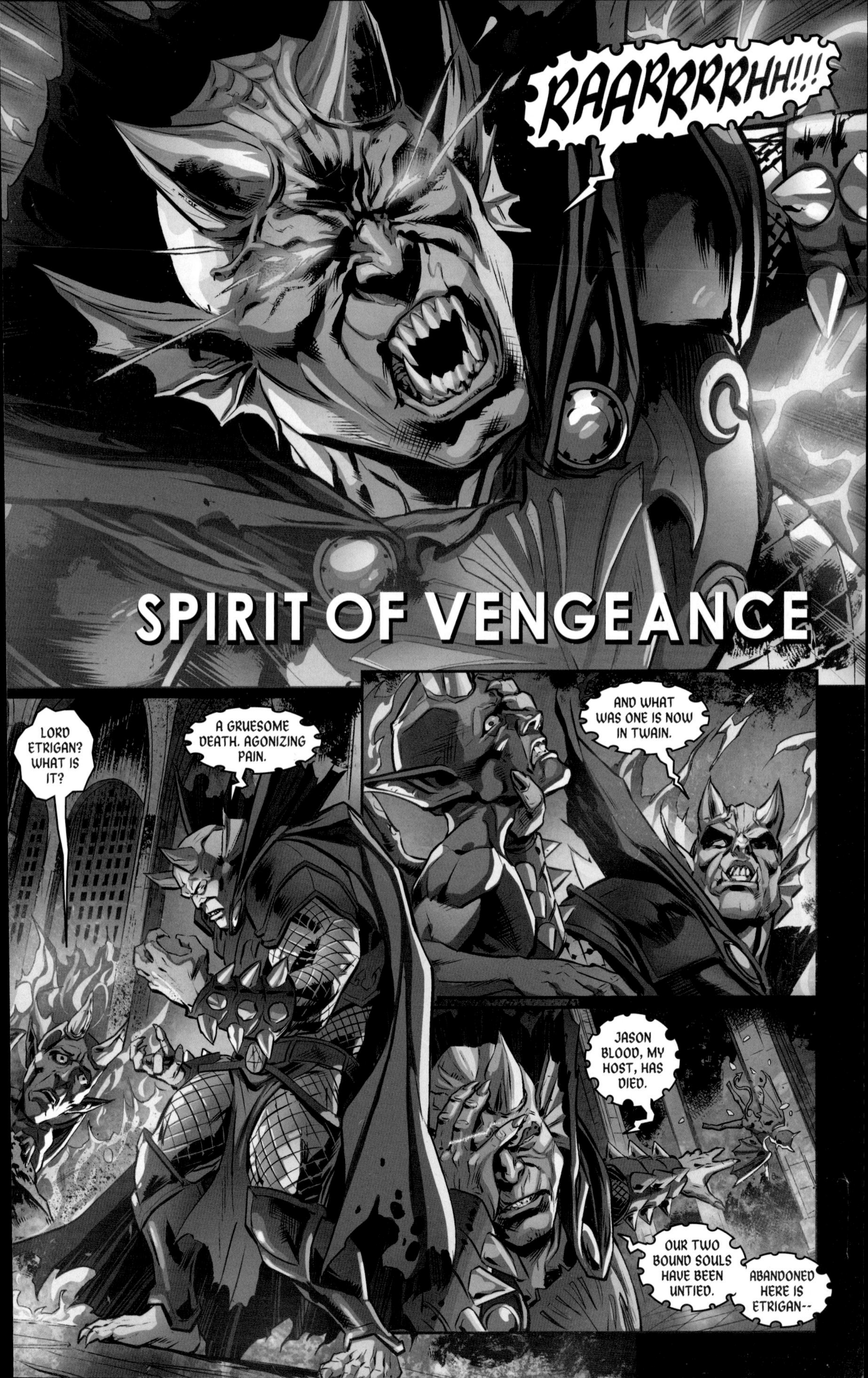
RAARRRRHH!!!
SPIRIT OF VENGEANCE
LORD ETRIGAN? WHAT IS IT?
A GRUESOME DEATH. AGONIZING PAIN.
AND WHAT WAS ONE IS NOW IN TWAIN.
JASON BLOOD, MY HOST, HAS DIED.
OUR TWO BOUND SOULS HAVE BEEN UNTIED.
ABANDONED HERE IS ETRIGAN--

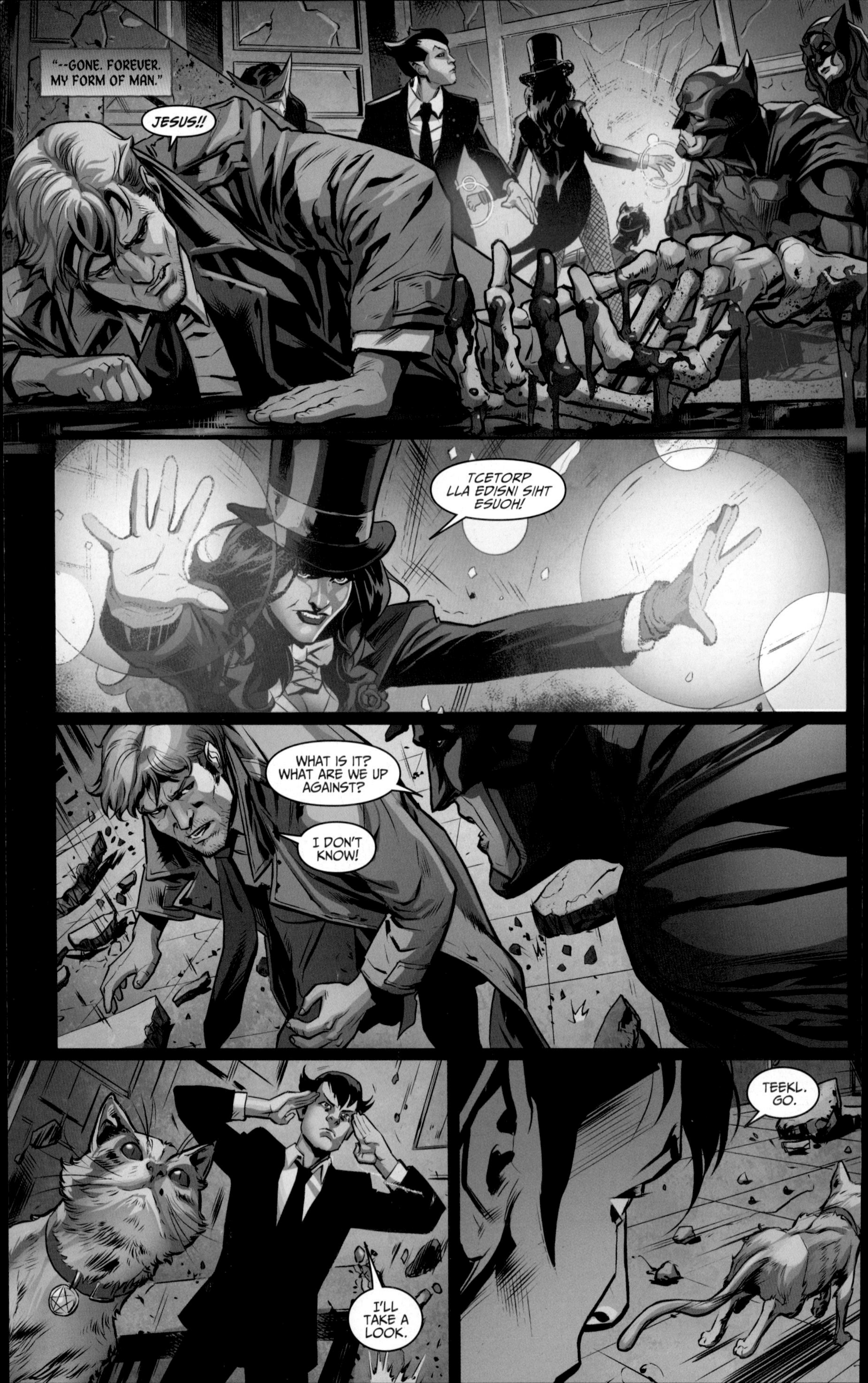
"--GONE. FOREVER. MY FORM OF MAN."
JESUS!!
TCETORP LLA EDISNI SIHT ESUOH!
WHAT IS IT? WHAT ARE WE UP AGAINST?
I DON'T KNOW!
I'LL TAKE A LOOK.
TEEKL. GO.

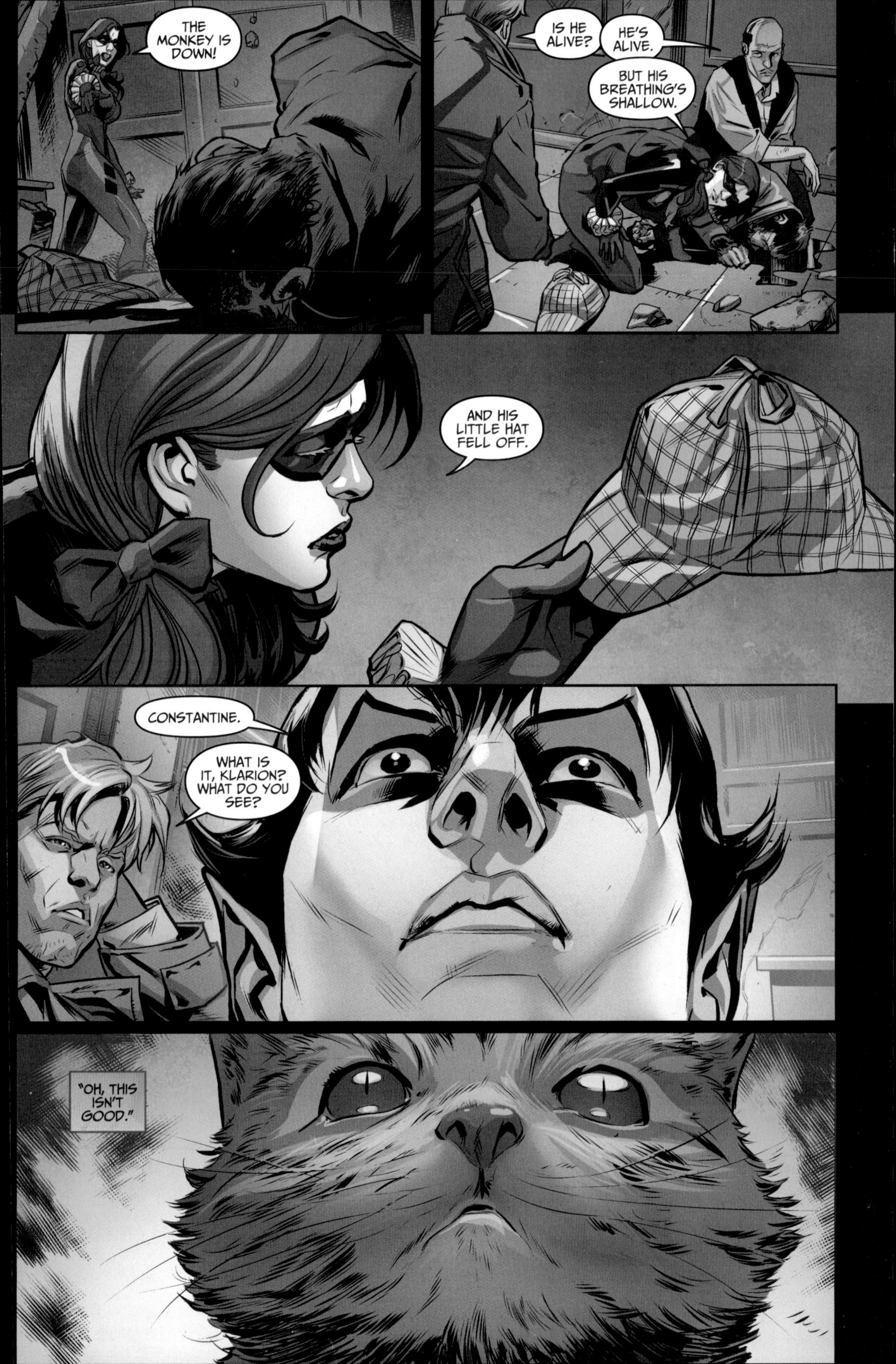
THE MONKEY IS DOWN!
IS HE ALIVE?
HE'S ALIVE.
BUT HIS BREATHING'S SHALLOW.
AND HIS LITTLE HAT FELL OFF.
CONSTANTINE.
WHAT IS IT, KLARION? WHAT DO YOU SEE?
"OH, THIS ISN'T GOOD."

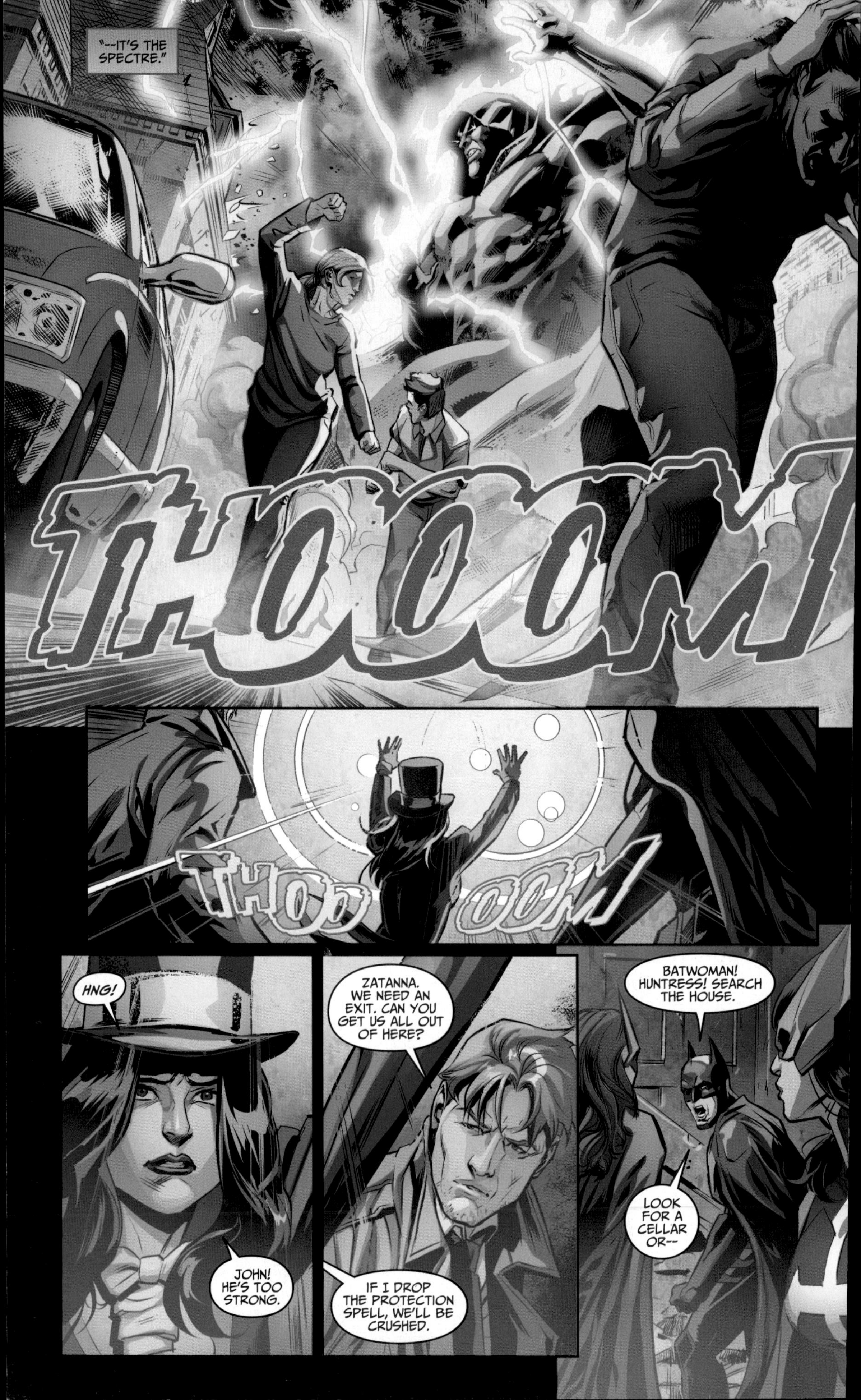
"--IT'S THE SPECTRE."
THOOOM
THOO OOM
HNG!
JOHN! HE'S TOO STRONG.
ZATANNA. WE NEED AN EXIT. CAN YOU GET US ALL OUT OF HERE?
IF I DROP THE PROTECTION SPELL, WE'LL BE CRUSHED.
BATWOMAN! HUNTRESS! SEARCH THE HOUSE.
LOOK FOR A CELLAR OR--

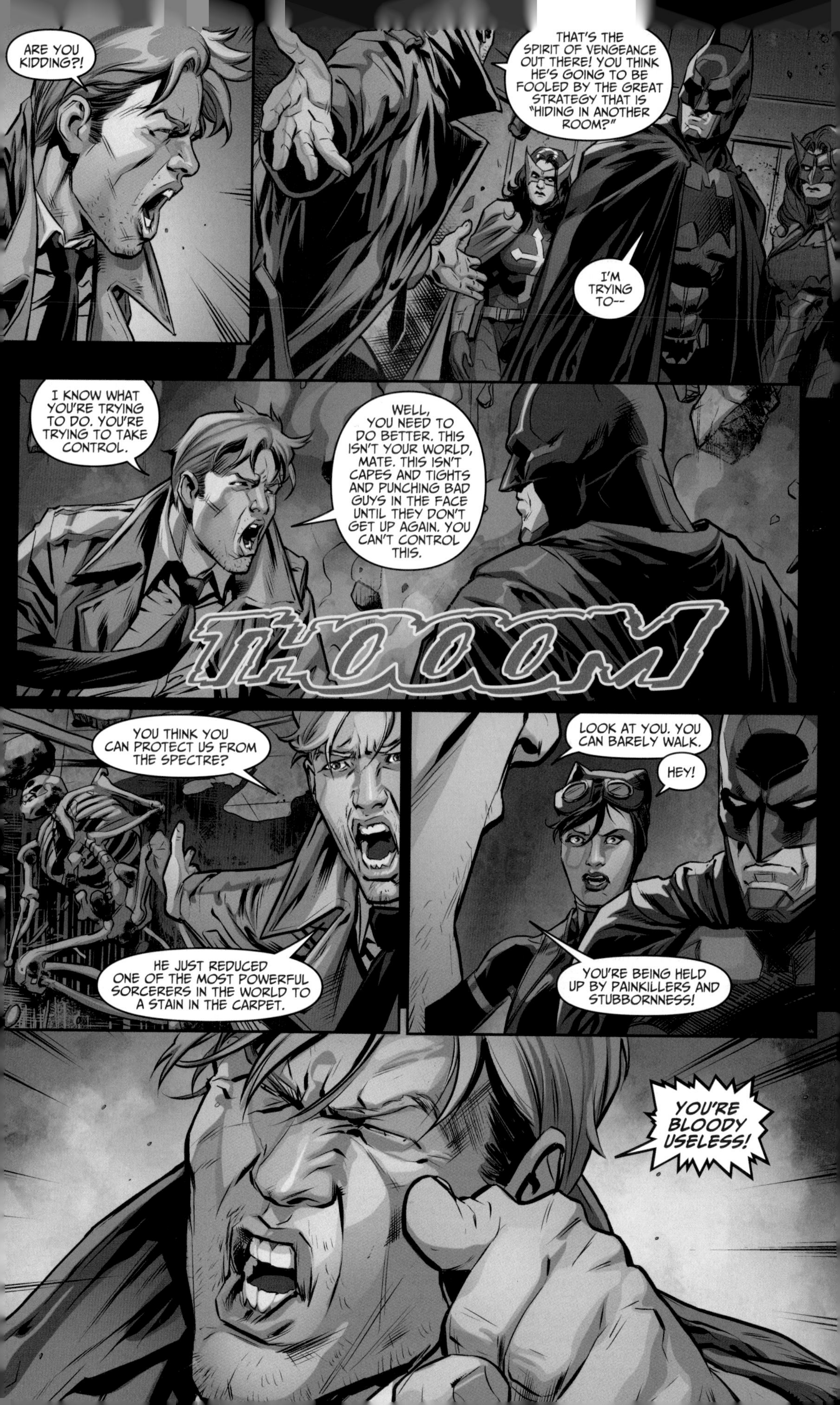
ARE YOU KIDDING?!
THAT'S THE SPIRIT OF VENGEANCE OUT THERE! YOU THINK HE'S GOING TO BE FOOLED BY THE GREAT STRATEGY THAT IS "HIDING IN ANOTHER ROOM?"
I'M TRYING TO--
I KNOW WHAT YOU'RE TRYING TO DO. YOU'RE TRYING TO TAKE CONTROL.
WELL, YOU NEED TO DO BETTER. THIS ISN'T YOUR WORLD, MATE. THIS ISN'T CAPES AND TIGHTS AND PUNCHING BAD GUYS IN THE FACE UNTIL THEY DON'T GET UP AGAIN. YOU CAN'T CONTROL THIS.
THOOOM
YOU THINK YOU CAN PROTECT US FROM THE SPECTRE?
HE JUST REDUCED ONE OF THE MOST POWERFUL SORCERERS IN THE WORLD TO A STAIN IN THE CARPET.
LOOK AT YOU. YOU CAN BARELY WALK.
HEY!
YOU'RE BEING HELD UP BY PAINKILLERS AND STUBBORNNESS!
YOU'RE BLOODY USELESS!

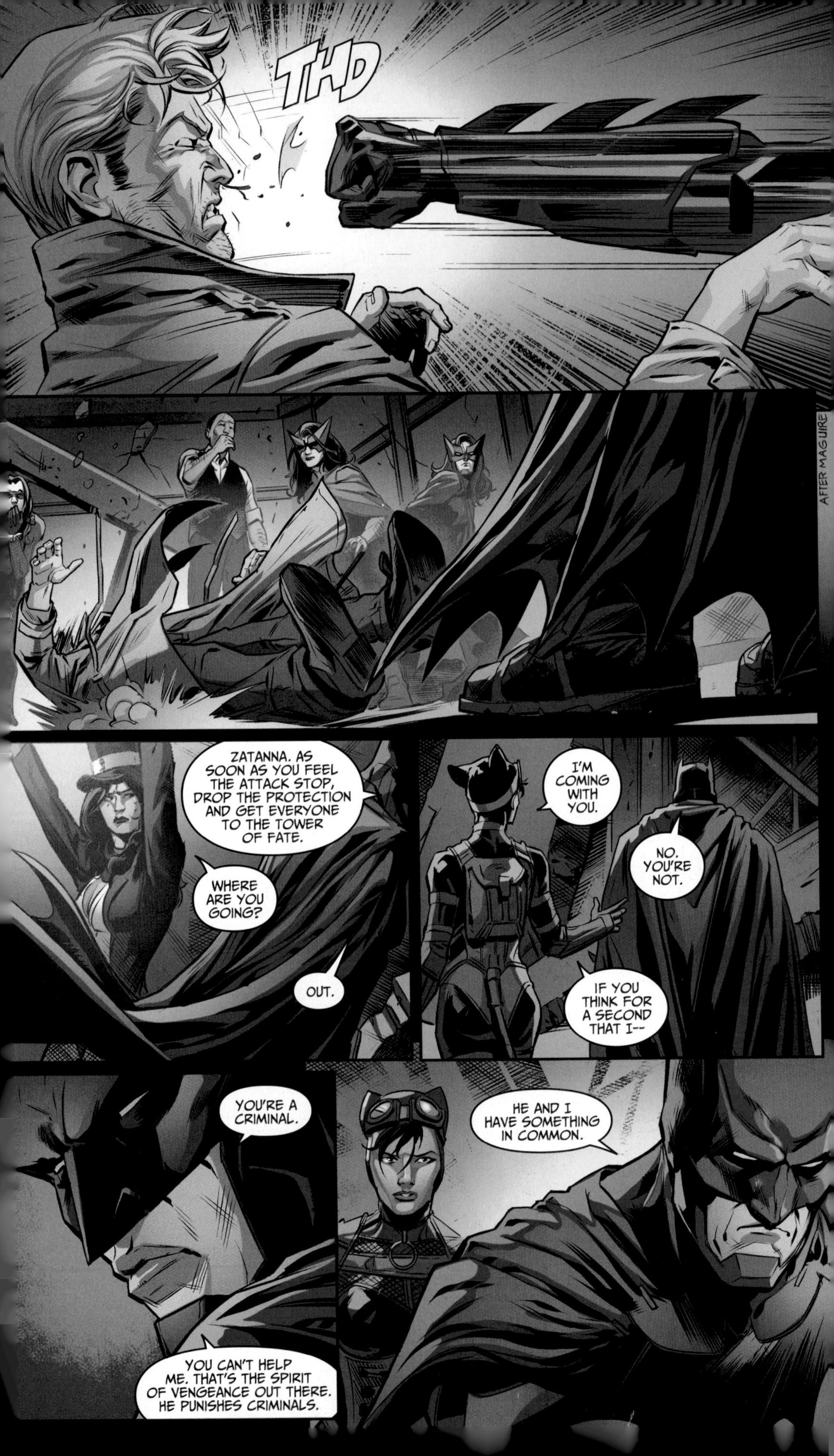

THD
AFTER MAGUIRE
ZATANNA. AS SOON AS YOU FEEL THE ATTACK STOP, DROP THE PROTECTION AND GET EVERYONE TO THE TOWER OF FATE.
WHERE ARE YOU GOING?
OUT.
I'M COMING WITH YOU.
NO. YOU'RE NOT.
IF YOU THINK FOR A SECOND THAT I--
YOU'RE A CRIMINAL.
HE AND I HAVE SOMETHING IN COMMON.
YOU CAN'T HELP ME. THAT'S THE SPIRIT OF VENGEANCE OUT THERE. HE PUNISHES CRIMINALS.

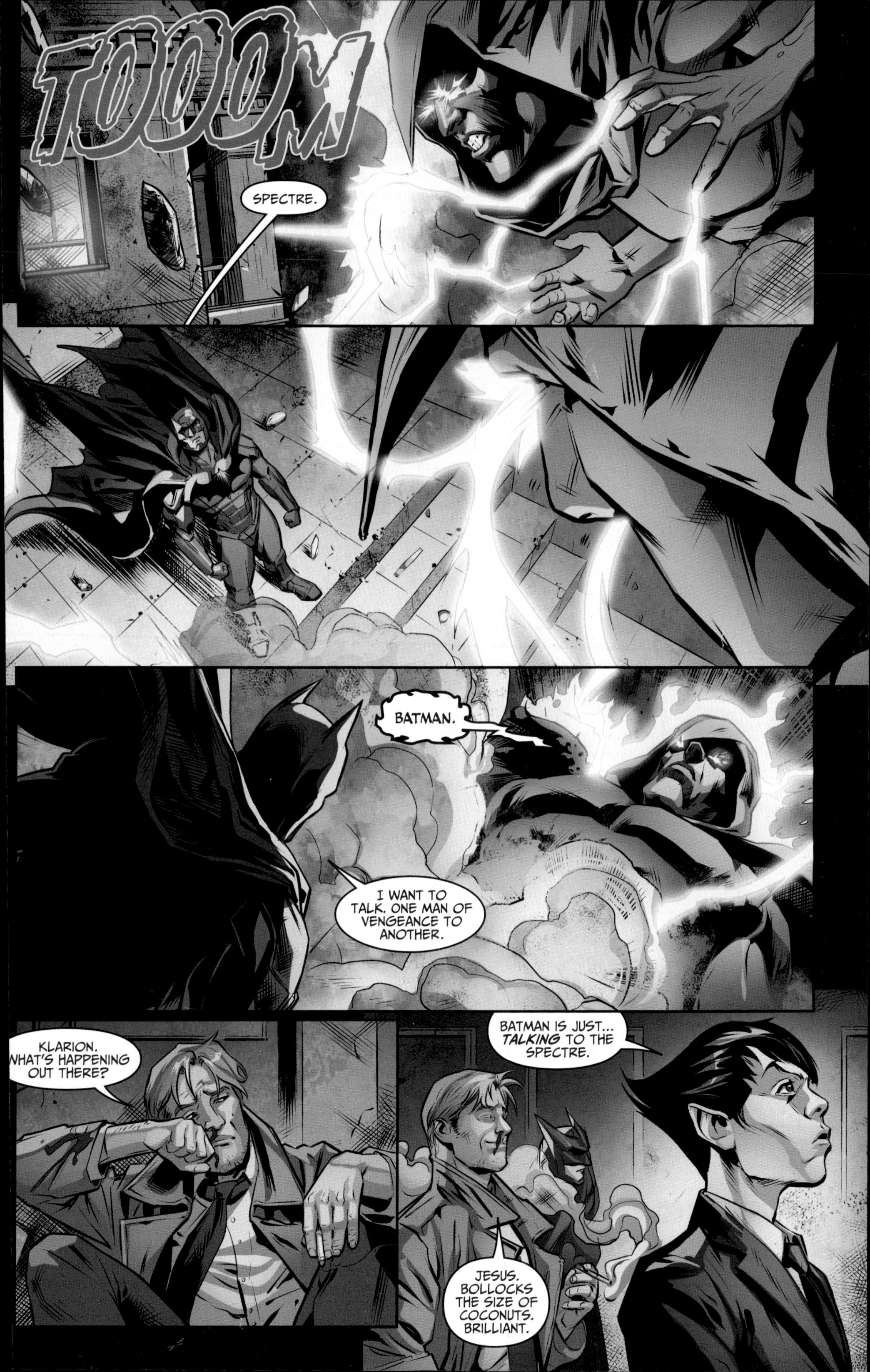
TOOOOM
SPECTRE.
BATMAN.
I WANT TO TALK. ONE MAN OF VENGEANCE TO ANOTHER.
KLARION. WHAT'S HAPPENING OUT THERE?
BATMAN IS JUST... *TALKING* TO THE SPECTRE.
JESUS. BOLLOCKS THE SIZE OF COCONUTS. BRILLIANT.

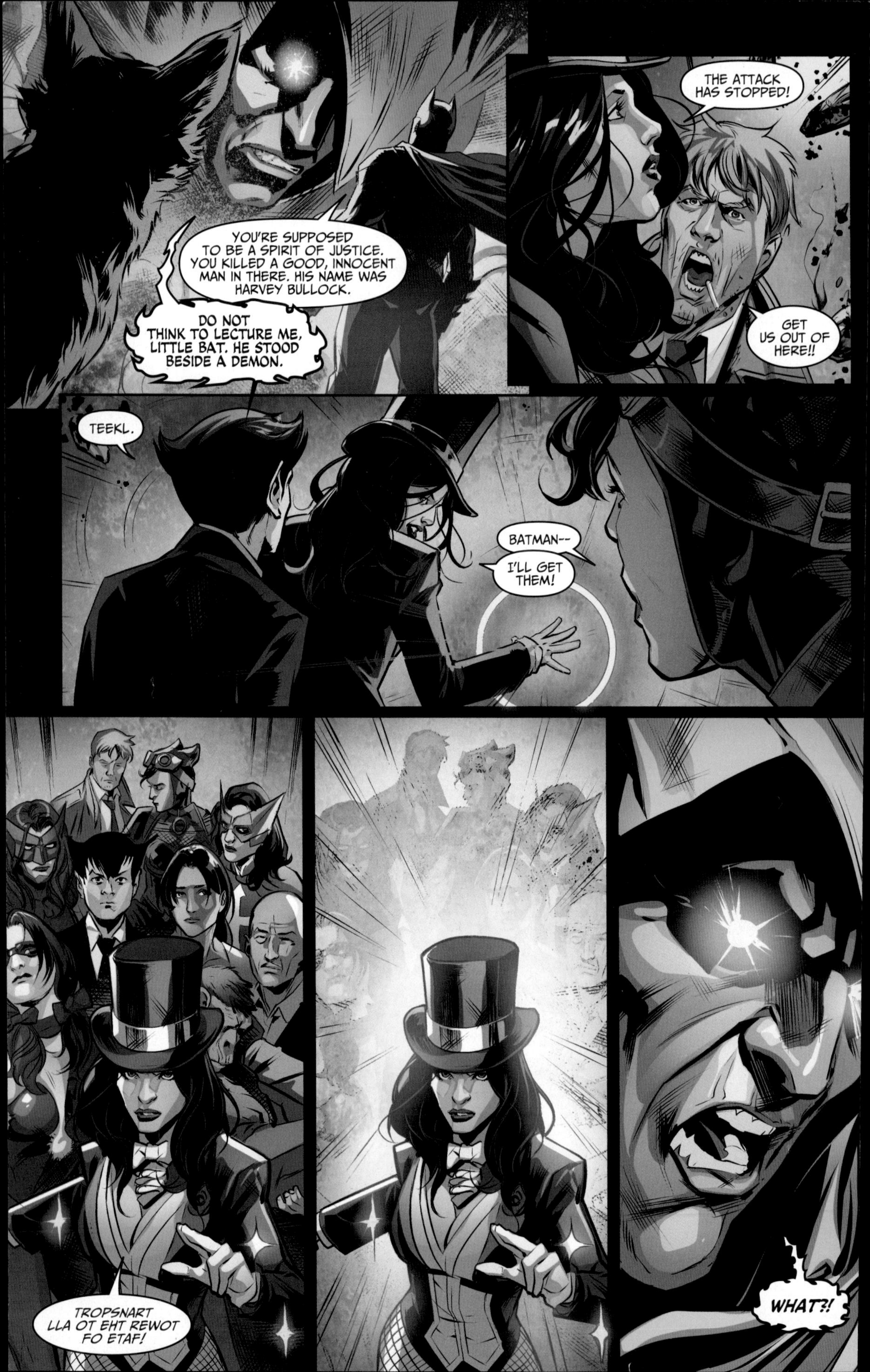
THE ATTACK HAS STOPPED!
YOU'RE SUPPOSED TO BE A SPIRIT OF JUSTICE. YOU KILLED A GOOD, INNOCENT MAN IN THERE. HIS NAME WAS HARVEY BULLOCK.
DO NOT THINK TO LECTURE ME, LITTLE BAT. HE STOOD BESIDE A DEMON.
GET US OUT OF HERE!!
TEEKL.
BATMAN--
I'LL GET THEM!
TROPSNART LLA OT EHT REWOT FO ETAF!
WHAT?!

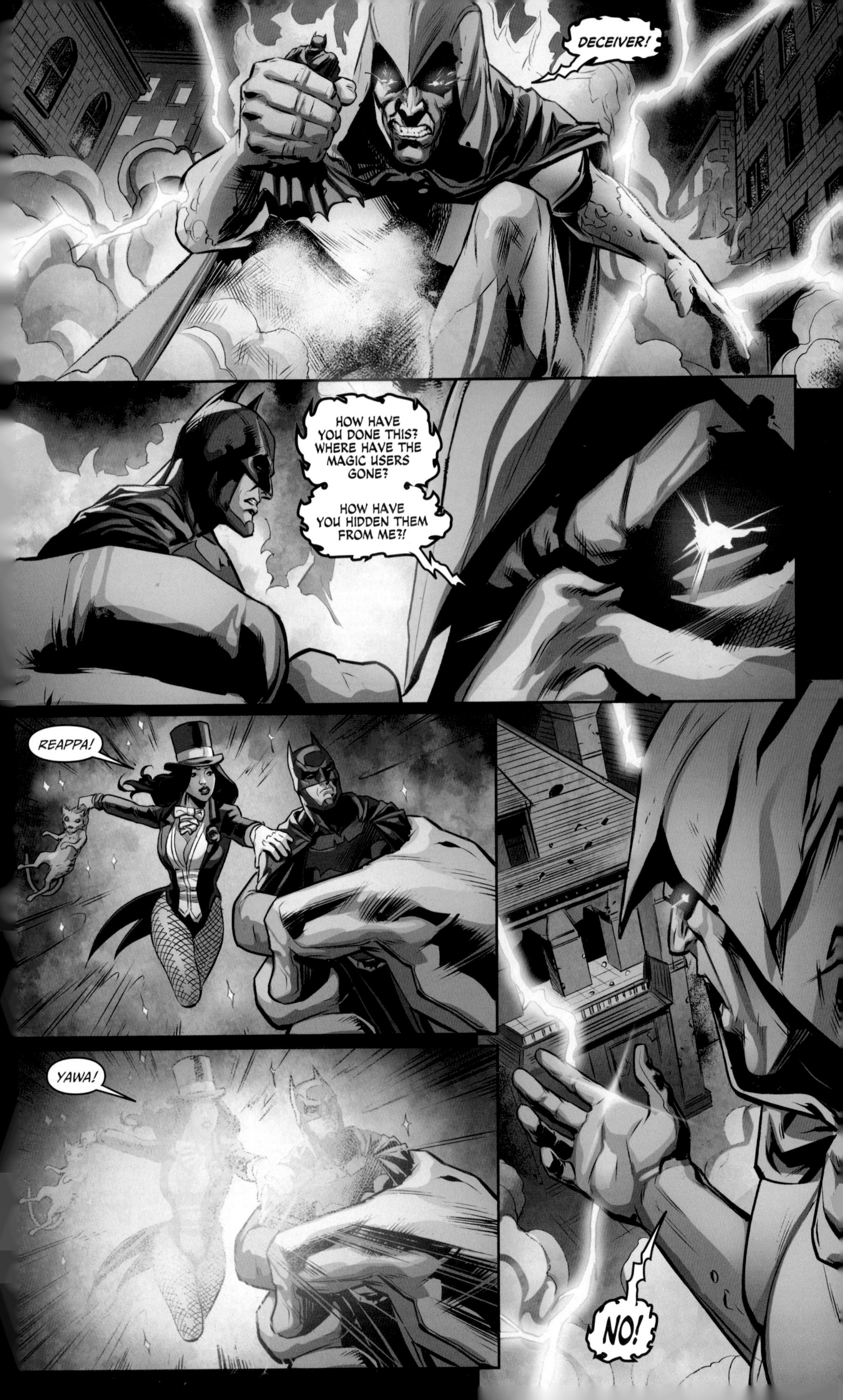
DECEIVER!
HOW HAVE YOU DONE THIS? WHERE HAVE THE MAGIC USERS GONE?
HOW HAVE YOU HIDDEN THEM FROM ME?!
REAPPA!
YAWA!
NO!

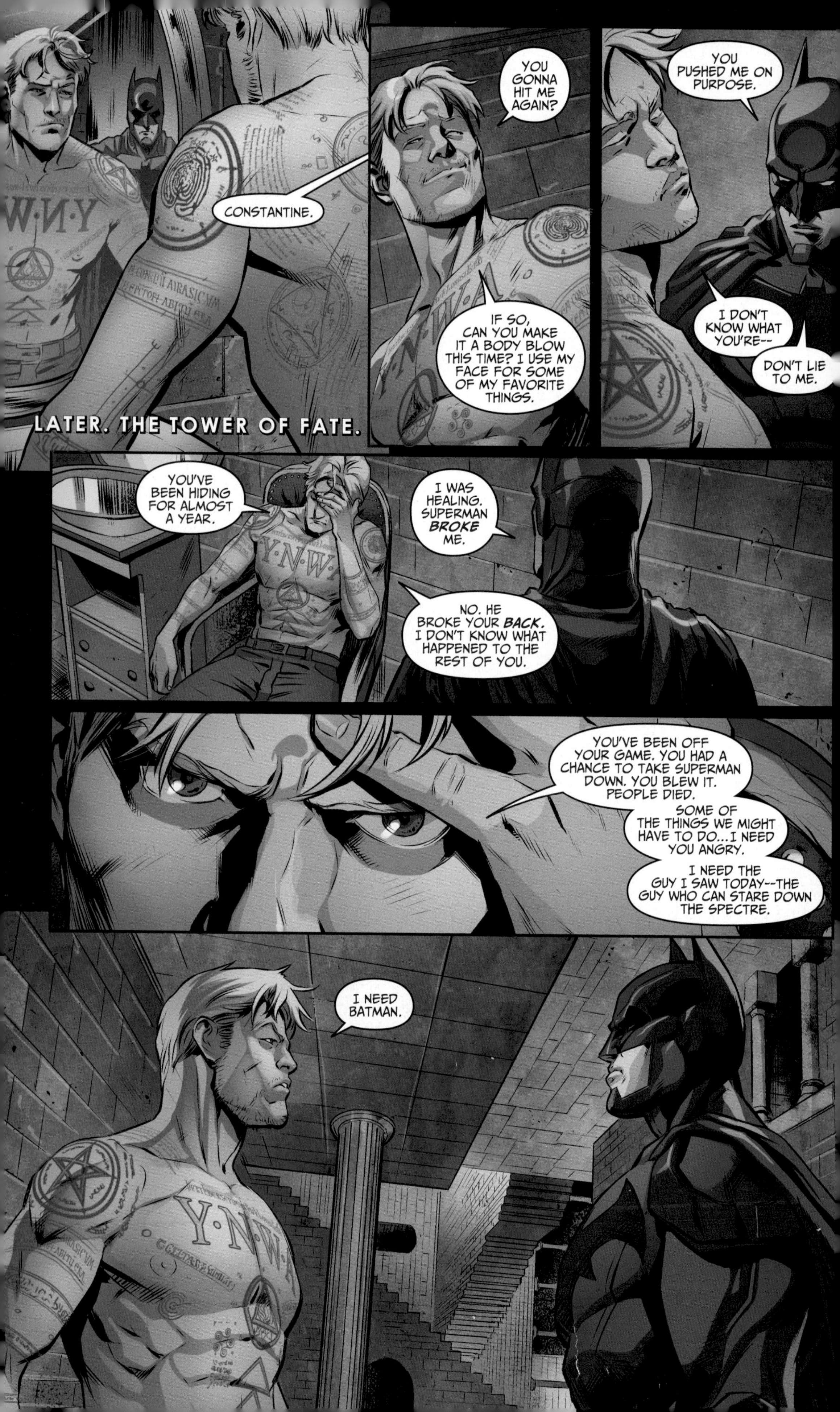
CONSTANTINE.
LATER. THE TOWER OF FATE.
YOU GONNA HIT ME AGAIN?
IF SO, CAN YOU MAKE IT A BODY BLOW THIS TIME? I USE MY FACE FOR SOME OF MY FAVORITE THINGS.
YOU PUSHED ME ON PURPOSE.
I DON'T KNOW WHAT YOU'RE--
DON'T LIE TO ME.
YOU'VE BEEN HIDING FOR ALMOST A YEAR.
I WAS HEALING. SUPERMAN BROKE ME.
NO. HE BROKE YOUR BACK. I DON'T KNOW WHAT HAPPENED TO THE REST OF YOU.
YOU'VE BEEN OFF YOUR GAME. YOU HAD A CHANCE TO TAKE SUPERMAN DOWN. YOU BLEW IT. PEOPLE DIED.
SOME OF THE THINGS WE MIGHT HAVE TO DO...I NEED YOU ANGRY.
I NEED THE GUY I SAW TODAY--THE GUY WHO CAN STARE DOWN THE SPECTRE.
I NEED BATMAN.

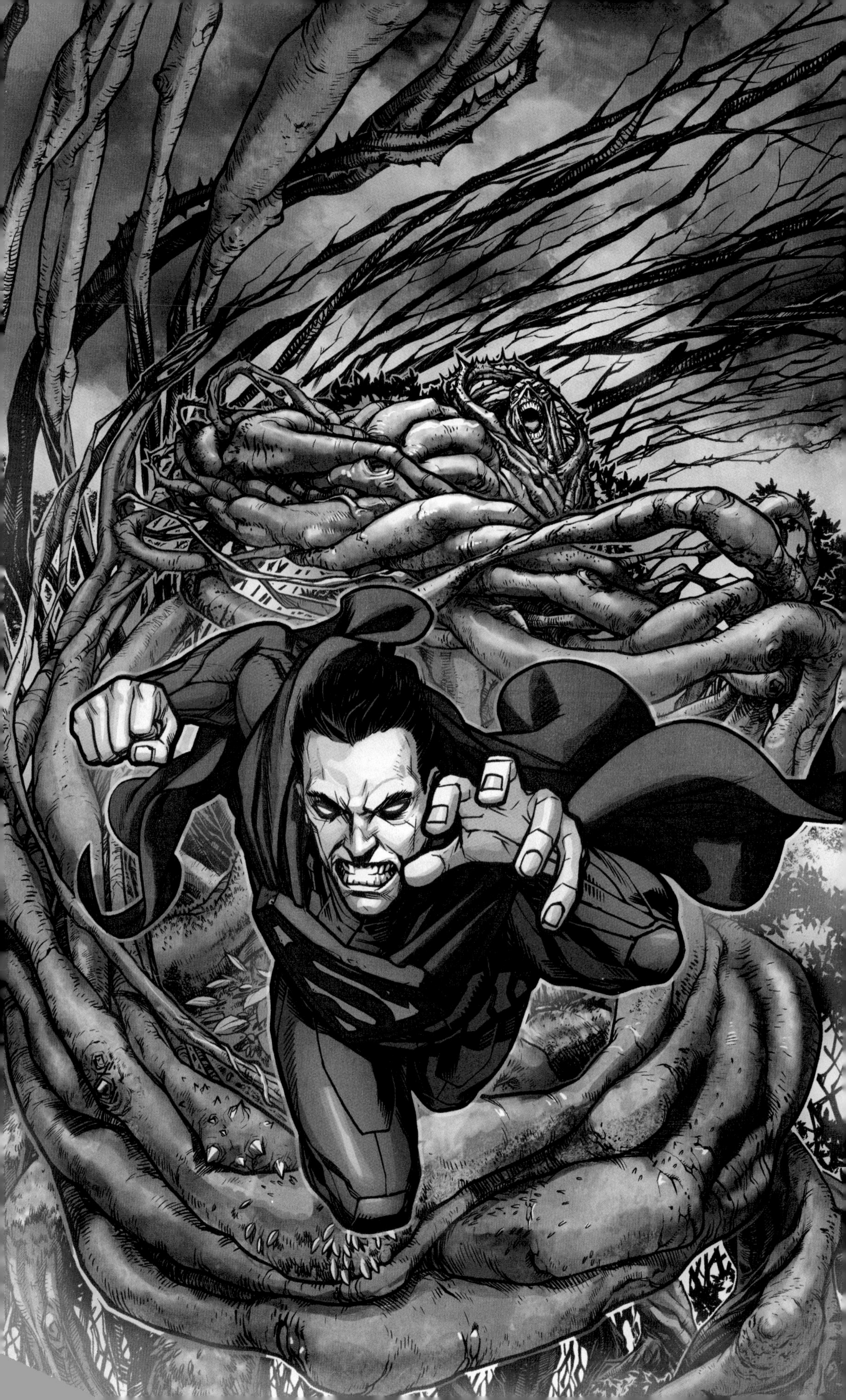

"The Coin" Mike S. Miller Artist J. Nanjan Colorist
"Xanadu" Bruno Redondo, Xermanico, & Juan Albarran Artists Rex Lokus Colorist
Cover Art by Neil Googe & Rex Lokus

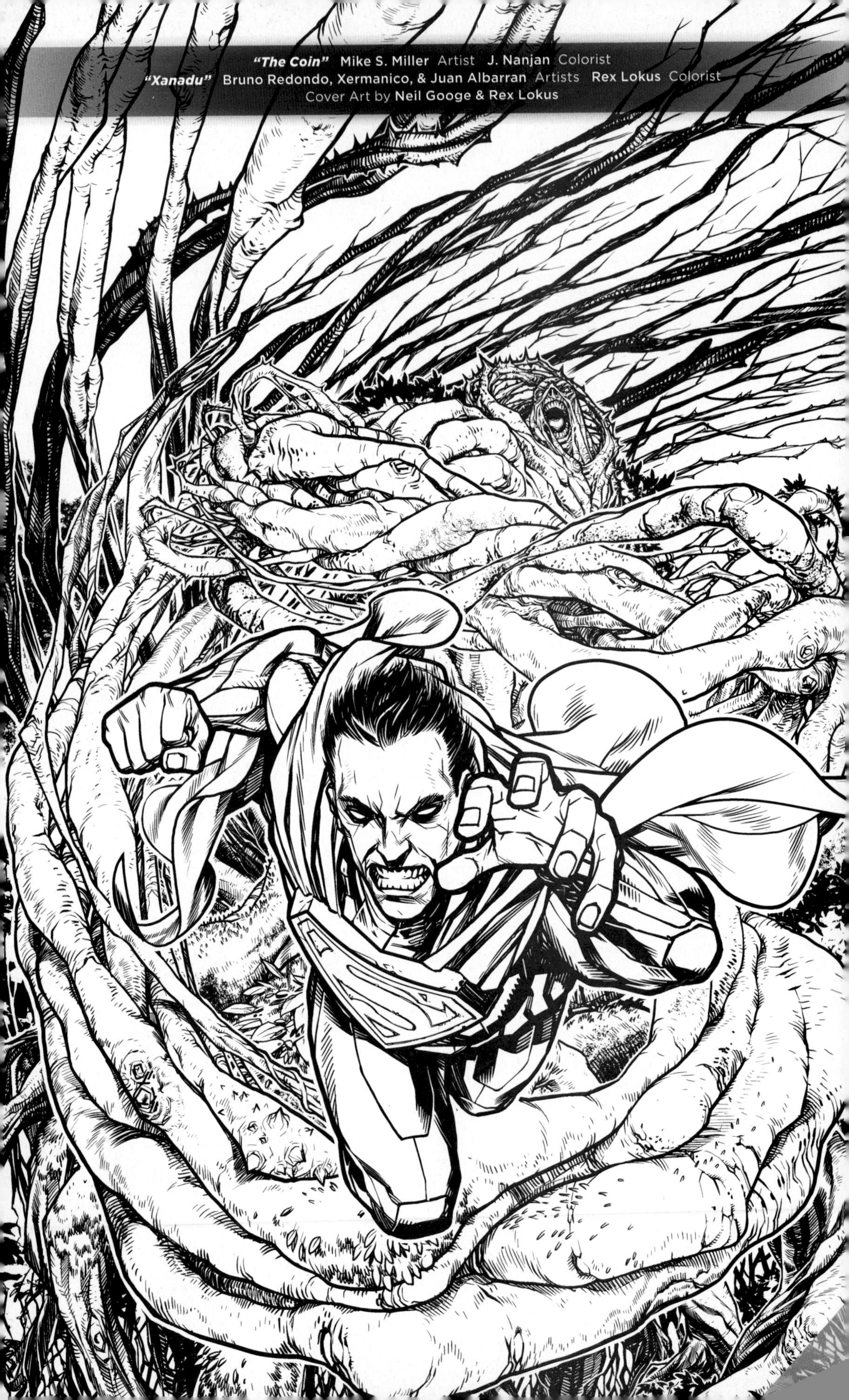

THE COIN

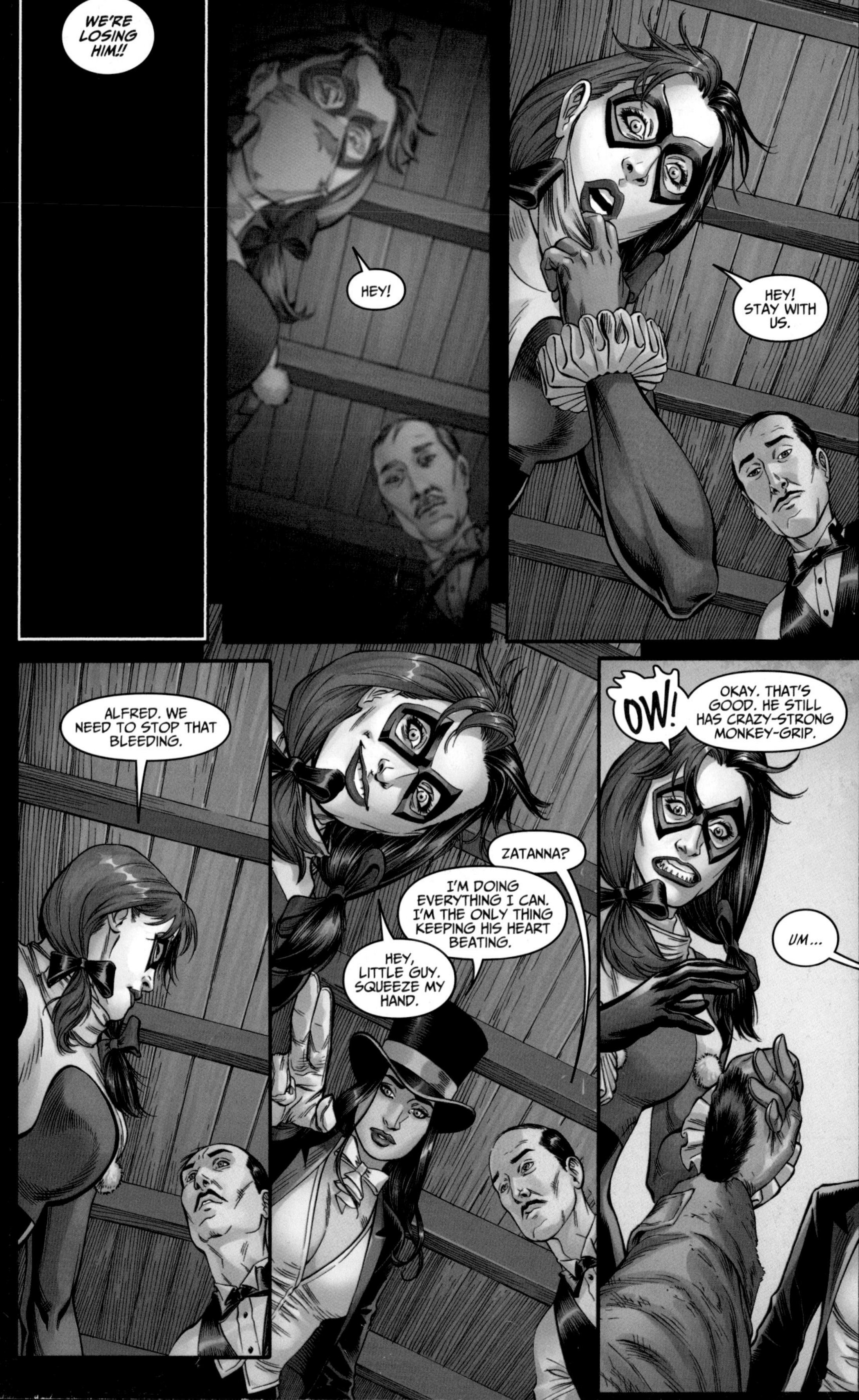

WE'RE LOSING HIM!!
HEY!
HEY! STAY WITH US.
ALFRED. WE NEED TO STOP THAT BLEEDING.
ZATANNA?
I'M DOING EVERYTHING I CAN. I'M THE ONLY THING KEEPING HIS HEART BEATING.
HEY, LITTLE GUY. SQUEEZE MY HAND.
OW!
OKAY. THAT'S GOOD. HE STILL HAS CRAZY-STRONG MONKEY-GRIP.
UM...

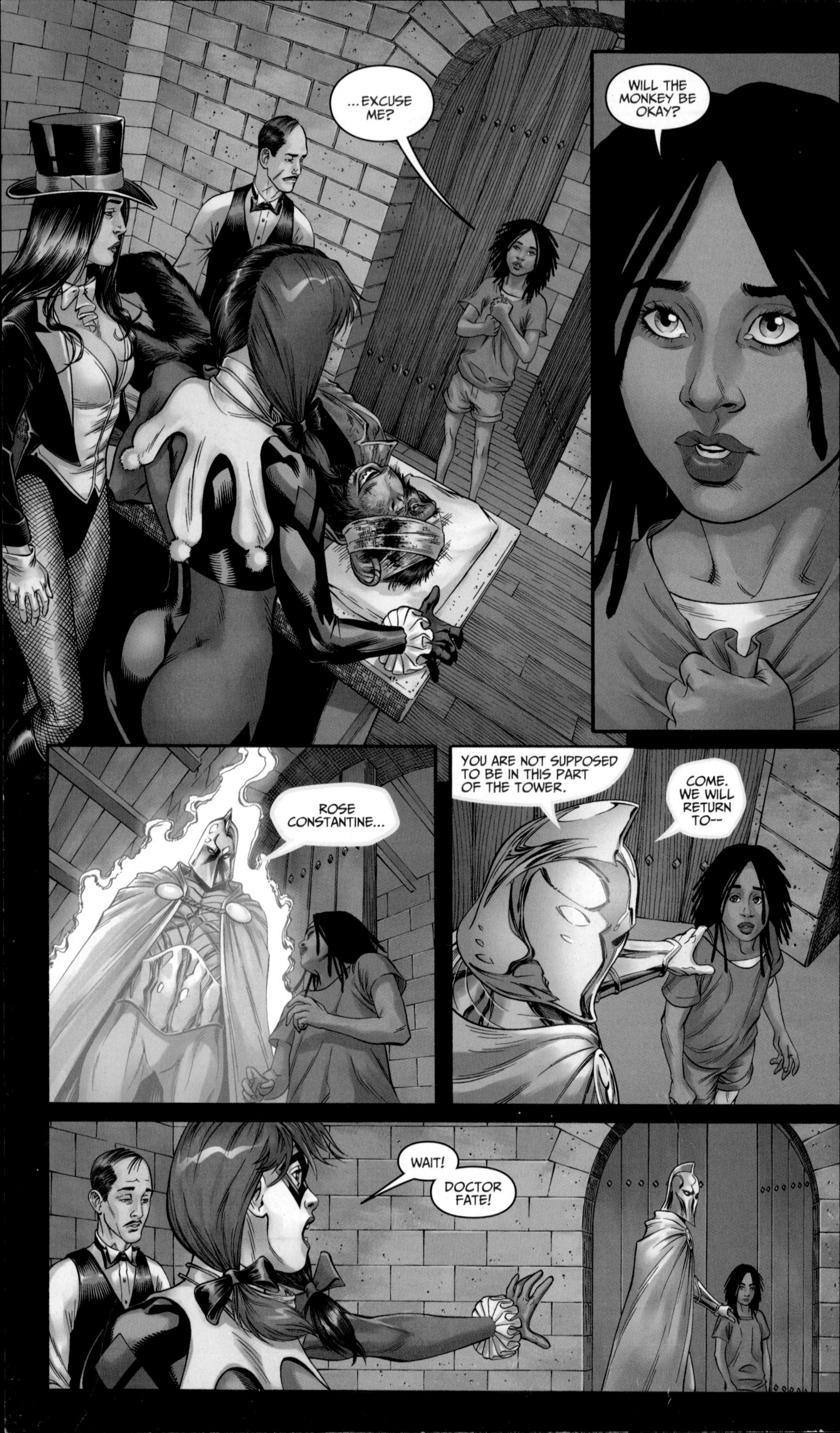
...EXCUSE ME?
WILL THE MONKEY BE OKAY?
ROSE CONSTANTINE...
YOU ARE NOT SUPPOSED TO BE IN THIS PART OF THE TOWER.
COME. WE WILL RETURN TO--
WAIT!
DOCTOR FATE!

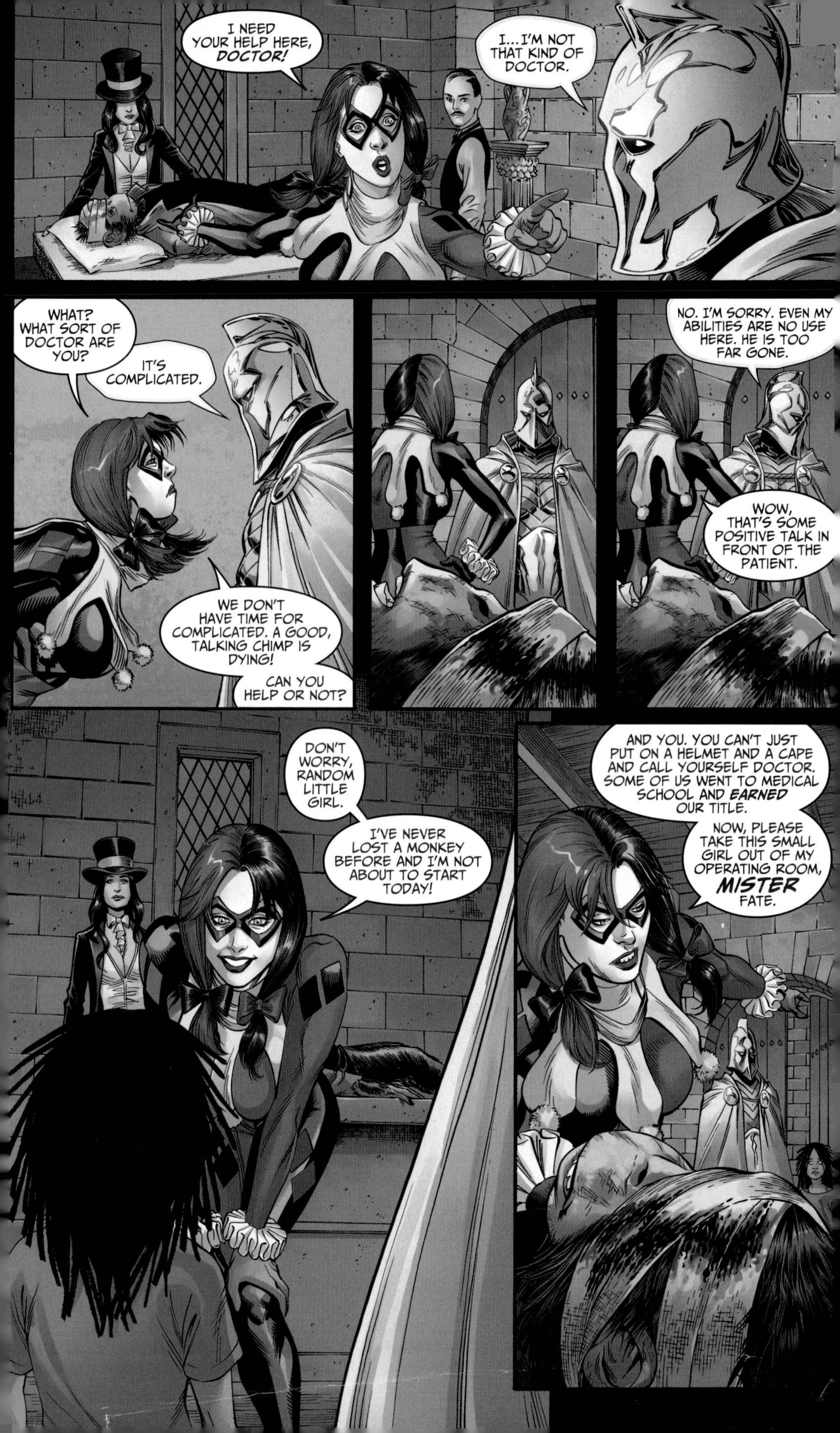
I NEED YOUR HELP HERE, DOCTOR!
I...I'M NOT THAT KIND OF DOCTOR.
WHAT? WHAT SORT OF DOCTOR ARE YOU?
IT'S COMPLICATED.
WE DON'T HAVE TIME FOR COMPLICATED. A GOOD, TALKING CHIMP IS DYING!
CAN YOU HELP OR NOT?
NO. I'M SORRY. EVEN MY ABILITIES ARE NO USE HERE. HE IS TOO FAR GONE.
WOW, THAT'S SOME POSITIVE TALK IN FRONT OF THE PATIENT.
DON'T WORRY, RANDOM LITTLE GIRL.
I'VE NEVER LOST A MONKEY BEFORE AND I'M NOT ABOUT TO START TODAY!
AND YOU. YOU CAN'T JUST PUT ON A HELMET AND A CAPE AND CALL YOURSELF DOCTOR. SOME OF US WENT TO MEDICAL SCHOOL AND EARNED OUR TITLE.
NOW, PLEASE TAKE THIS SMALL GIRL OUT OF MY OPERATING ROOM, MISTER FATE.

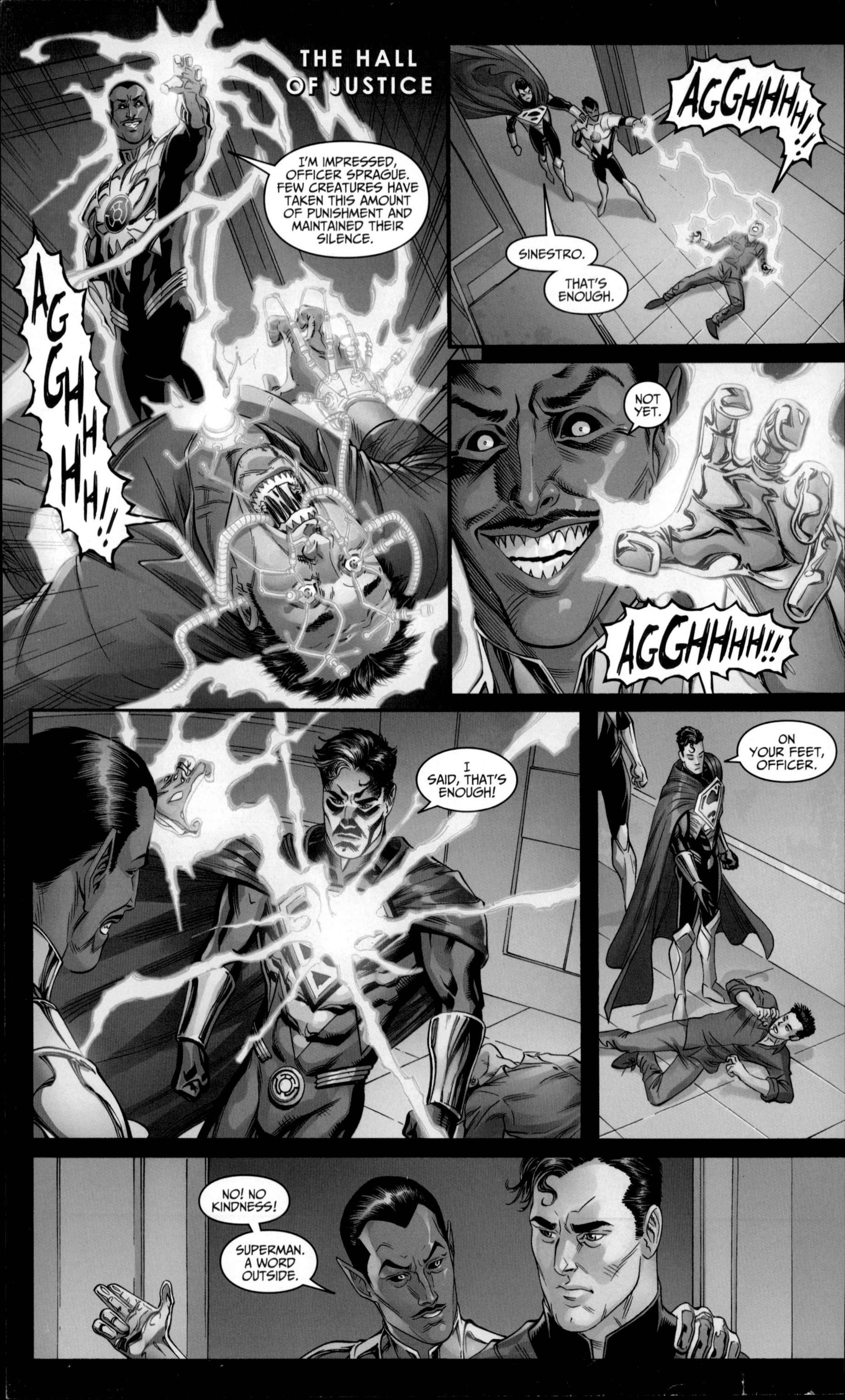
THE HALL OF JUSTICE
I'M IMPRESSED, OFFICER SPRAGUE. FEW CREATURES HAVE TAKEN THIS AMOUNT OF PUNISHMENT AND MAINTAINED THEIR SILENCE.
AGGHHHHH!!
AGGHHHH!!
SINESTRO.
THAT'S ENOUGH.
NOT YET.
AGGHHHH!!
I SAID, THAT'S ENOUGH!
ON YOUR FEET, OFFICER.
NO! NO KINDNESS!
SUPERMAN. A WORD OUTSIDE.

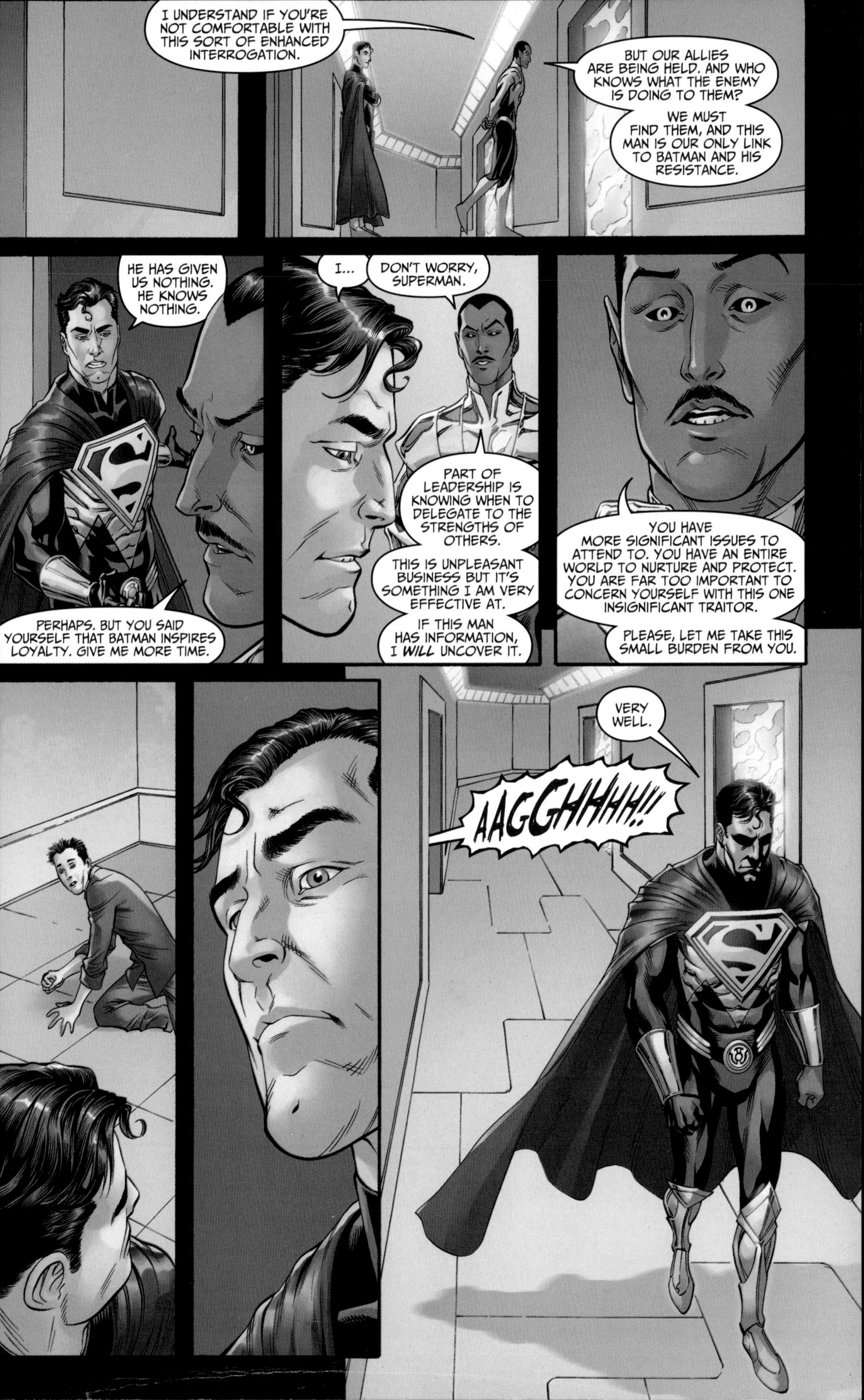
I UNDERSTAND IF YOU'RE NOT COMFORTABLE WITH THIS SORT OF ENHANCED INTERROGATION.
BUT OUR ALLIES ARE BEING HELD. AND WHO KNOWS WHAT THE ENEMY IS DOING TO THEM?
WE MUST FIND THEM, AND THIS MAN IS OUR ONLY LINK TO BATMAN AND HIS RESISTANCE.
HE HAS GIVEN US NOTHING. HE KNOWS NOTHING.
PERHAPS. BUT YOU SAID YOURSELF THAT BATMAN INSPIRES LOYALTY. GIVE ME MORE TIME.
I...
DON'T WORRY, SUPERMAN.
PART OF LEADERSHIP IS KNOWING WHEN TO DELEGATE TO THE STRENGTHS OF OTHERS.
THIS IS UNPLEASANT BUSINESS BUT IT'S SOMETHING I AM VERY EFFECTIVE AT.
IF THIS MAN HAS INFORMATION, I WILL UNCOVER IT.
YOU HAVE MORE SIGNIFICANT ISSUES TO ATTEND TO. YOU HAVE AN ENTIRE WORLD TO NURTURE AND PROTECT. YOU ARE FAR TOO IMPORTANT TO CONCERN YOURSELF WITH THIS ONE INSIGNIFICANT TRAITOR.
PLEASE, LET ME TAKE THIS SMALL BURDEN FROM YOU.
VERY WELL.
AAGGHHHH!!

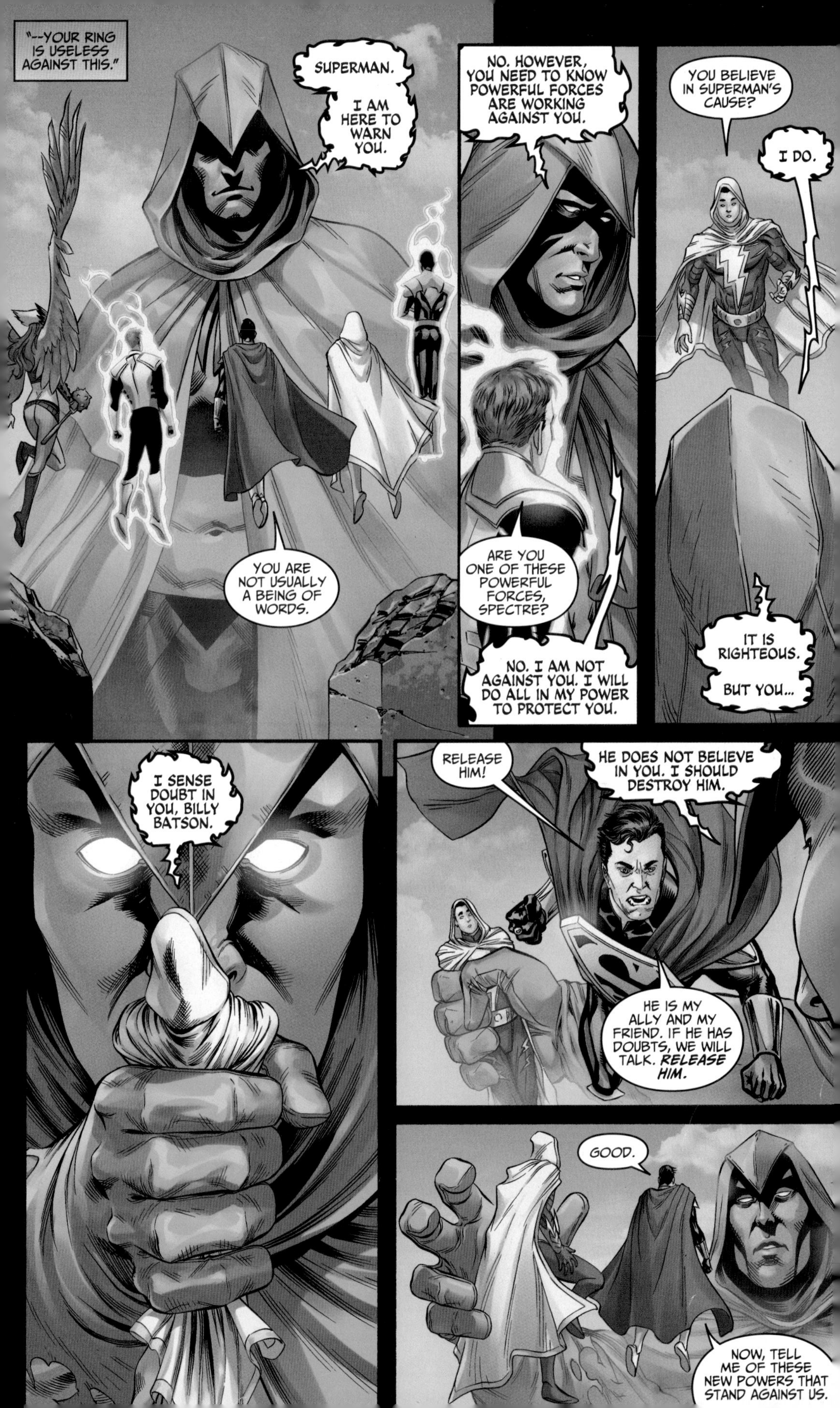
"--YOUR RING IS USELESS AGAINST THIS."
SUPERMAN.
I AM HERE TO WARN YOU.
YOU ARE NOT USUALLY A BEING OF WORDS.
NO. HOWEVER, YOU NEED TO KNOW POWERFUL FORCES ARE WORKING AGAINST YOU.
ARE YOU ONE OF THESE POWERFUL FORCES, SPECTRE?
NO. I AM NOT AGAINST YOU. I WILL DO ALL IN MY POWER TO PROTECT YOU.
YOU BELIEVE IN SUPERMAN'S CAUSE?
I DO.
IT IS RIGHTEOUS.
BUT YOU...
I SENSE DOUBT IN YOU, BILLY BATSON.
RELEASE HIM!
HE DOES NOT BELIEVE IN YOU. I SHOULD DESTROY HIM.
HE IS MY ALLY AND MY FRIEND. IF HE HAS DOUBTS, WE WILL TALK. *RELEASE HIM.*
GOOD.
NOW, TELL ME OF THESE NEW POWERS THAT STAND AGAINST US.

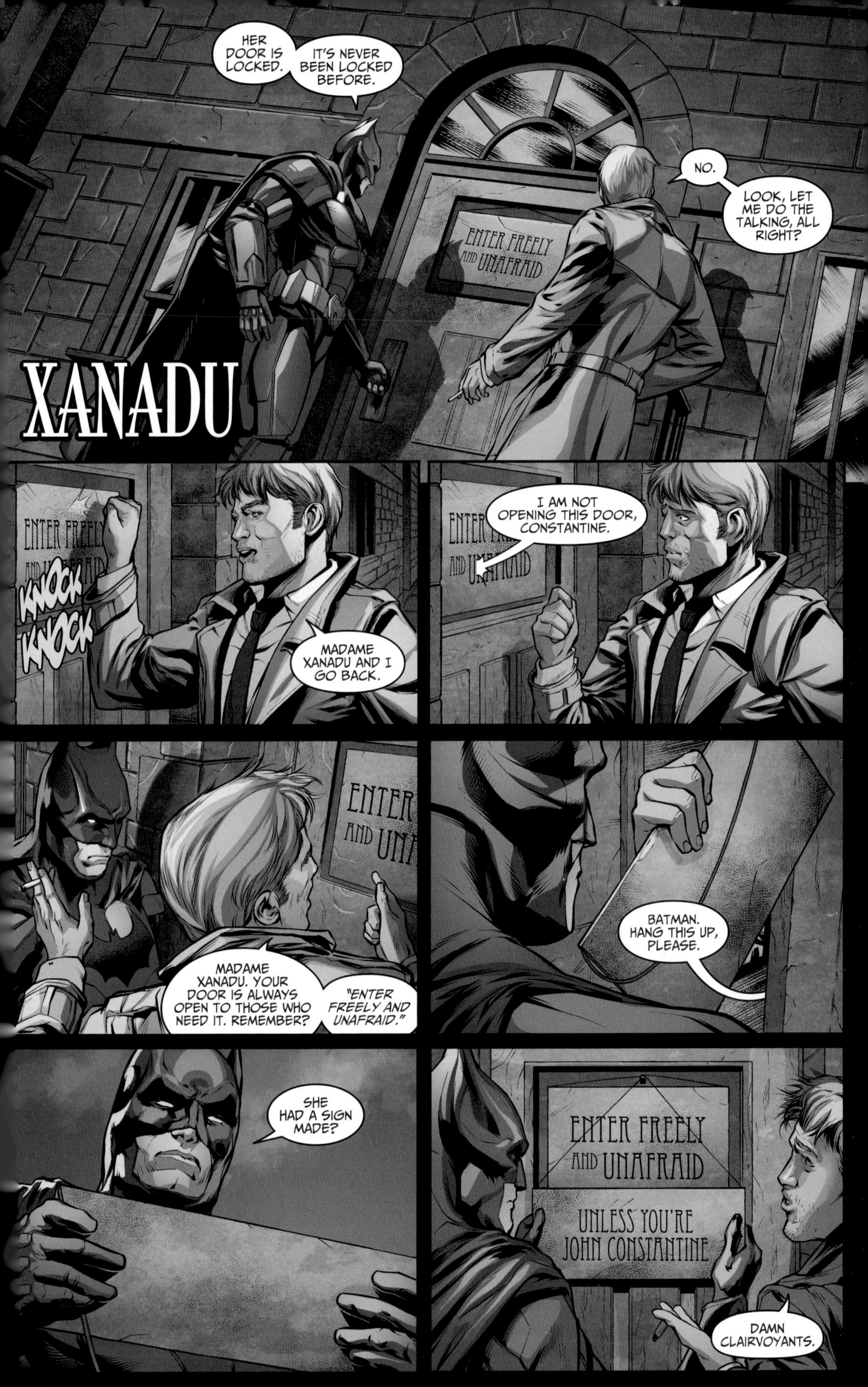
HER DOOR IS LOCKED.
IT'S NEVER BEEN LOCKED BEFORE.
NO.
LOOK, LET ME DO THE TALKING, ALL RIGHT?
ENTER FREELY AND UNAFRAID
XANADU
KNOCK KNOCK
MADAME XANADU AND I GO BACK.
I AM NOT OPENING THIS DOOR, CONSTANTINE.
MADAME XANADU. YOUR DOOR IS ALWAYS OPEN TO THOSE WHO NEED IT. REMEMBER?
"ENTER FREELY AND UNAFRAID."
BATMAN. HANG THIS UP, PLEASE.
SHE HAD A SIGN MADE?
ENTER FREELY AND UNAFRAID
UNLESS YOU'RE JOHN CONSTANTINE
DAMN CLAIRVOYANTS.

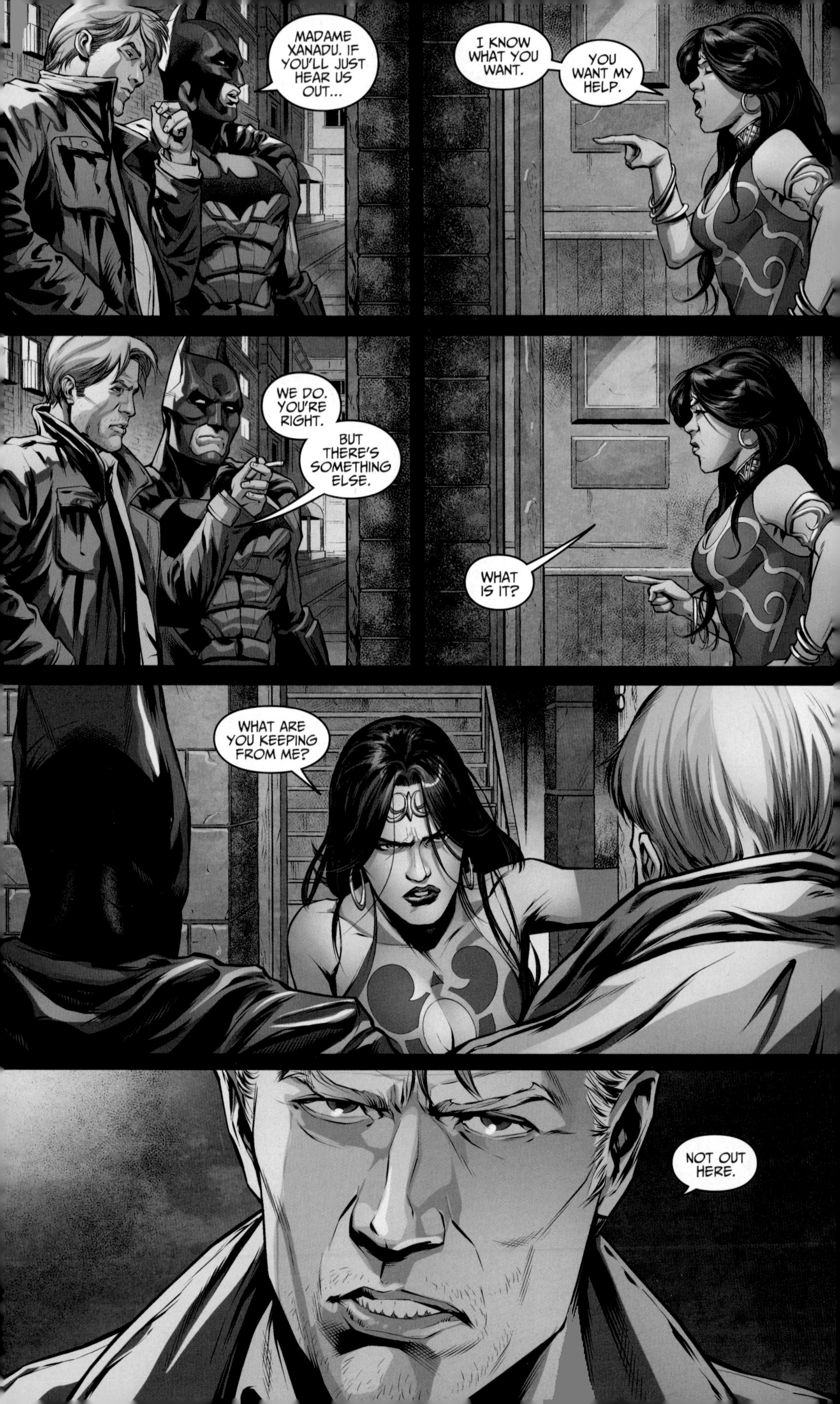
MADAME XANADU. IF YOU'LL JUST HEAR US OUT...
I KNOW WHAT YOU WANT.
YOU WANT MY HELP.
WE DO. YOU'RE RIGHT.
BUT THERE'S SOMETHING ELSE.
WHAT IS IT?
WHAT ARE YOU KEEPING FROM ME?
NOT OUT HERE.

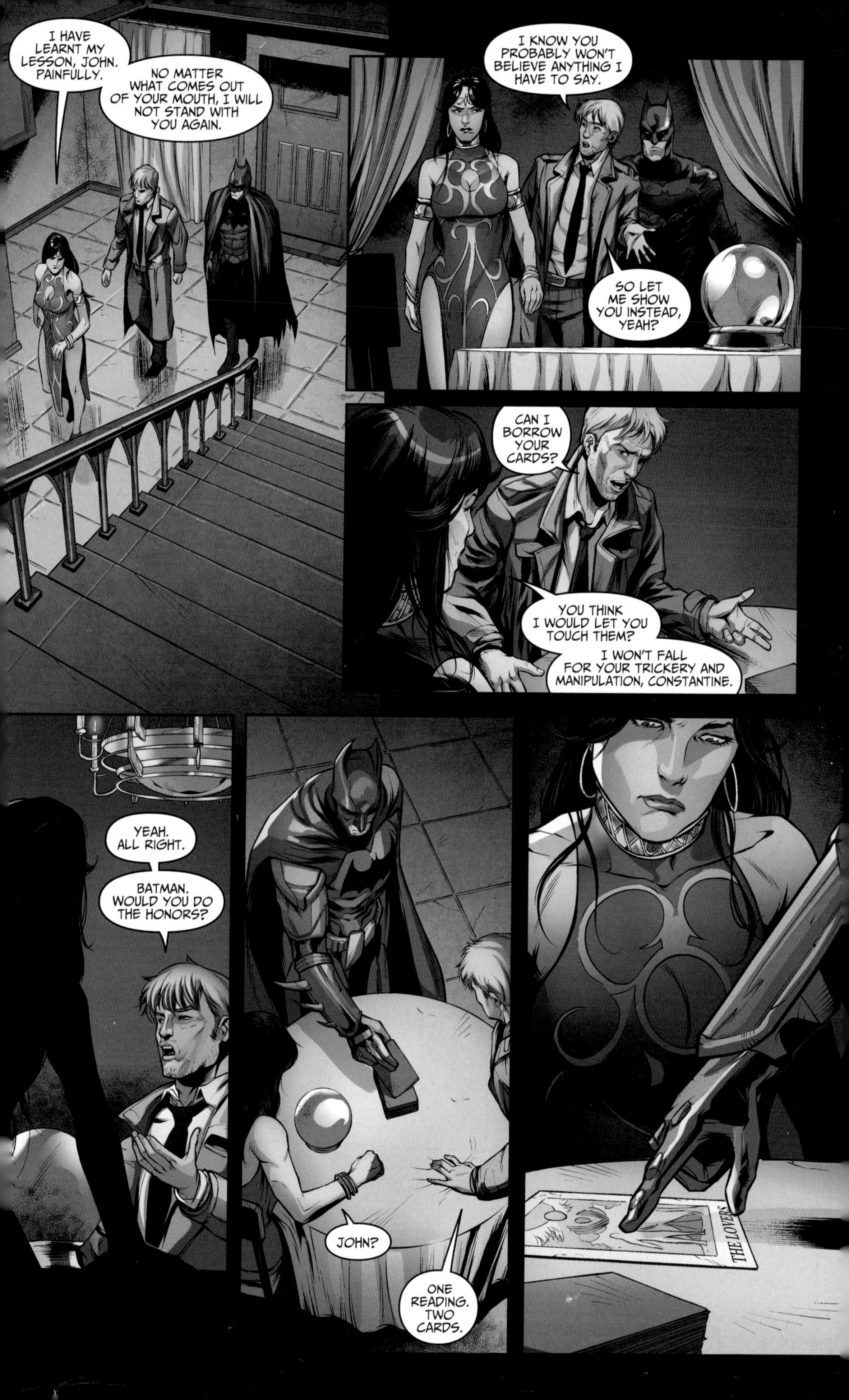
I HAVE LEARNT MY LESSON, JOHN. PAINFULLY.
NO MATTER WHAT COMES OUT OF YOUR MOUTH, I WILL NOT STAND WITH YOU AGAIN.
I KNOW YOU PROBABLY WON'T BELIEVE ANYTHING I HAVE TO SAY.
SO LET ME SHOW YOU INSTEAD, YEAH?
CAN I BORROW YOUR CARDS?
YOU THINK I WOULD LET YOU TOUCH THEM?
I WON'T FALL FOR YOUR TRICKERY AND MANIPULATION, CONSTANTINE.
YEAH. ALL RIGHT.
BATMAN. WOULD YOU DO THE HONORS?
JOHN?
ONE READING. TWO CARDS.
THE LOVERS

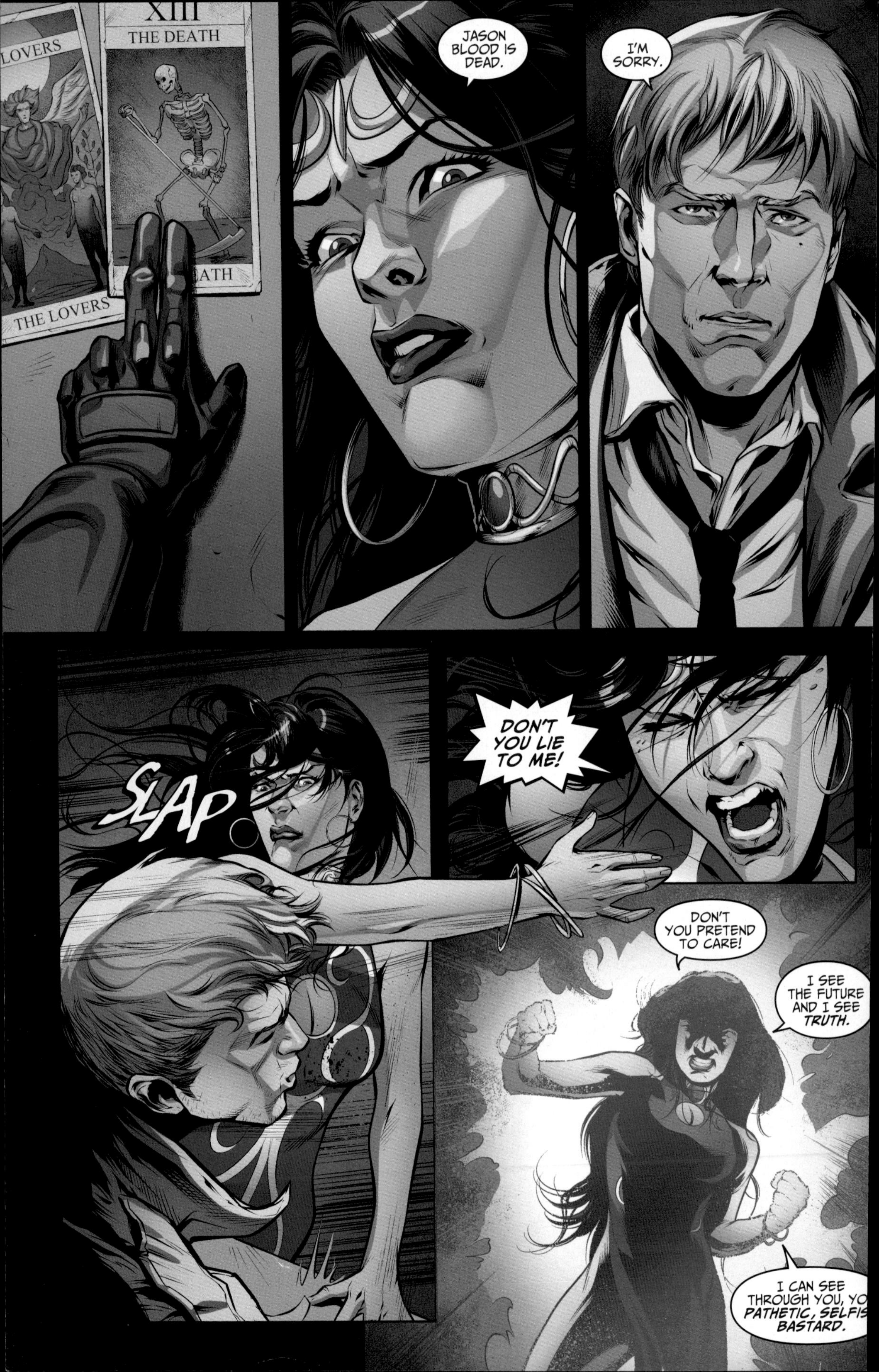
XIII
THE DEATH
LOVERS
DEATH
THE LOVERS
JASON BLOOD IS DEAD.
I'M SORRY.
SLAP
DON'T YOU LIE TO ME!
DON'T YOU PRETEND TO CARE!
I SEE THE FUTURE AND I SEE *TRUTH.*
I CAN SEE THROUGH YOU, YO
PATHETIC, SELFIS
BASTARD.

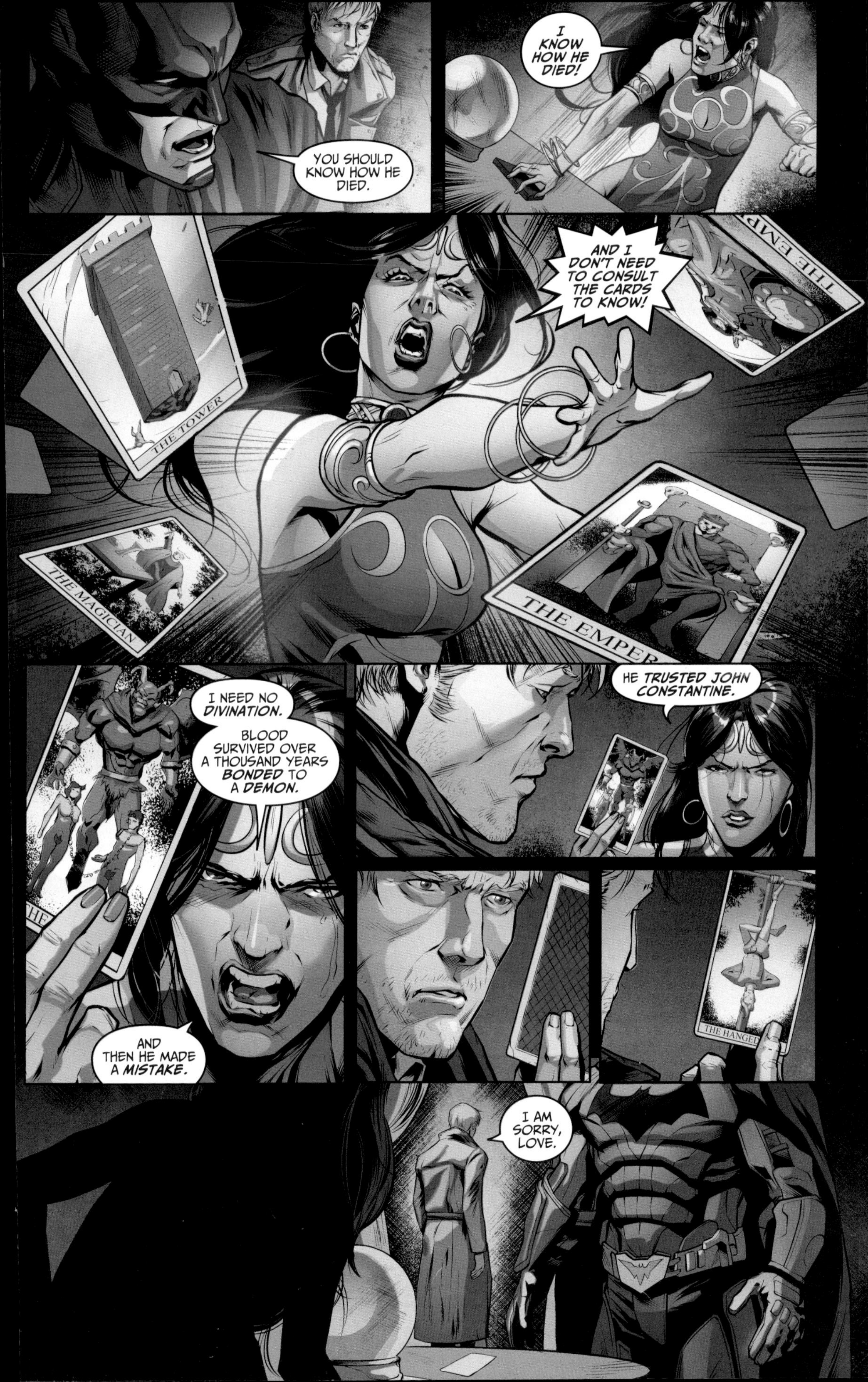

YOU SHOULD KNOW HOW HE DIED.
I KNOW HOW HE DIED!
AND I DON'T NEED TO CONSULT THE CARDS TO KNOW!
THE TOWER
THE MAGICIAN
THE EMPER
I NEED NO DIVINATION.
BLOOD SURVIVED OVER A THOUSAND YEARS BONDED TO A DEMON.
AND THEN HE MADE A MISTAKE.
HE TRUSTED JOHN CONSTANTINE.
THE HANGED
I AM SORRY, LOVE.

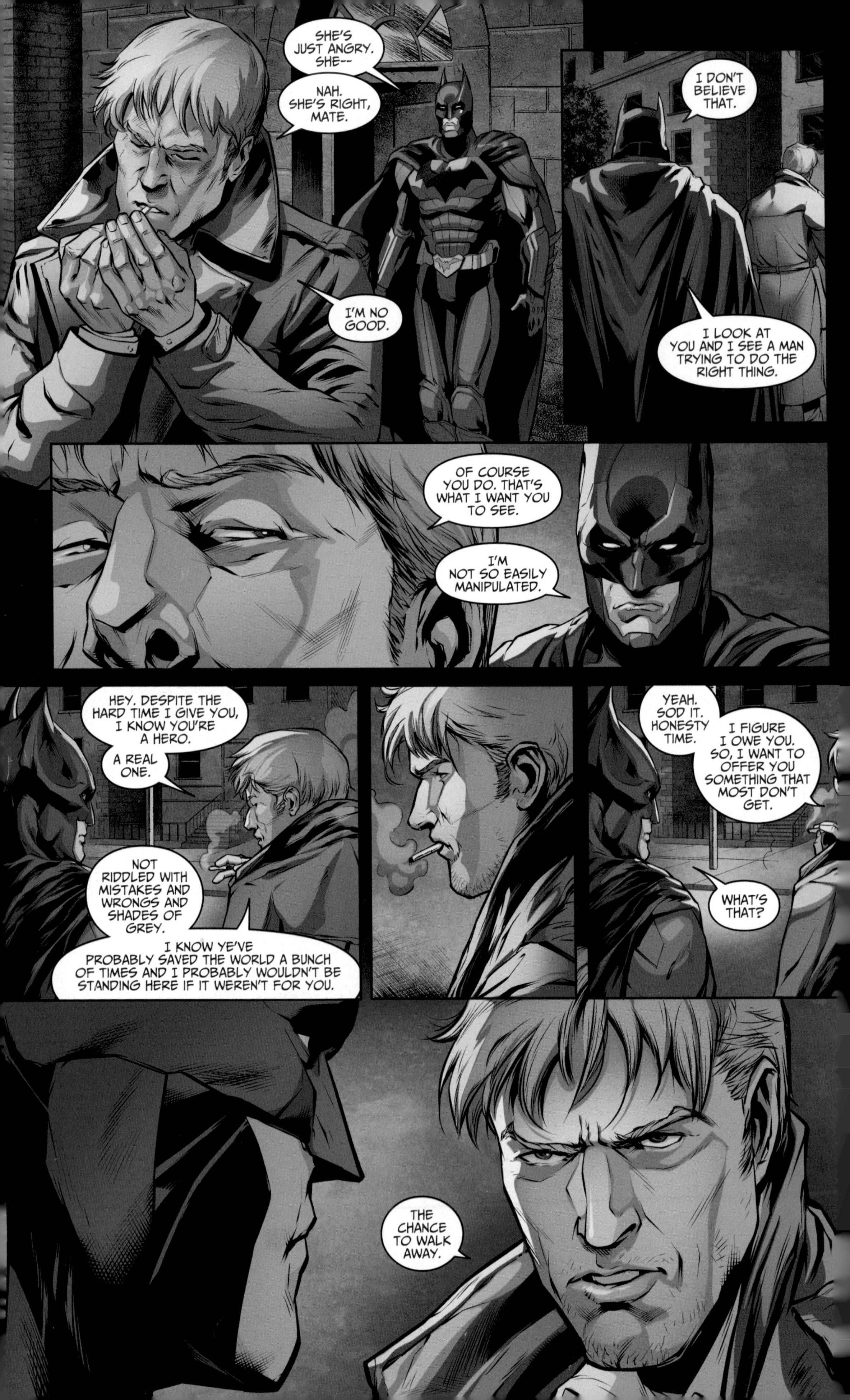
SHE'S JUST ANGRY. SHE--
NAH. SHE'S RIGHT, MATE.
I'M NO GOOD.
I DON'T BELIEVE THAT.
I LOOK AT YOU AND I SEE A MAN TRYING TO DO THE RIGHT THING.
OF COURSE YOU DO. THAT'S WHAT I WANT YOU TO SEE.
I'M NOT SO EASILY MANIPULATED.
HEY. DESPITE THE HARD TIME I GIVE YOU, I KNOW YOU'RE A HERO.
A REAL ONE.
NOT RIDDLED WITH MISTAKES AND WRONGS AND SHADES OF GREY.
I KNOW YE'VE PROBABLY SAVED THE WORLD A BUNCH OF TIMES AND I PROBABLY WOULDN'T BE STANDING HERE IF IT WEREN'T FOR YOU.
YEAH. SOD IT. HONESTY TIME.
I FIGURE I OWE YOU. SO, I WANT TO OFFER YOU SOMETHING THAT MOST DON'T GET.
WHAT'S THAT?
THE CHANCE TO WALK AWAY.

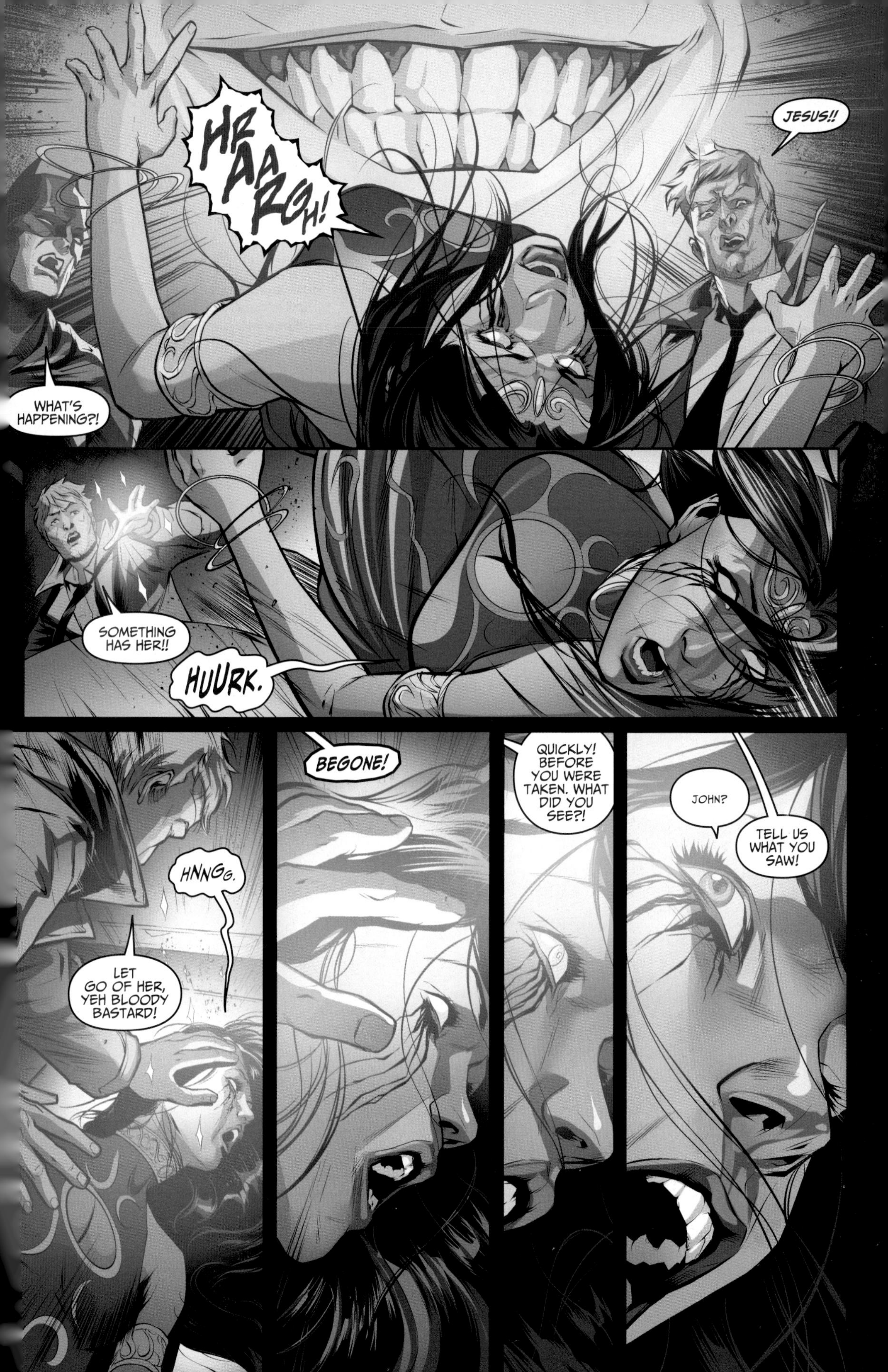
HRAARGH!
JESUS!!
WHAT'S HAPPENING?!
SOMETHING HAS HER!!
HUURK.
HNNGG.
LET GO OF HER, YEH BLOODY BASTARD!
BEGONE!
QUICKLY! BEFORE YOU WERE TAKEN. WHAT DID YOU SEE?!
JOHN?
TELL US WHAT YOU SAW!

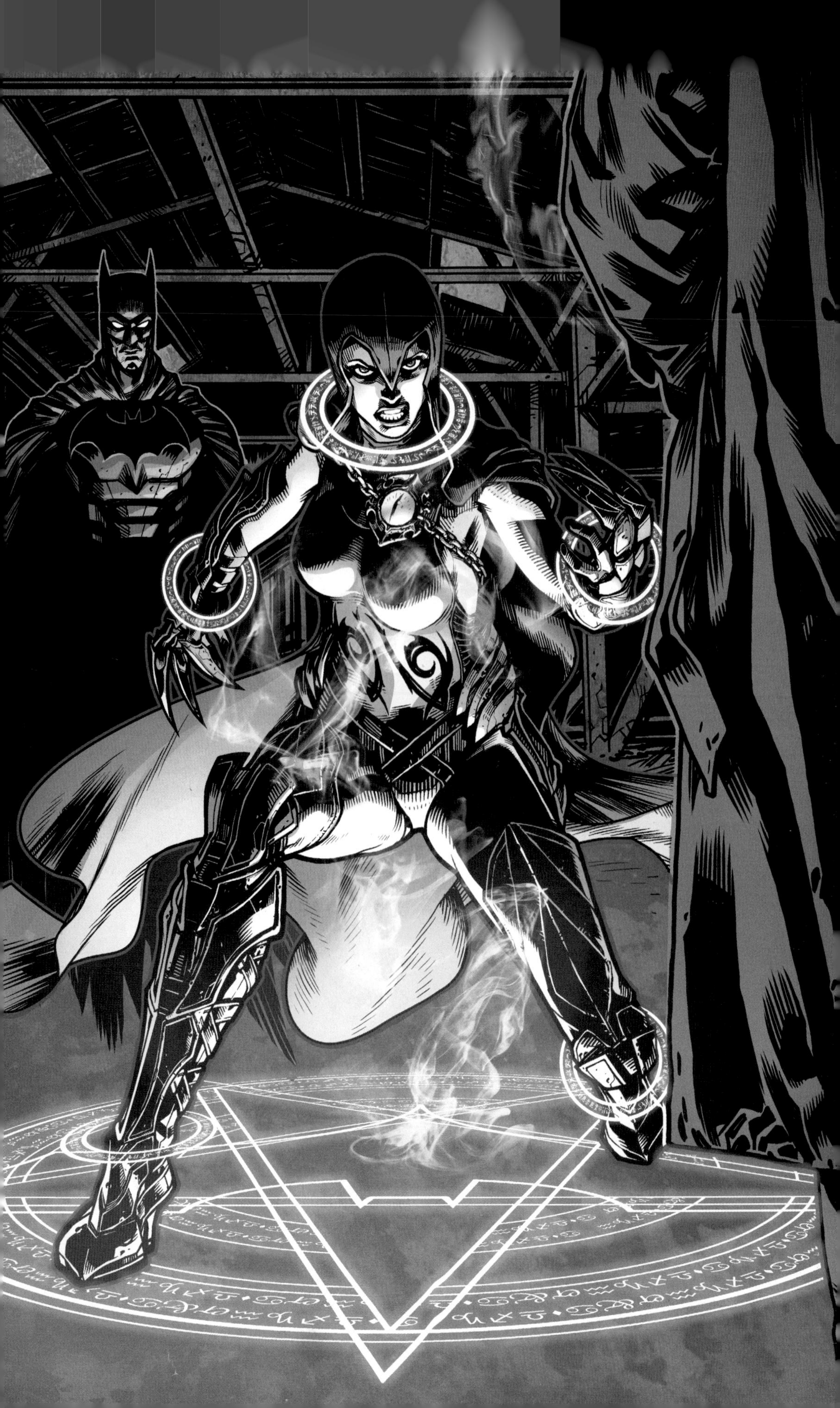

"Raven's Rescue" **Bruno Redondo & Xermanico** Artists **Rex Lokus** Colorist
"Ragman's Souls" **Mike S. Miller** Artist **J. Nanjan** Colorist
Cover Art by **Neil Googe & Rex Lokus**

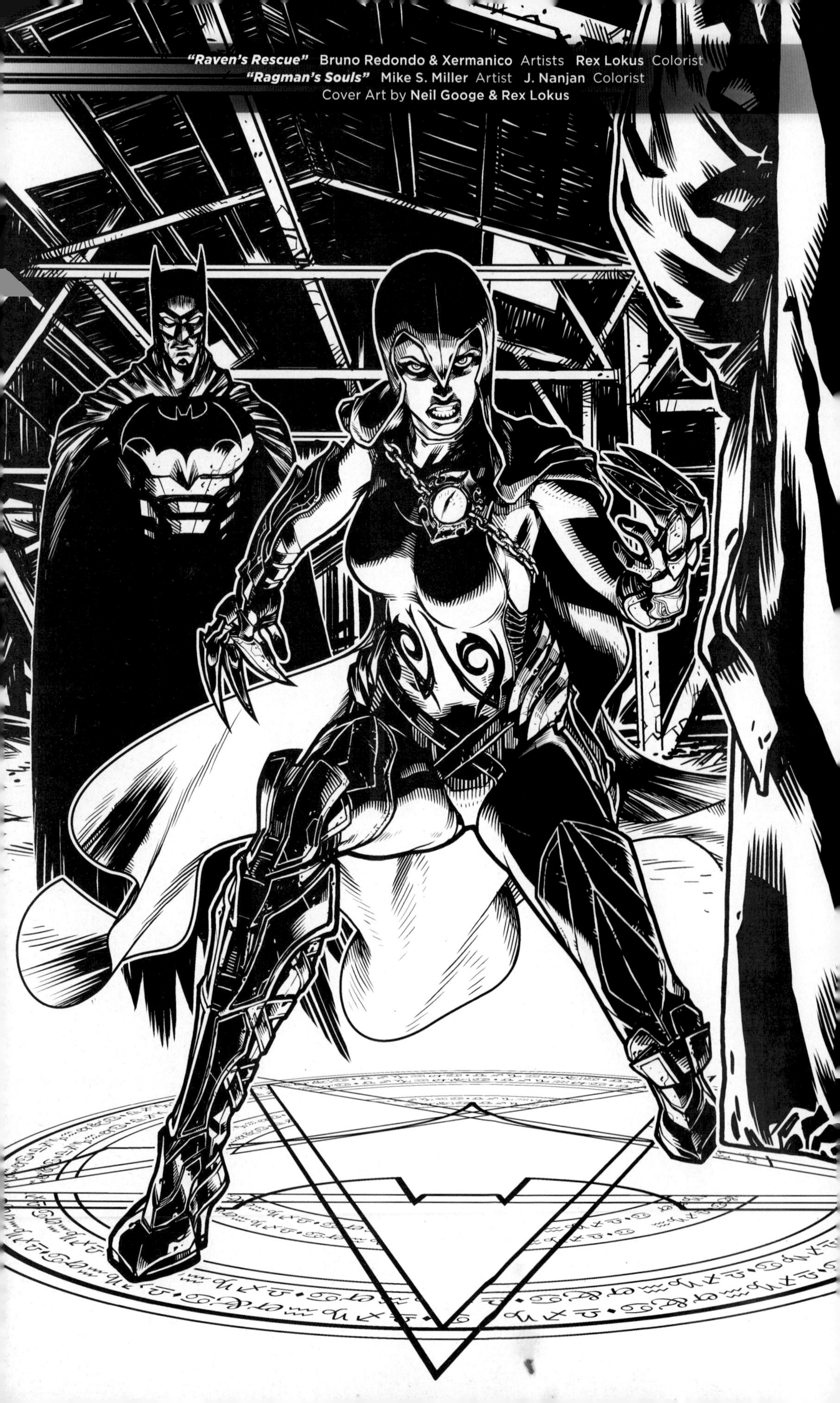

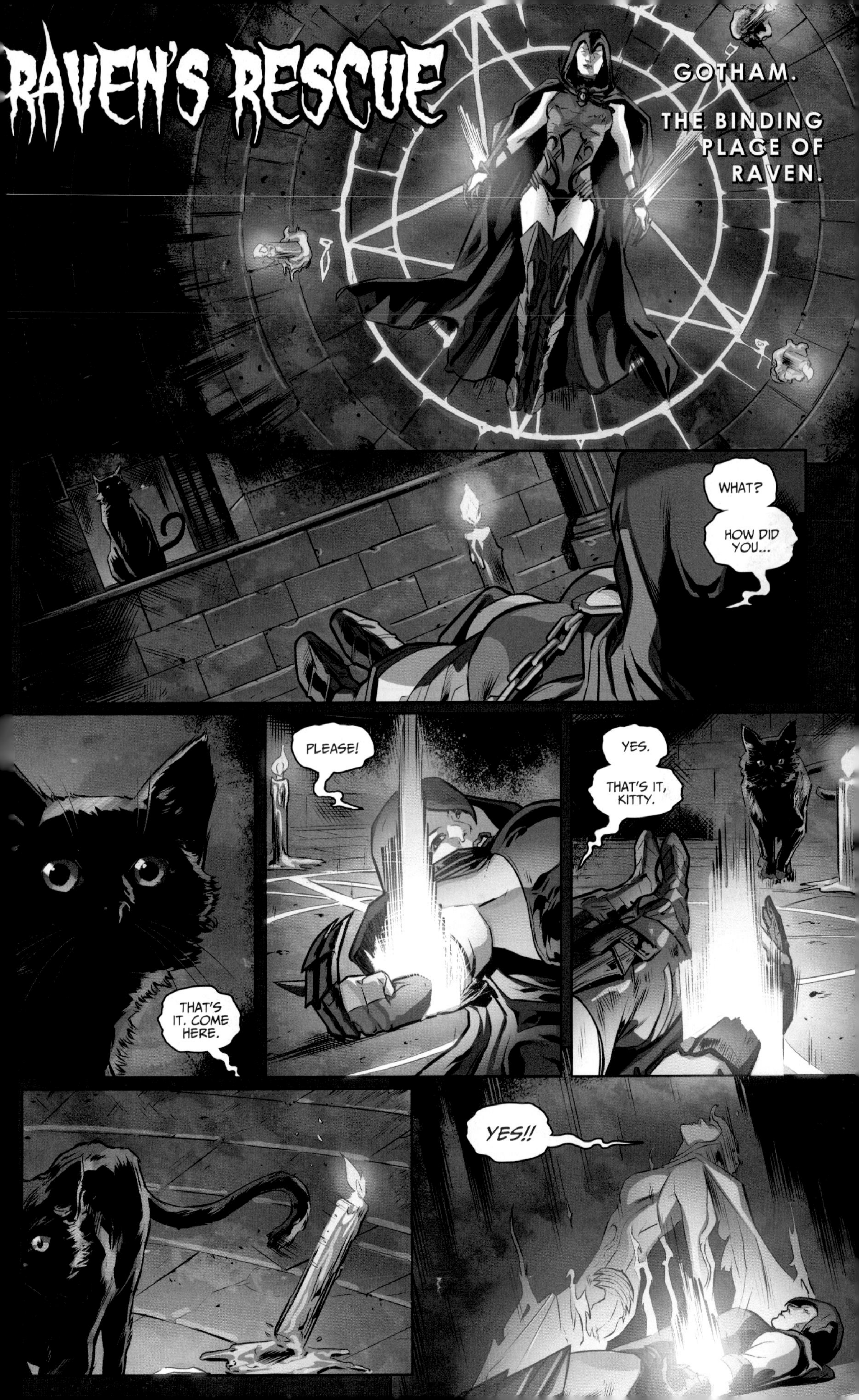
RAVEN'S RESCUE
GOTHAM.
THE BINDING PLACE OF RAVEN.
WHAT?
HOW DID YOU...
THAT'S IT. COME HERE.
PLEASE!
YES.
THAT'S IT, KITTY.
YES!!

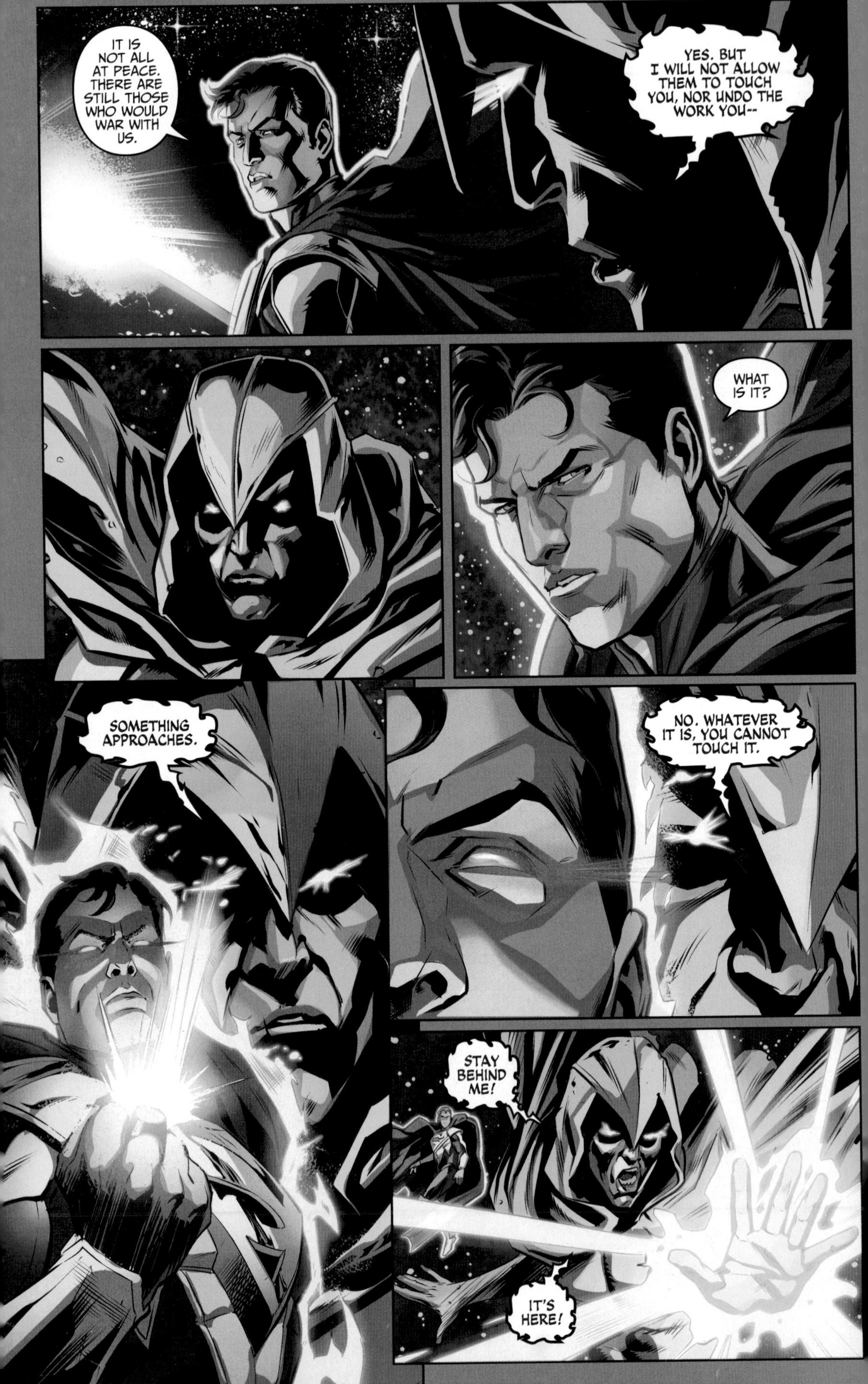
IT IS NOT ALL AT PEACE. THERE ARE STILL THOSE WHO WOULD WAR WITH US.
YES. BUT I WILL NOT ALLOW THEM TO TOUCH YOU, NOR UNDO THE WORK YOU--
WHAT IS IT?
SOMETHING APPROACHES.
NO. WHATEVER IT IS, YOU CANNOT TOUCH IT.
STAY BEHIND ME!
IT'S HERE!

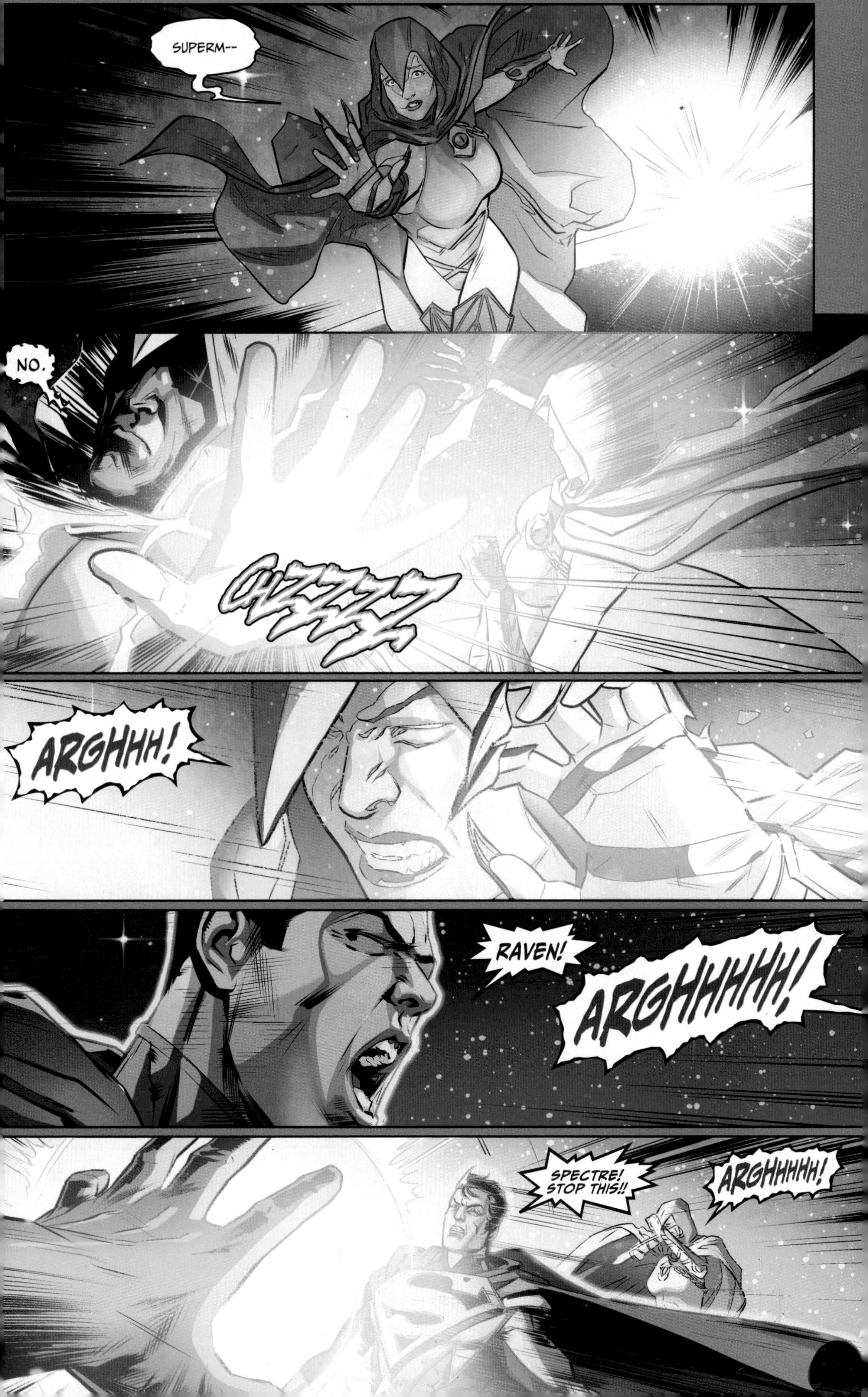

SUPERM--
NO.
CHZZZZ
ARGHHH!
RAVEN!
ARGHHHHH!
SPECTRE! STOP THIS!!
ARGHHHHH!

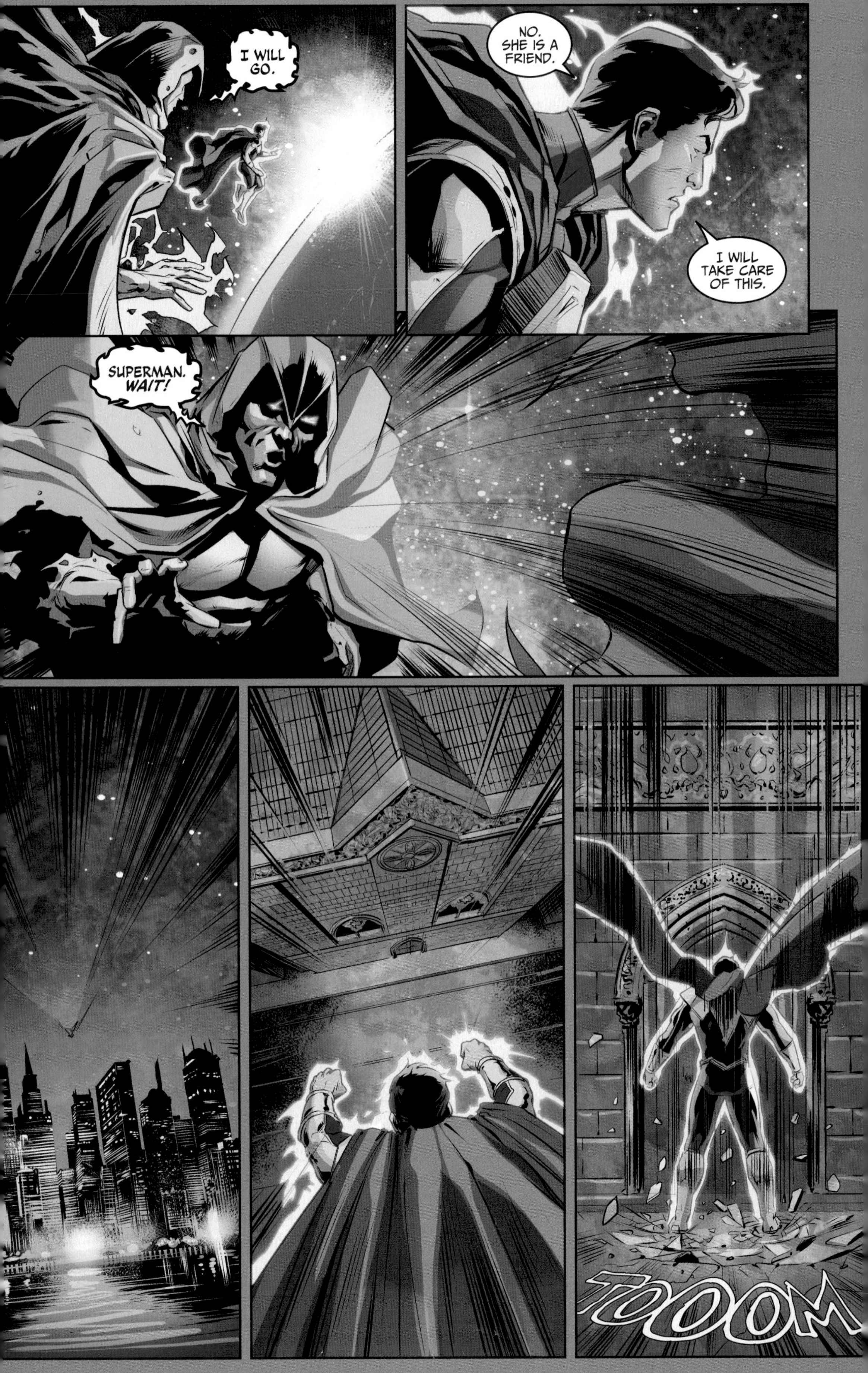
I WILL GO.
NO. SHE IS A FRIEND.
I WILL TAKE CARE OF THIS.
SUPERMAN. WAIT!
TOOOM

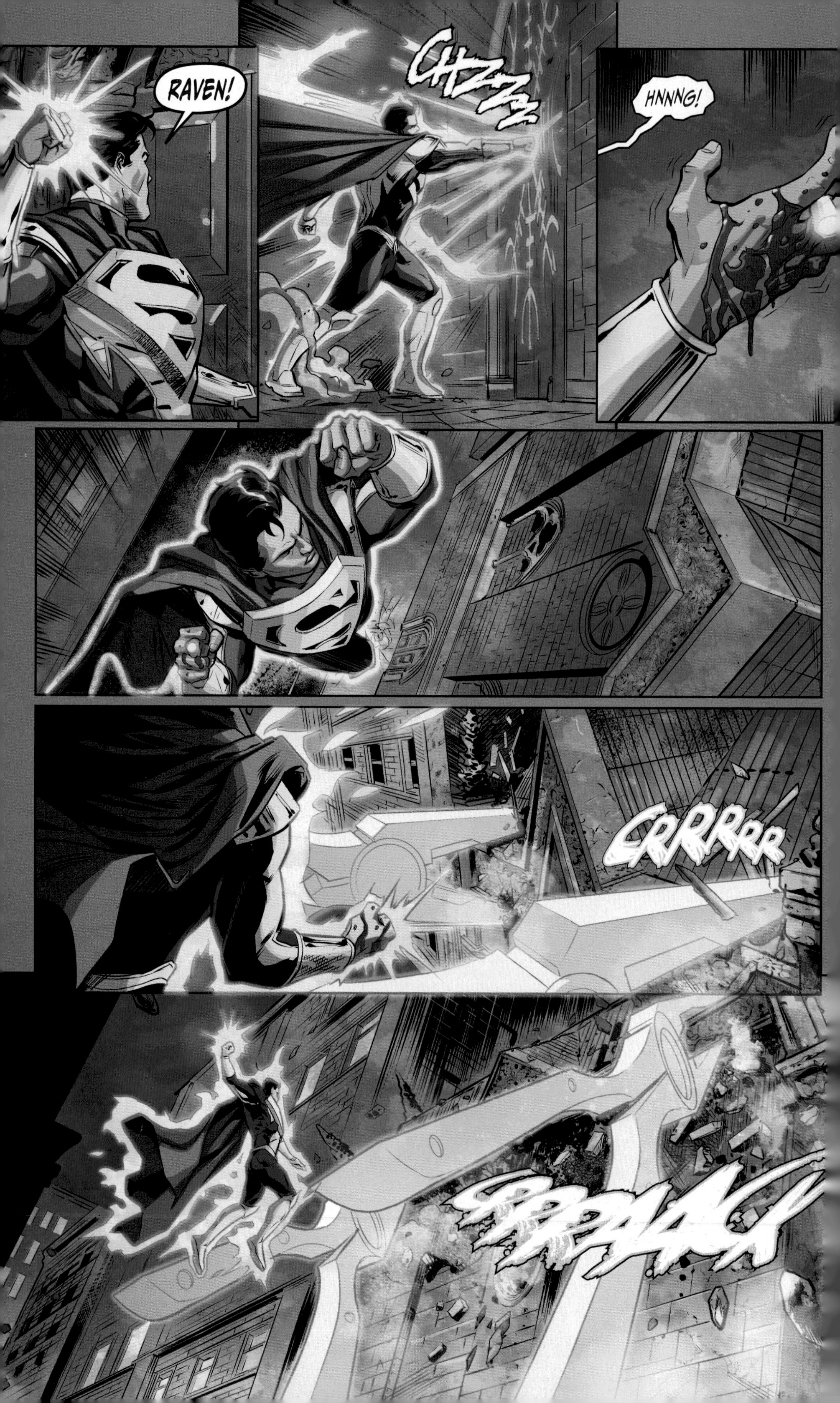
RAVEN!
CHZZZZ
HNNNG!
CRRRRR
SPRAAACK

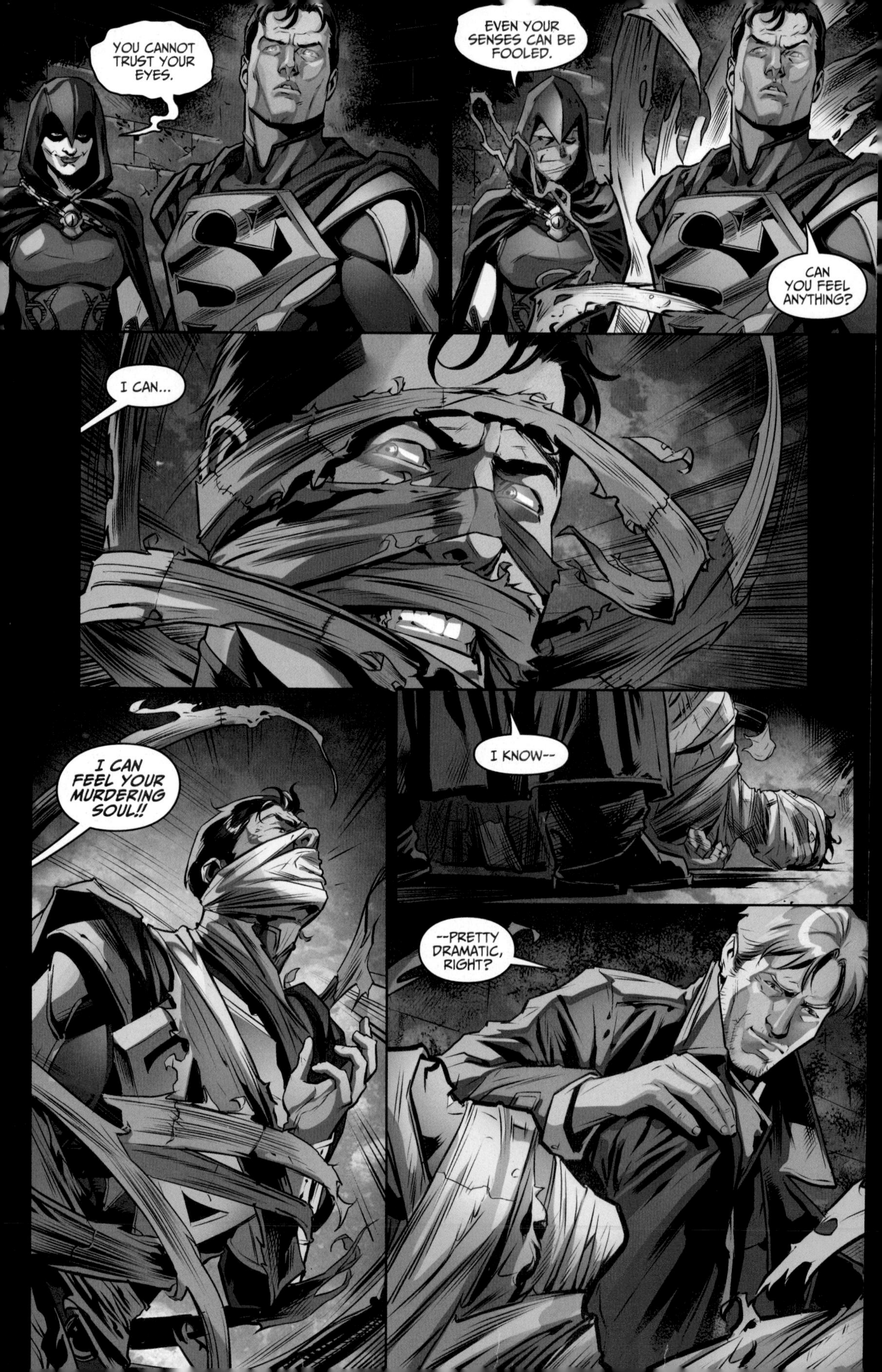
YOU CANNOT TRUST YOUR EYES.
EVEN YOUR SENSES CAN BE FOOLED.
CAN YOU FEEL ANYTHING?
I CAN...
I CAN FEEL YOUR MURDERING SOUL!!
I KNOW--
--PRETTY DRAMATIC, RIGHT?

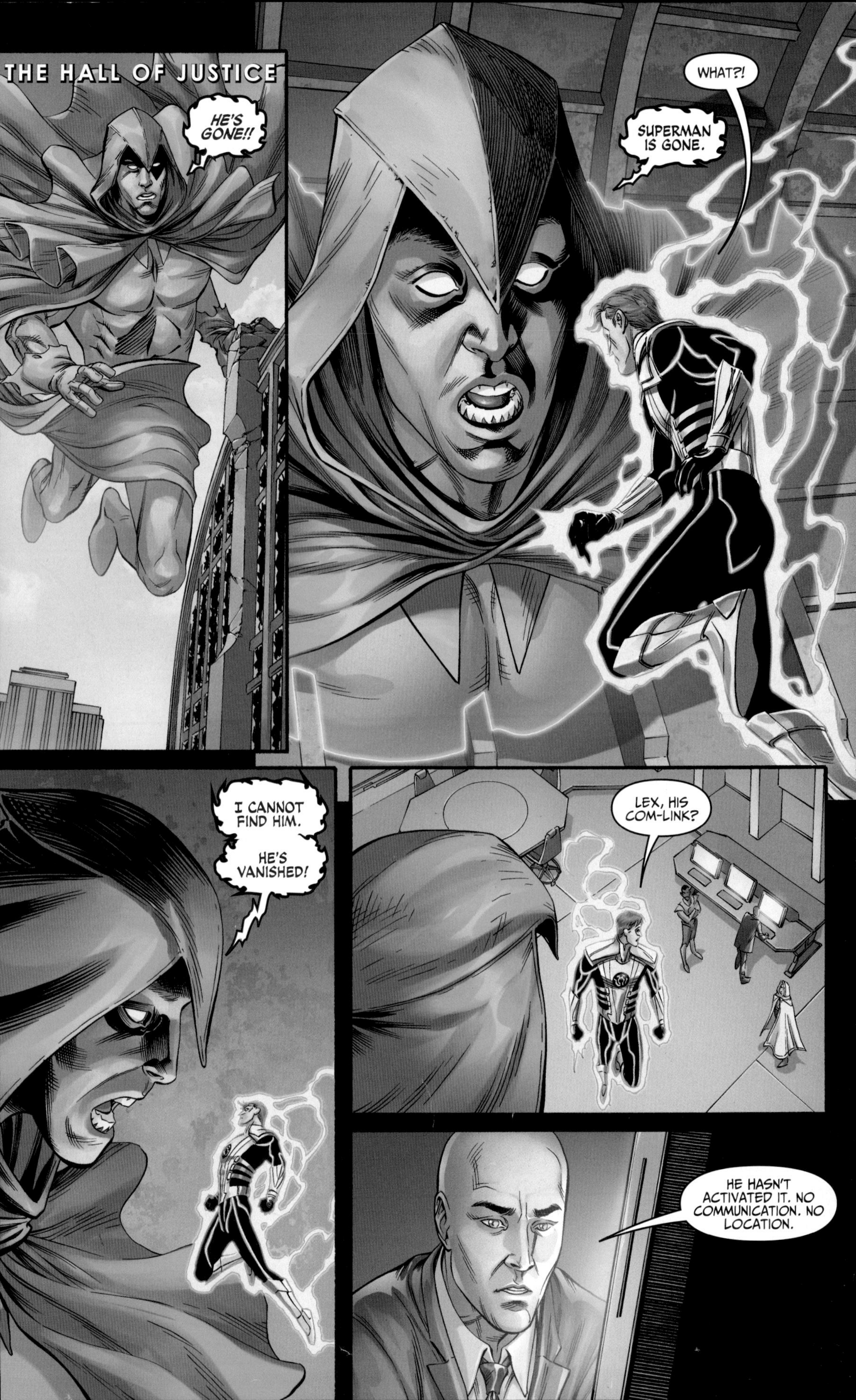
THE HALL OF JUSTICE
HE'S GONE!!
SUPERMAN IS GONE.
WHAT?!
I CANNOT FIND HIM.
HE'S VANISHED!
LEX, HIS COM-LINK?
HE HASN'T ACTIVATED IT. NO COMMUNICATION. NO LOCATION.

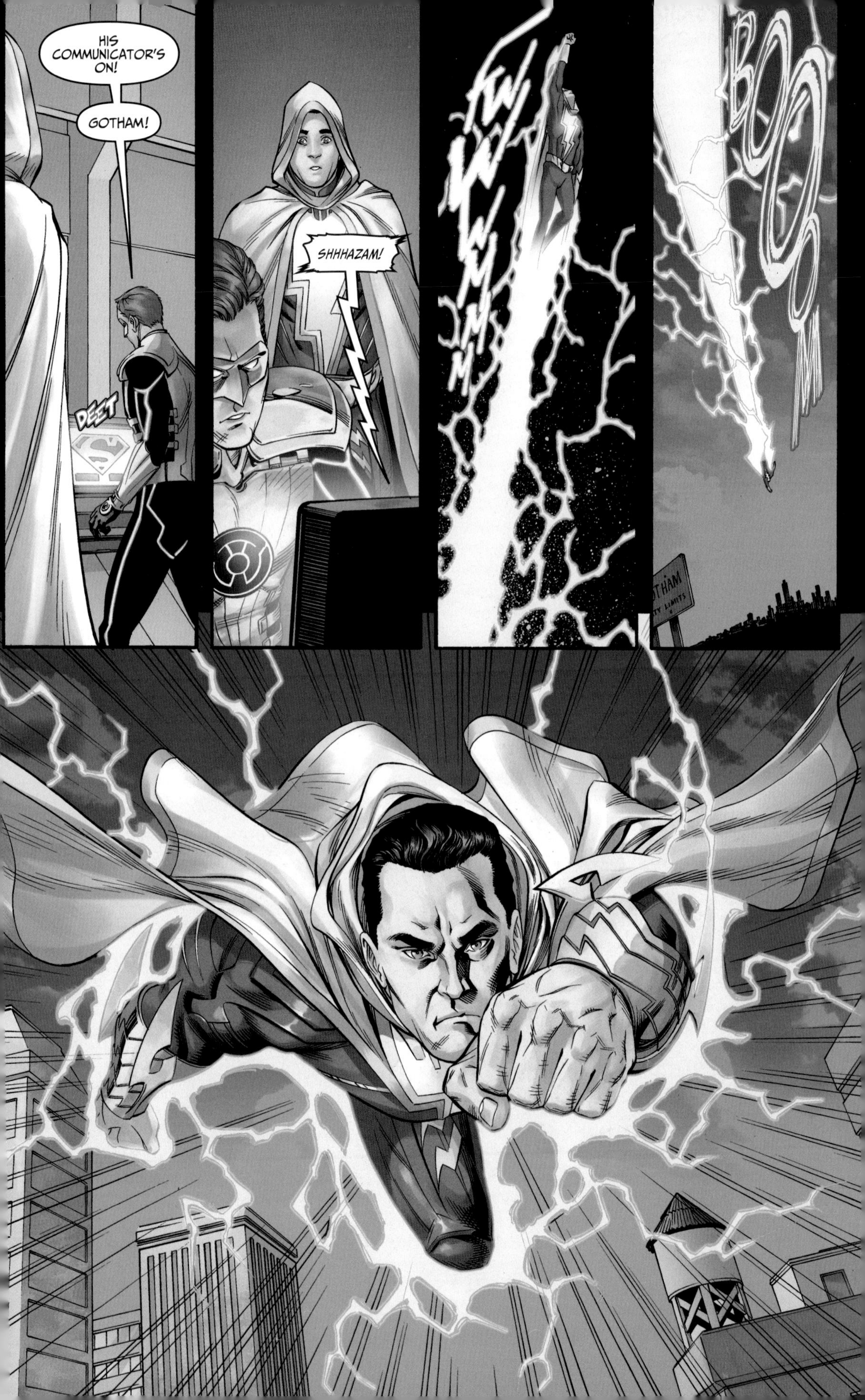
HIS COMMUNICATOR'S ON!
GOTHAM!
DEET
SHHHAZAM!
BOOOM

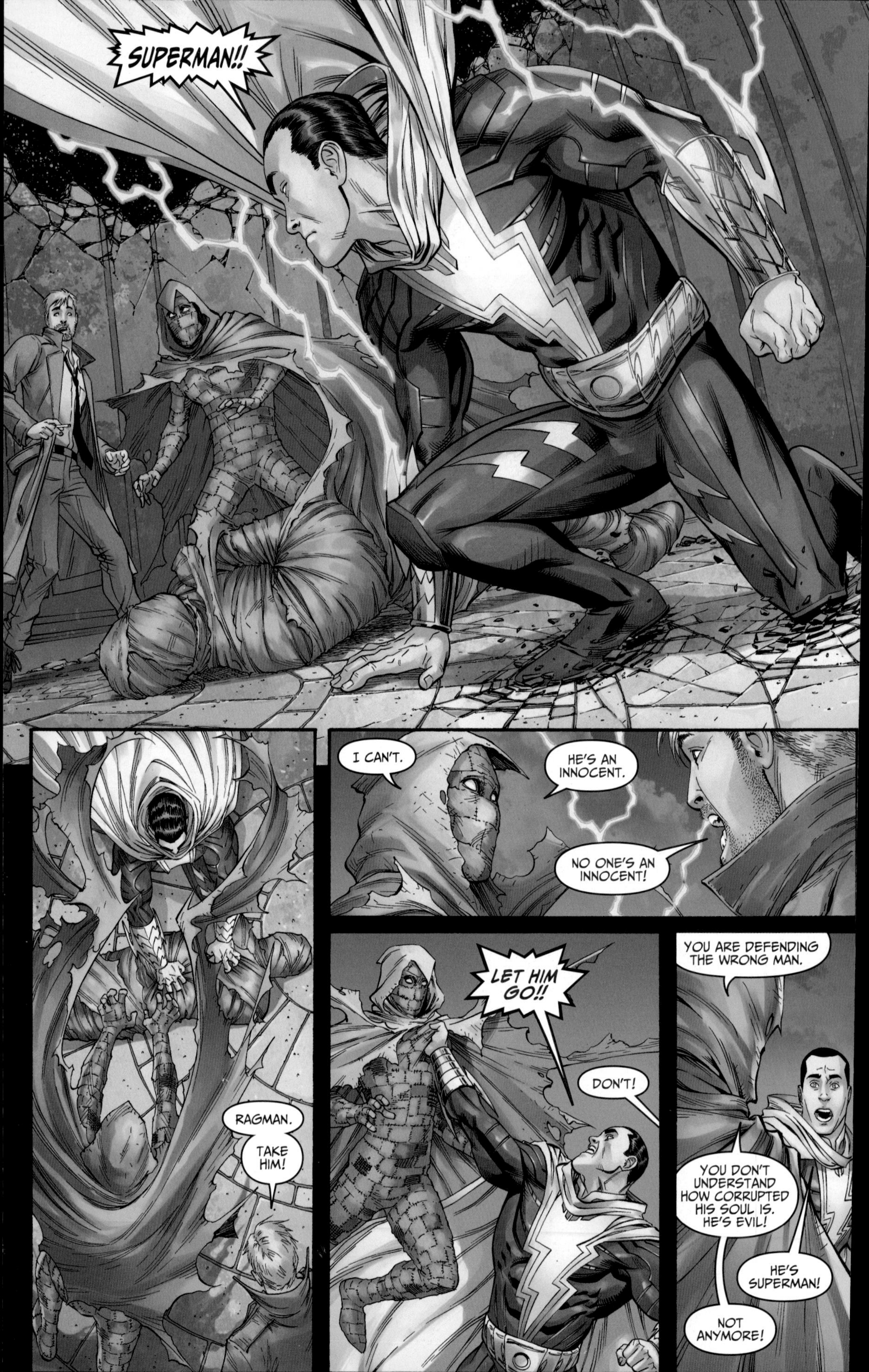
SUPERMAN!!
I CAN'T.
HE'S AN INNOCENT.
NO ONE'S AN INNOCENT!
RAGMAN.
TAKE HIM!
LET HIM GO!!
DON'T!
YOU ARE DEFENDING THE WRONG MAN.
YOU DON'T UNDERSTAND HOW CORRUPTED HIS SOUL IS. HE'S EVIL!
HE'S SUPERMAN!
NOT ANYMORE!

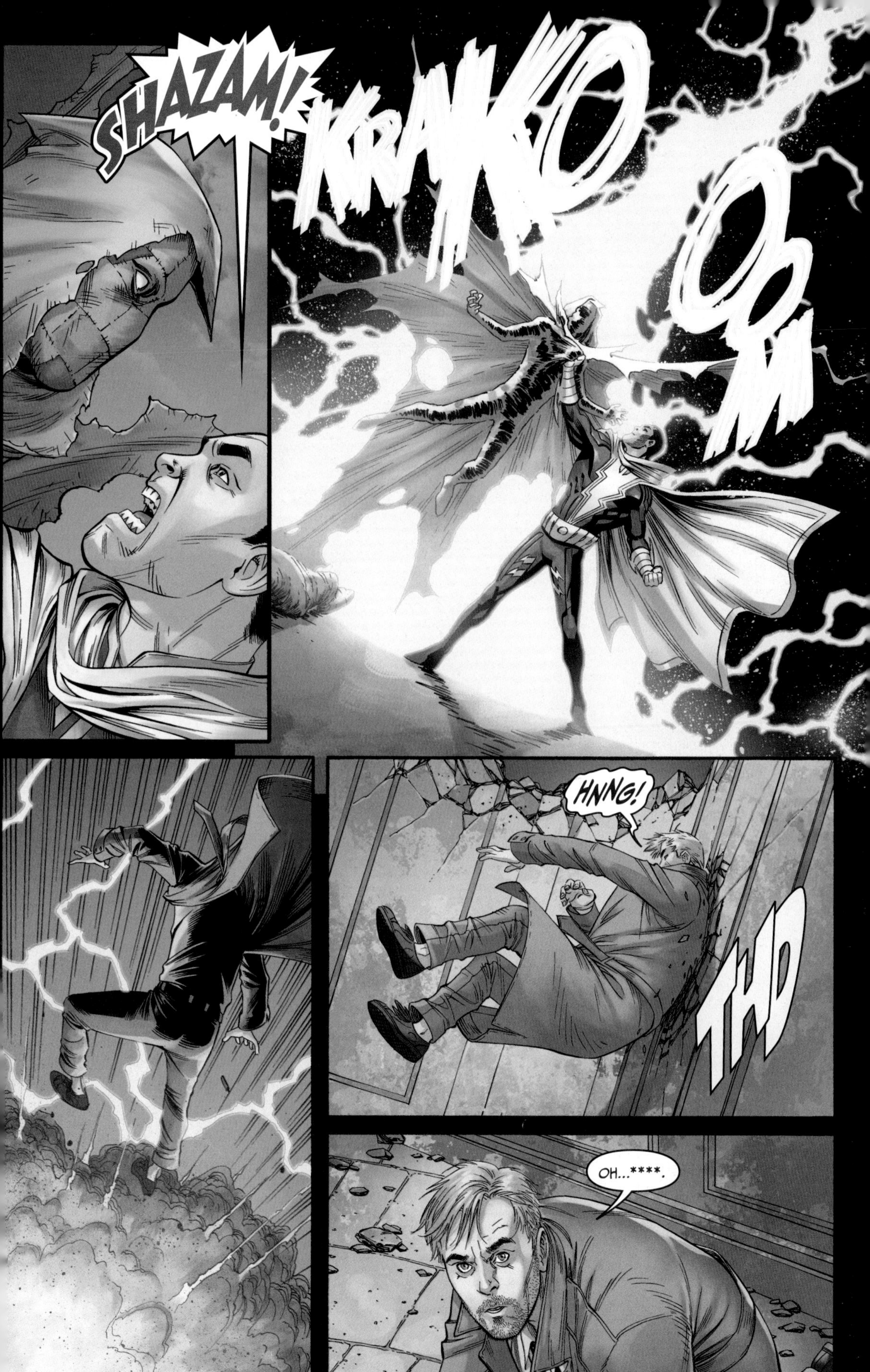
SHAZAM!
KRAKOOOM
HNNG!
THD
OH...****.

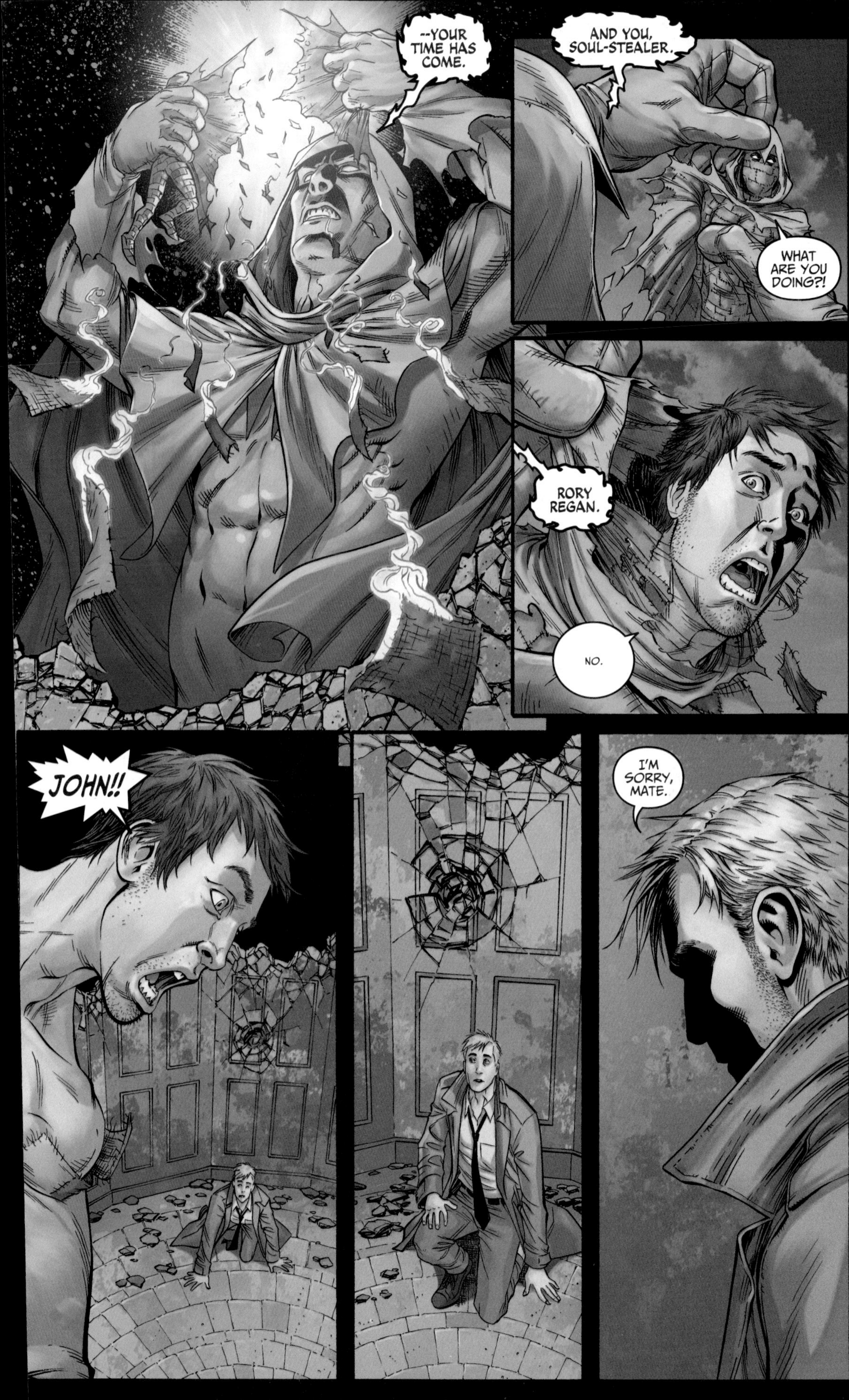
--YOUR TIME HAS COME.
AND YOU, SOUL-STEALER.
WHAT ARE YOU DOING?!
RORY REGAN.
NO.
JOHN!!
I'M SORRY, MATE.

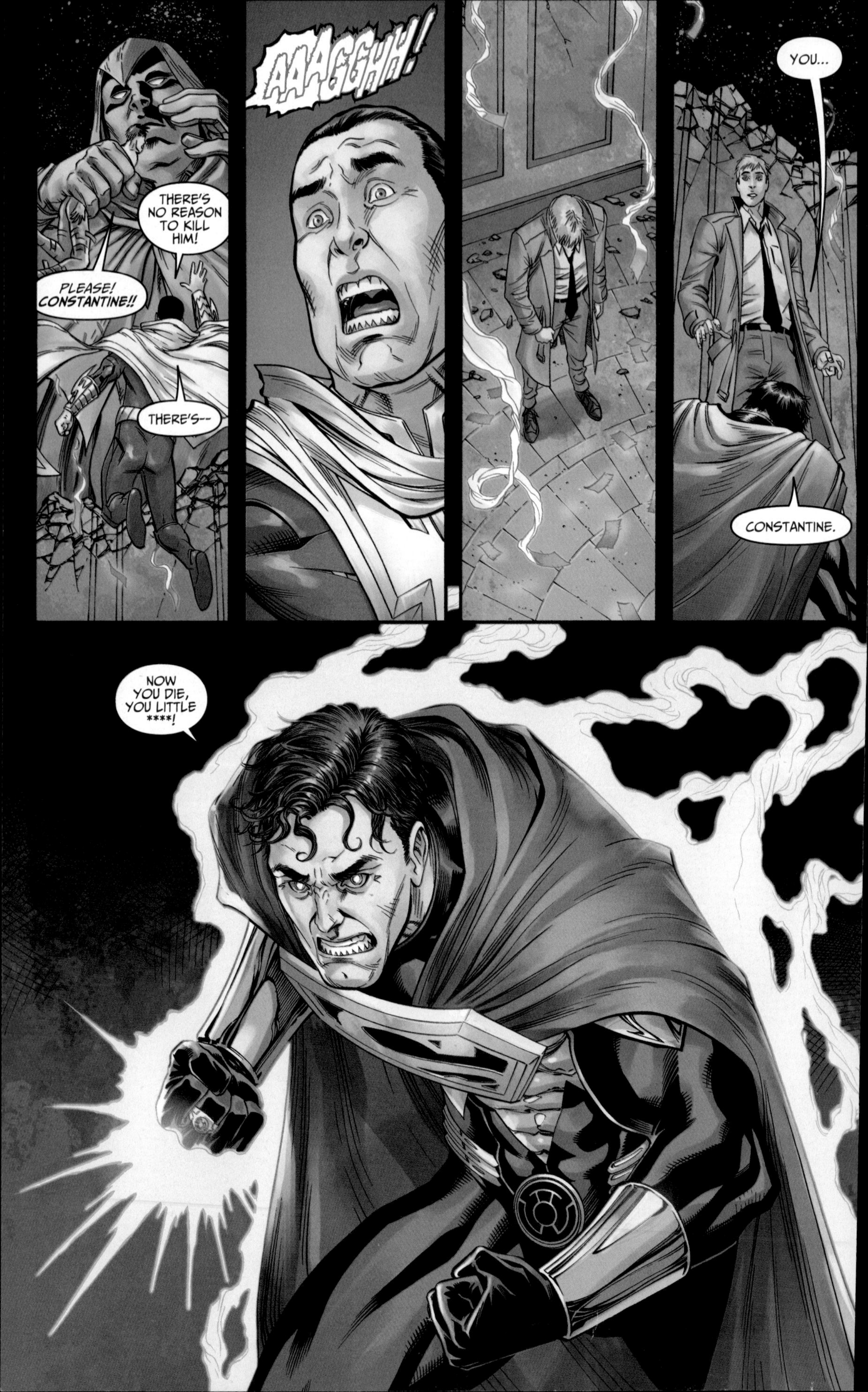
PLEASE! CONSTANTINE!!
THERE'S NO REASON TO KILL HIM!
THERE'S--
AAAGGHH!
YOU...
CONSTANTINE.
NOW YOU DIE, YOU LITTLE ****!

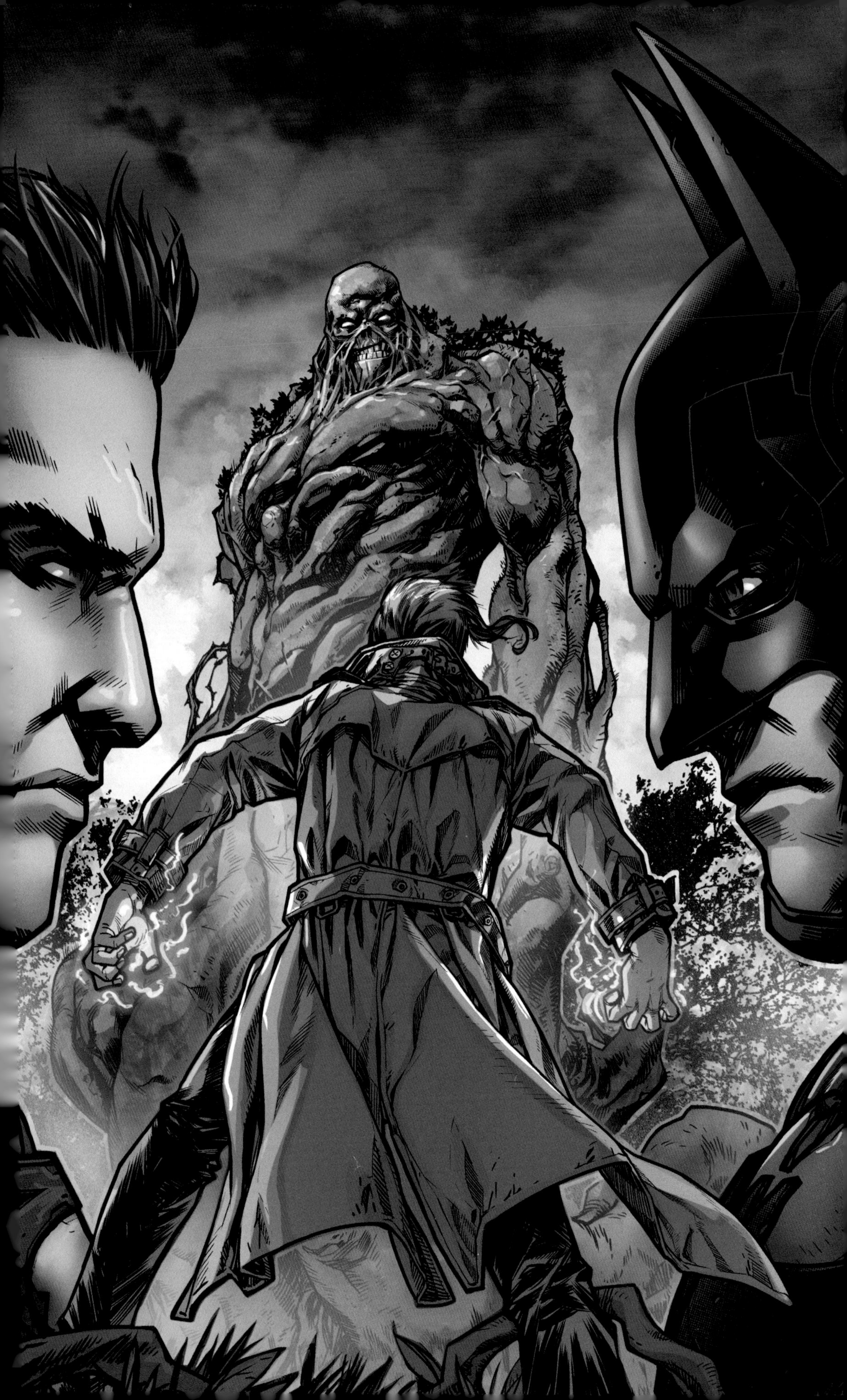

"Dead Man" Bruno Redondo & Juan Albarran Artists **Rex Lokus** Colorist
"Death of A Deadman" Mike S. Miller Artist J. Nanjan Colorist
Cover Art by **Neil Googe & Rex Lokus**

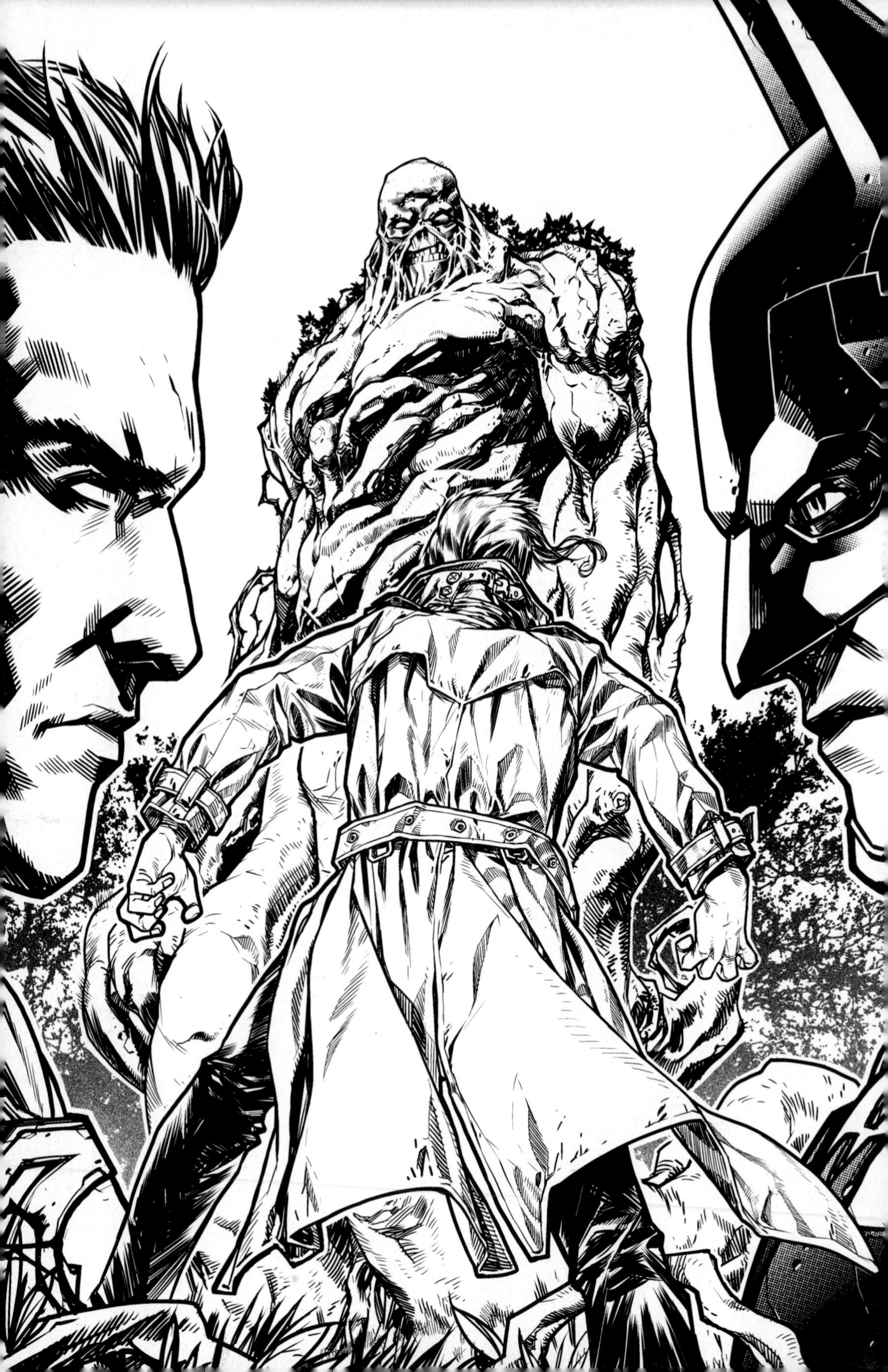

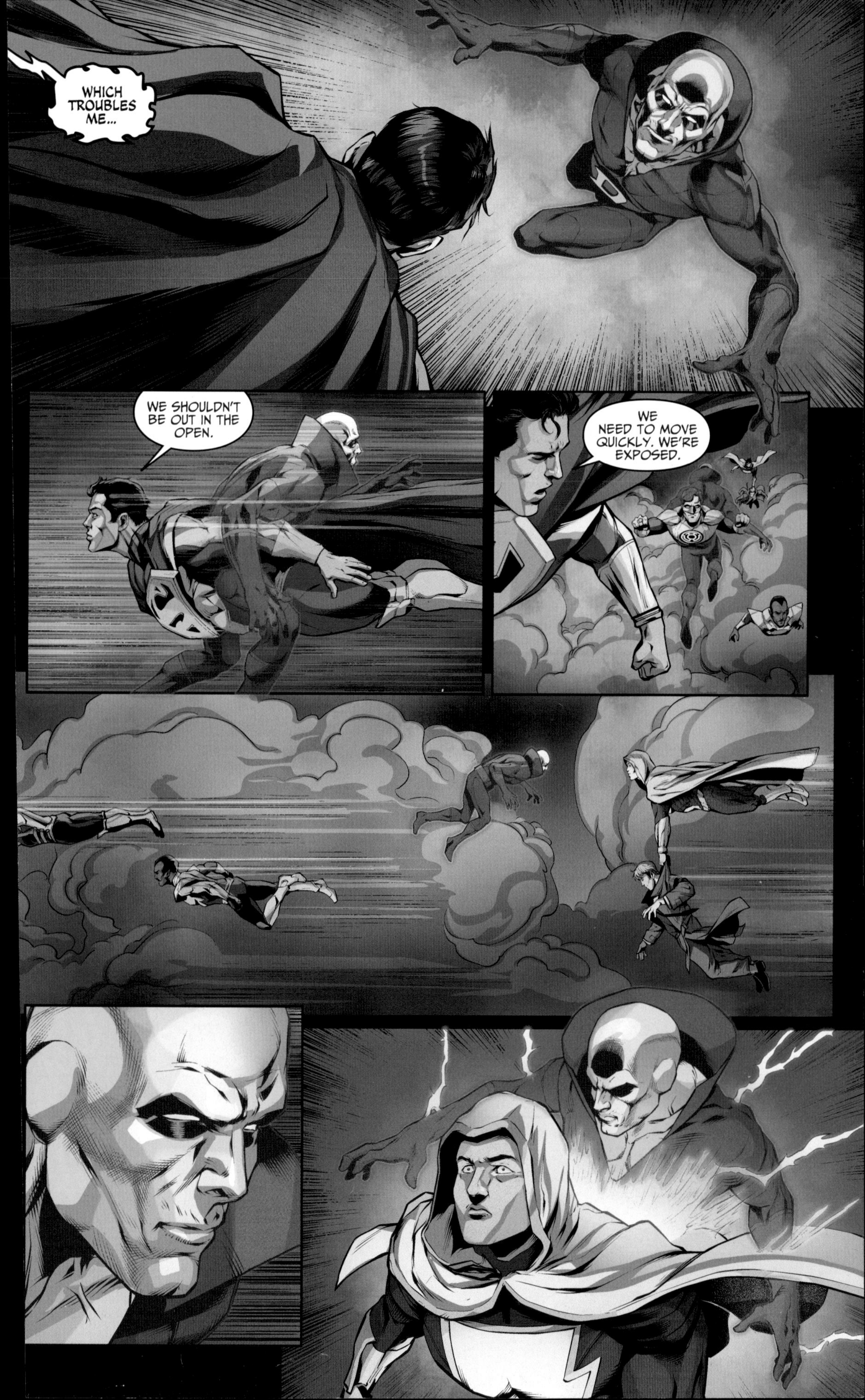
WHICH TROUBLES ME...
WE SHOULDN'T BE OUT IN THE OPEN.
WE NEED TO MOVE QUICKLY. WE'RE EXPOSED.

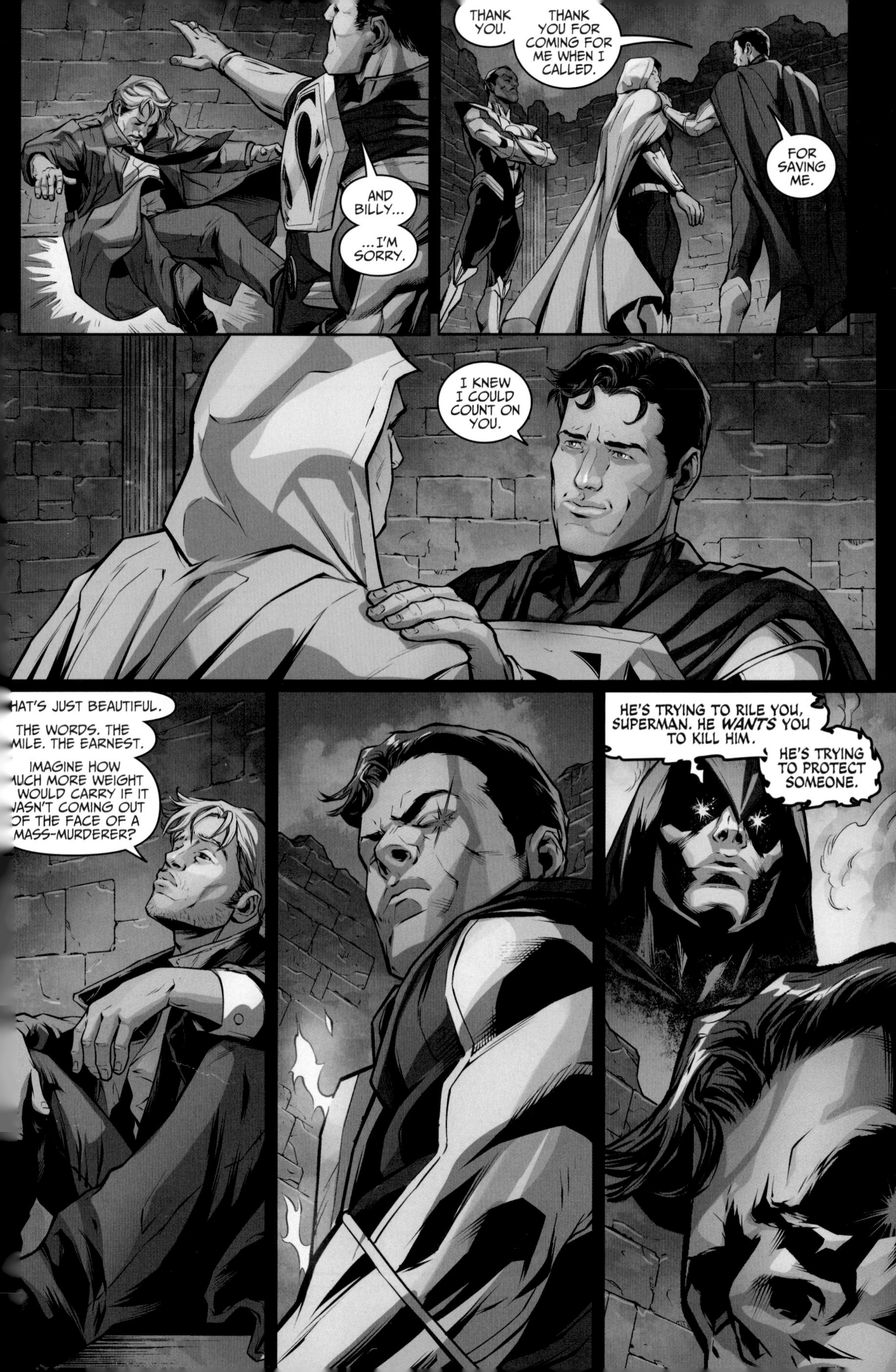
AND BILLY...
...I'M SORRY.
THANK YOU.
THANK YOU FOR COMING FOR ME WHEN I CALLED.
FOR SAVING ME.
I KNEW I COULD COUNT ON YOU.
HAT'S JUST BEAUTIFUL.
THE WORDS. THE MILE. THE EARNEST.
IMAGINE HOW UCH MORE WEIGHT WOULD CARRY IF IT VASN'T COMING OUT OF THE FACE OF A MASS-MURDERER?
HE'S TRYING TO RILE YOU, SUPERMAN. HE *WANTS* YOU TO KILL HIM.
HE'S TRYING TO PROTECT SOMEONE.

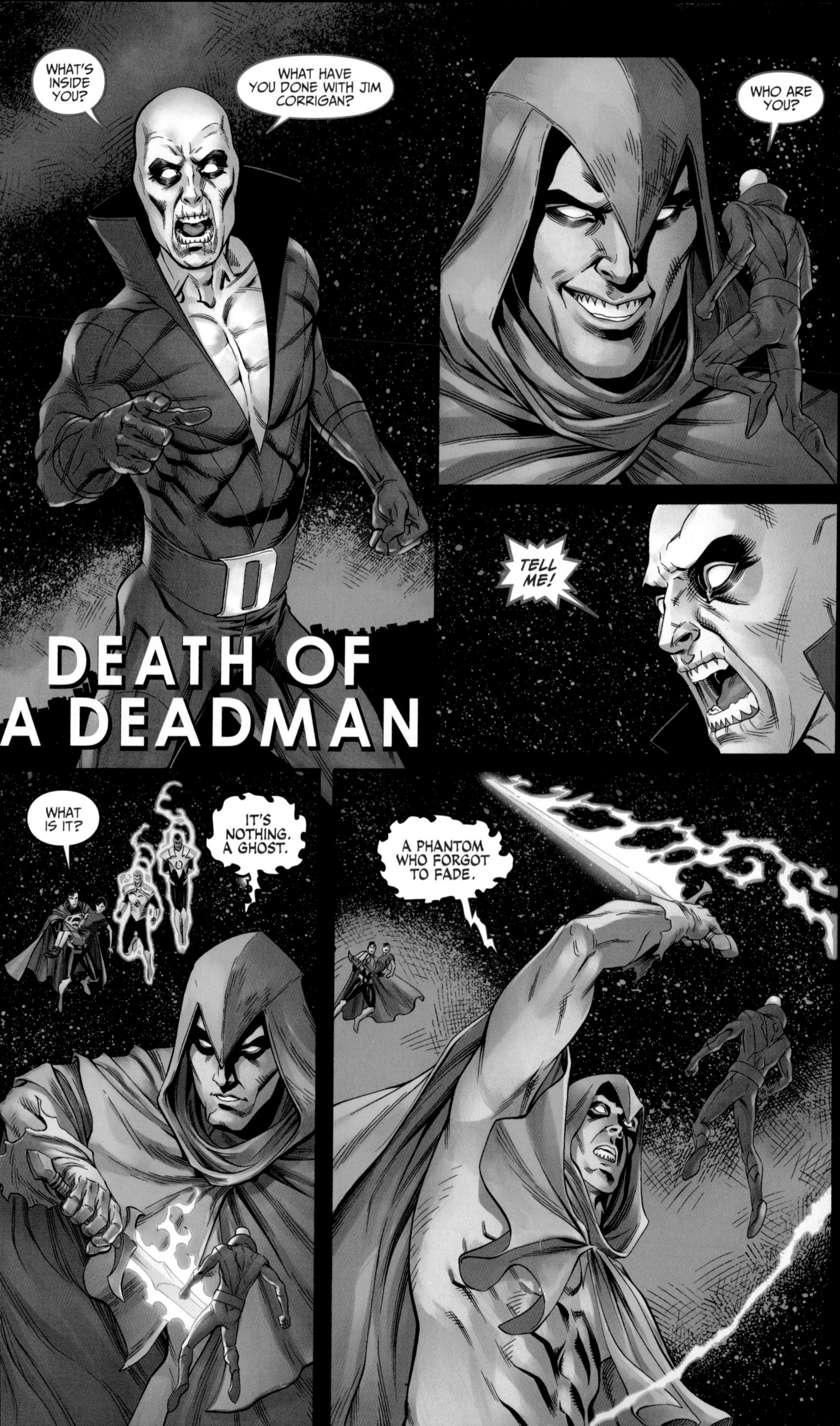
WHAT'S INSIDE YOU?
WHAT HAVE YOU DONE WITH JIM CORRIGAN?
DEATH OF A DEADMAN
WHO ARE YOU?
TELL ME!
WHAT IS IT?
IT'S NOTHING. A GHOST.
A PHANTOM WHO FORGOT TO FADE.

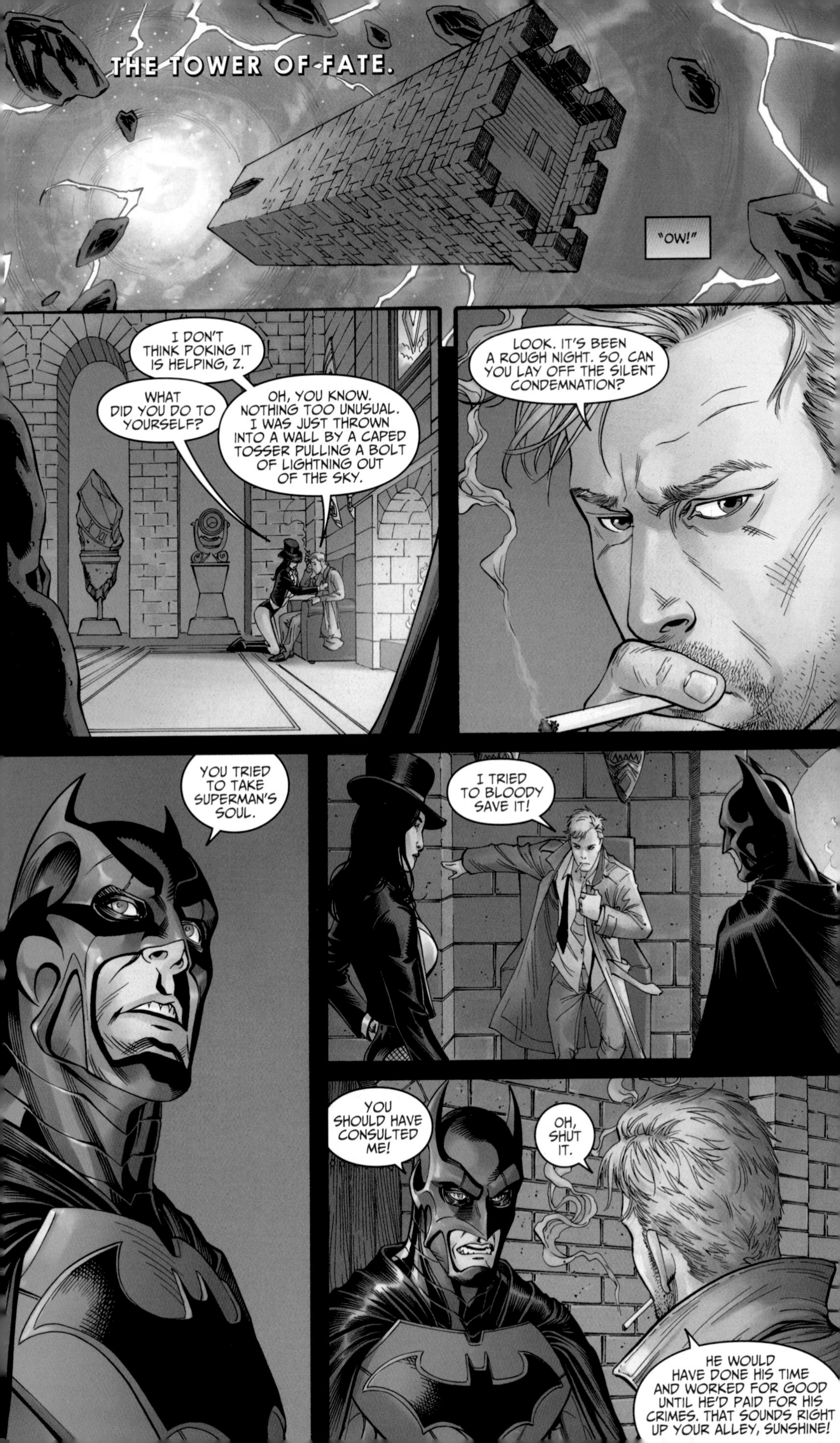
THE TOWER OF FATE.
"OW!"
I DON'T THINK POKING IT IS HELPING, Z.
WHAT DID YOU DO TO YOURSELF?
OH, YOU KNOW. NOTHING TOO UNUSUAL. I WAS JUST THROWN INTO A WALL BY A CAPED TOSSER PULLING A BOLT OF LIGHTNING OUT OF THE SKY.
LOOK. IT'S BEEN A ROUGH NIGHT. SO, CAN YOU LAY OFF THE SILENT CONDEMNATION?
YOU TRIED TO TAKE SUPERMAN'S SOUL.
I TRIED TO BLOODY SAVE IT!
YOU SHOULD HAVE CONSULTED ME!
OH, SHUT IT.
HE WOULD HAVE DONE HIS TIME AND WORKED FOR GOOD UNTIL HE'D PAID FOR HIS CRIMES. THAT SOUNDS RIGHT UP YOUR ALLEY, SUNSHINE!

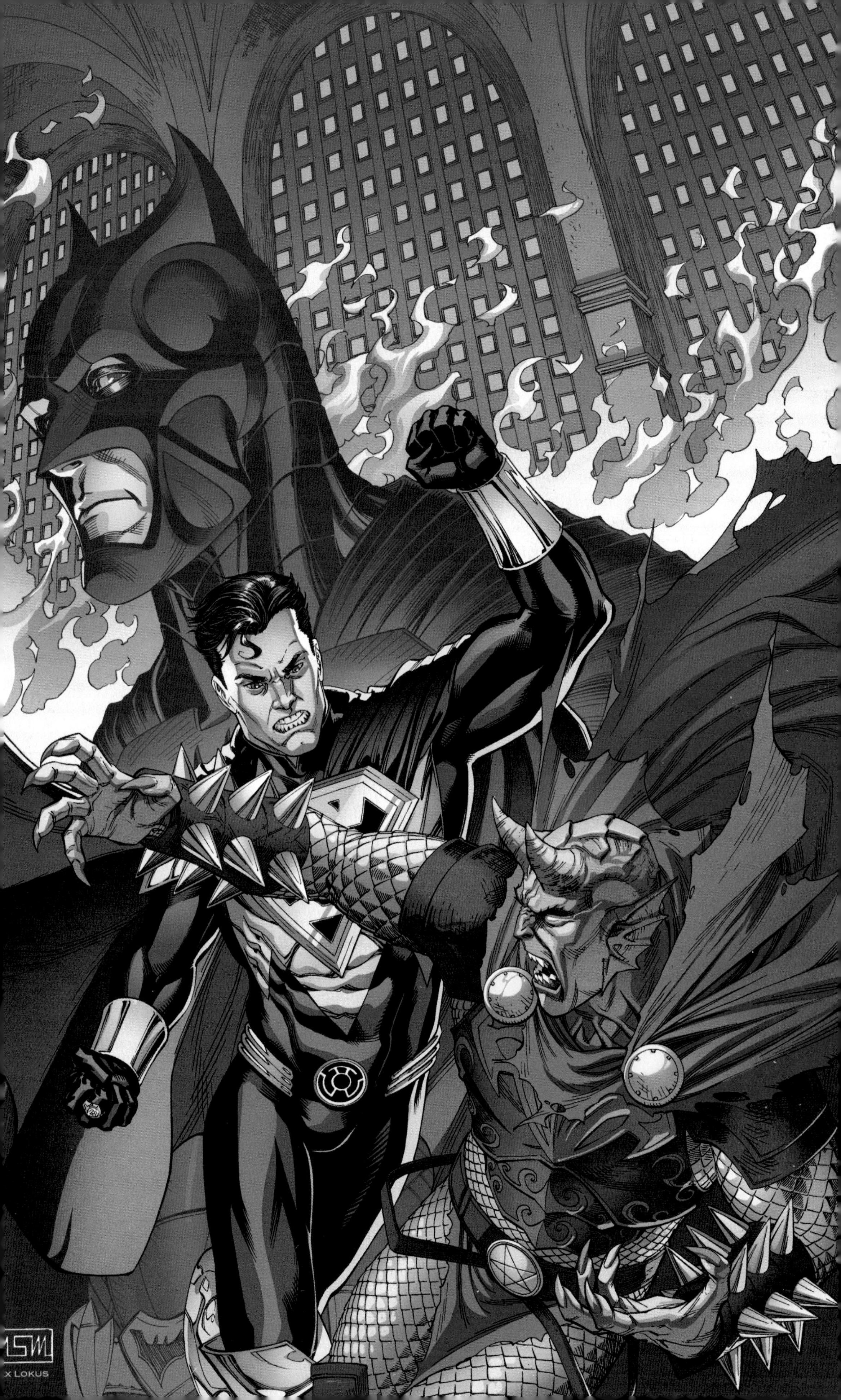
X LOKUS

"Raise the Demon" **Bruno Redondo & Xermanico** Artists **Rex Lokus** Colorist
"Secret Weapon" Mike S. Miller, Bruno Redondo & Juan Albarran Artist **Rex Lokus** Colorist
Cover Art by **Mike S. Miller & Rex Lokus**

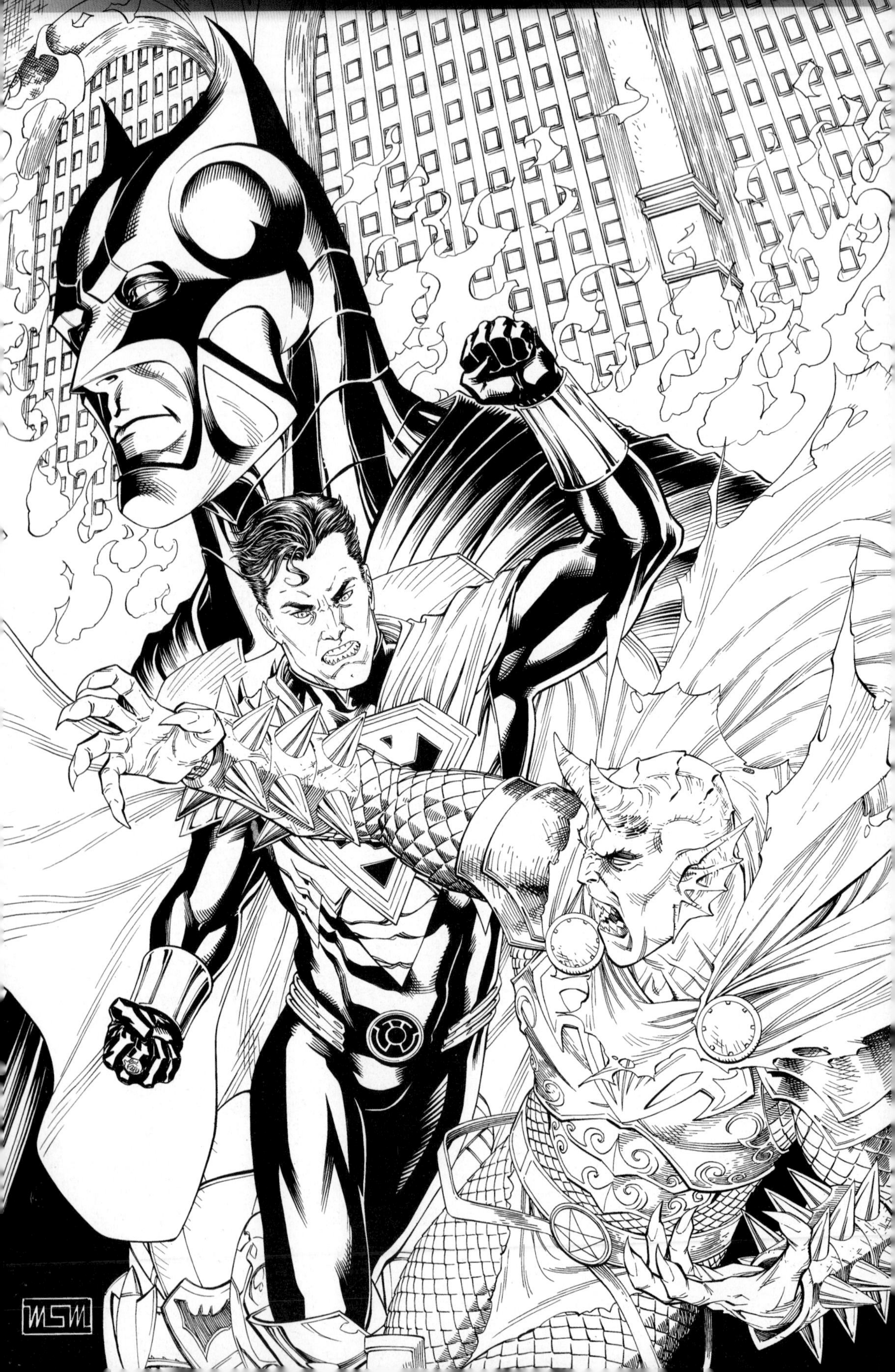

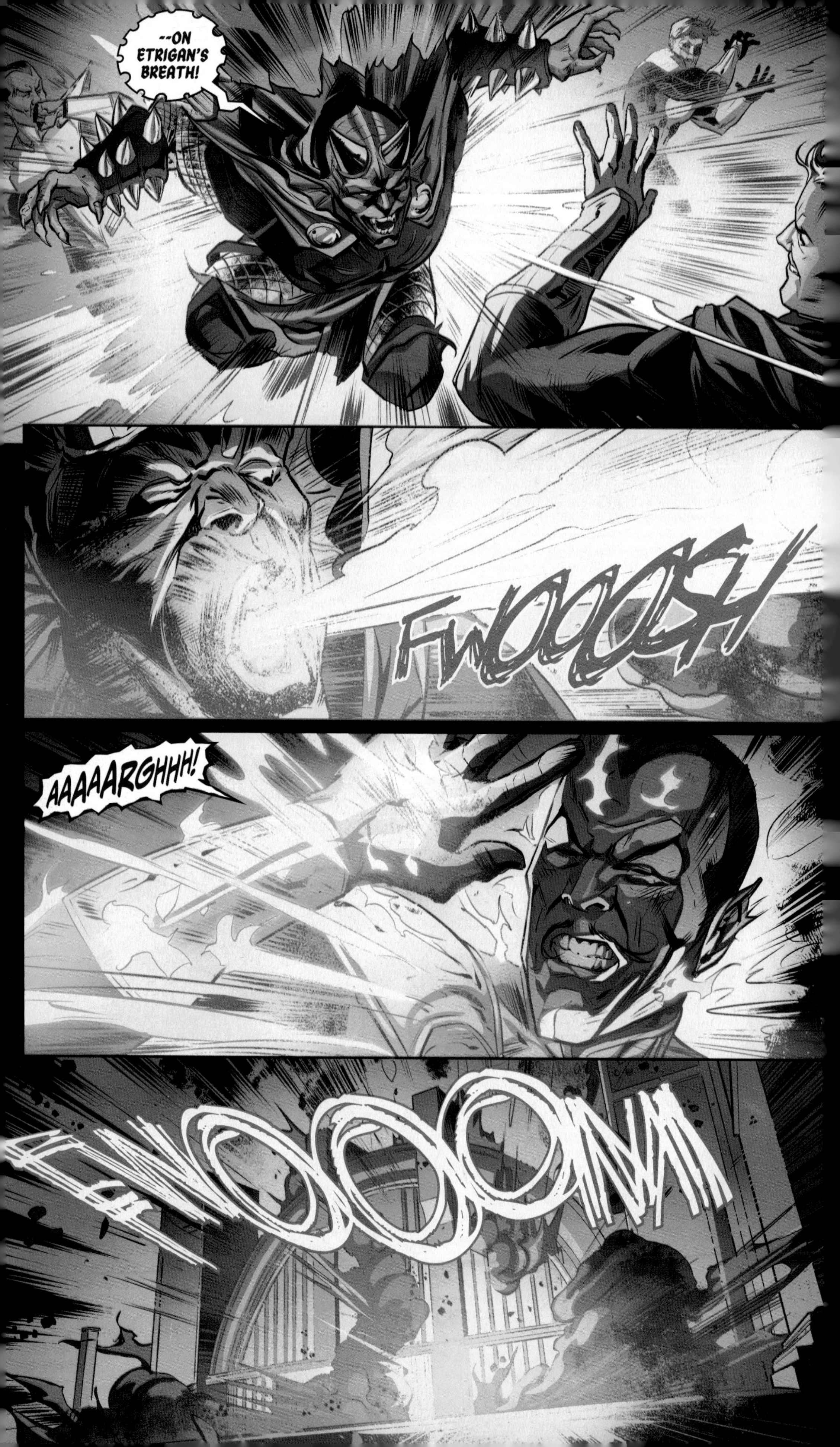
--ON ETRIGAN'S BREATH!
FWOOOSH
AAAAARGHHH!
KA-WHOOOOM

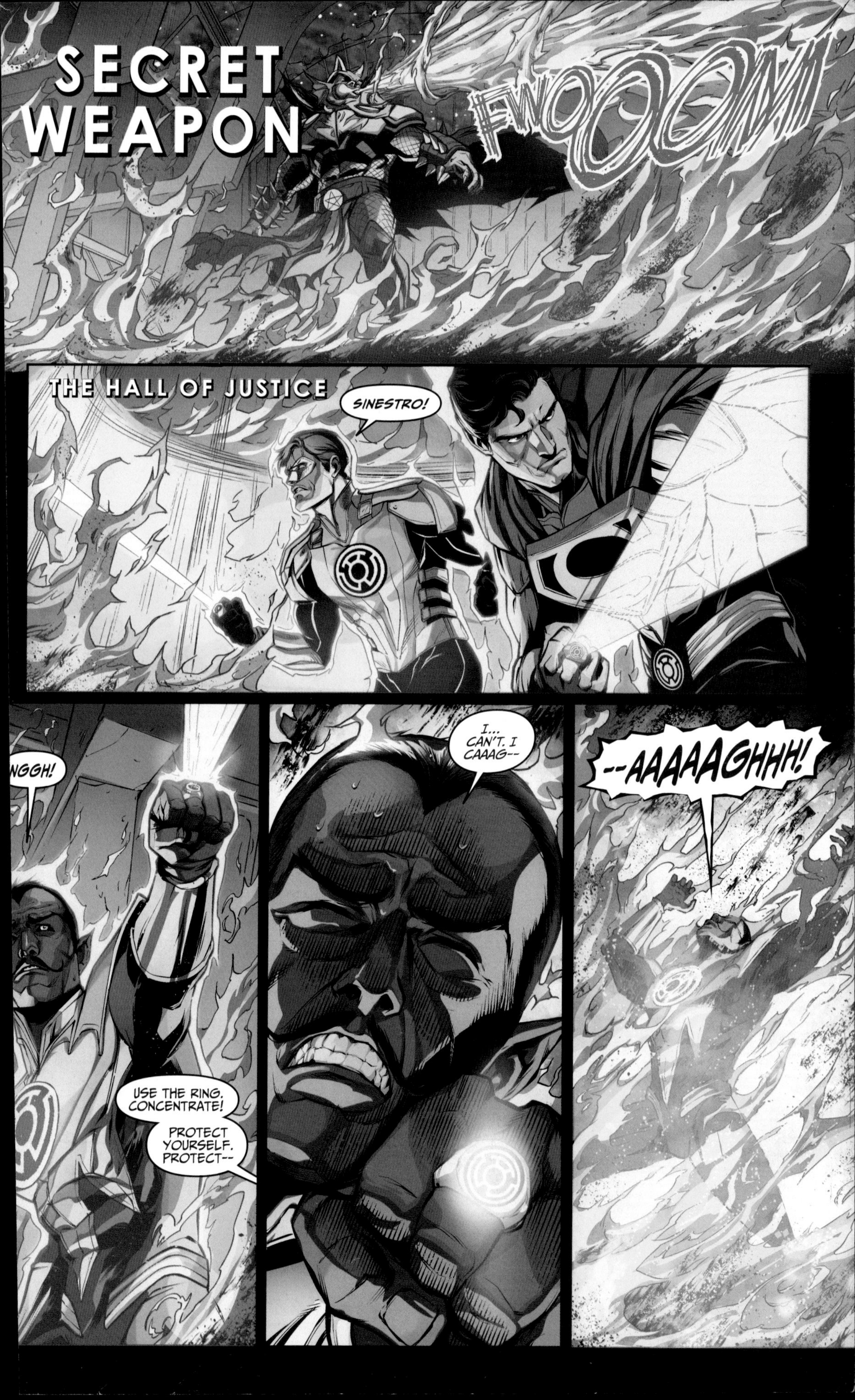
SECRET WEAPON
FWOOOOOM!
THE HALL OF JUSTICE
SINESTRO!
NGGH!
USE THE RING. CONCENTRATE!
PROTECT YOURSELF. PROTECT--
I... CAN'T. I CAAAG--
--AAAAAGHHH!

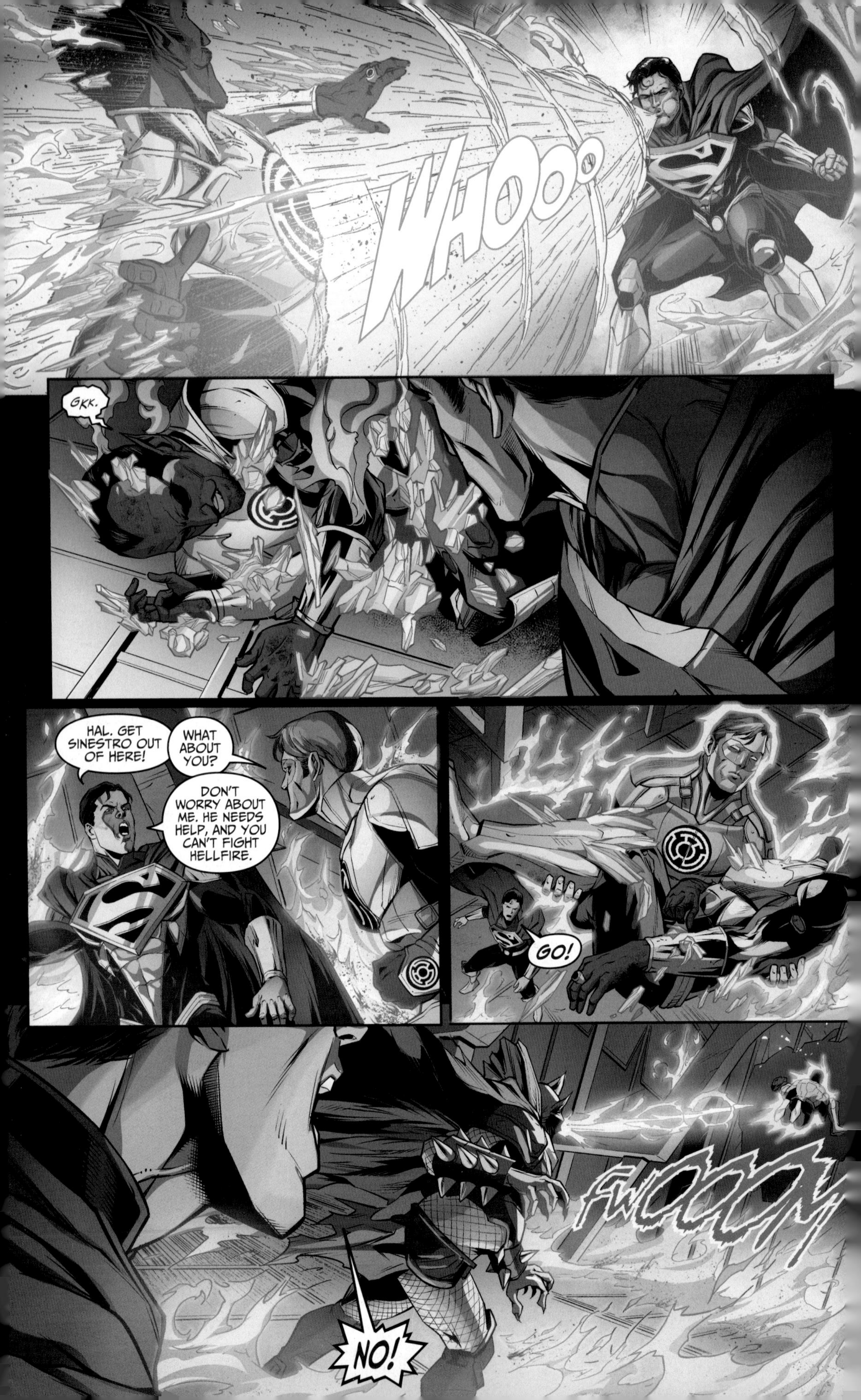
WHOOO
GKK.
HAL. GET SINESTRO OUT OF HERE!
WHAT ABOUT YOU?
DON'T WORRY ABOUT ME. HE NEEDS HELP, AND YOU CAN'T FIGHT HELLFIRE.
GO!
FWOOOM
NO!

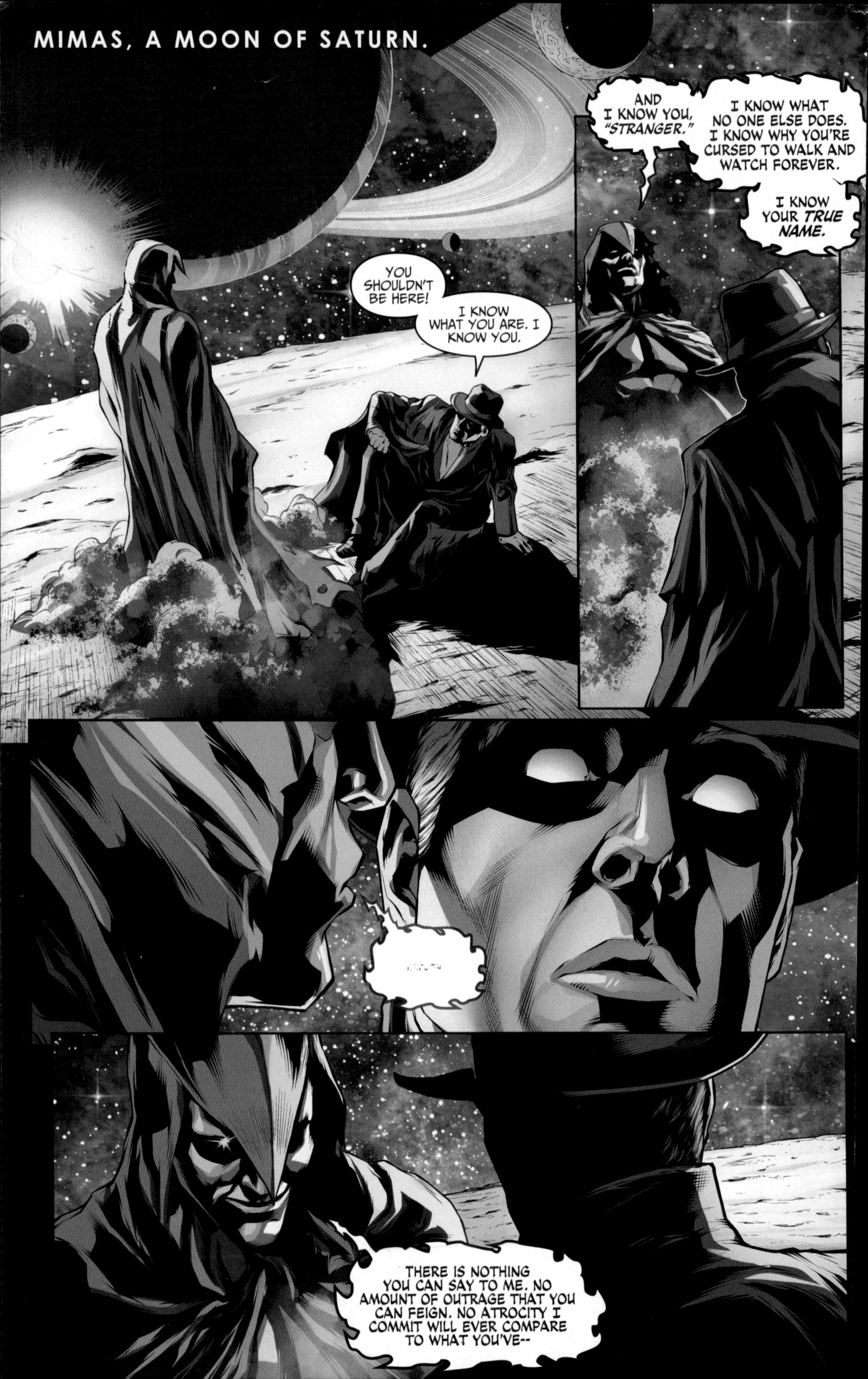
MIMAS, A MOON OF SATURN.
YOU SHOULDN'T BE HERE!
I KNOW WHAT YOU ARE. I KNOW YOU.
AND I KNOW YOU, "STRANGER."
I KNOW WHAT NO ONE ELSE DOES. I KNOW WHY YOU'RE CURSED TO WALK AND WATCH FOREVER.
I KNOW YOUR *TRUE NAME.*
THERE IS NOTHING YOU CAN SAY TO ME. NO AMOUNT OF OUTRAGE THAT YOU CAN FEIGN. NO ATROCITY I COMMIT WILL EVER COMPARE TO WHAT YOU'VE--

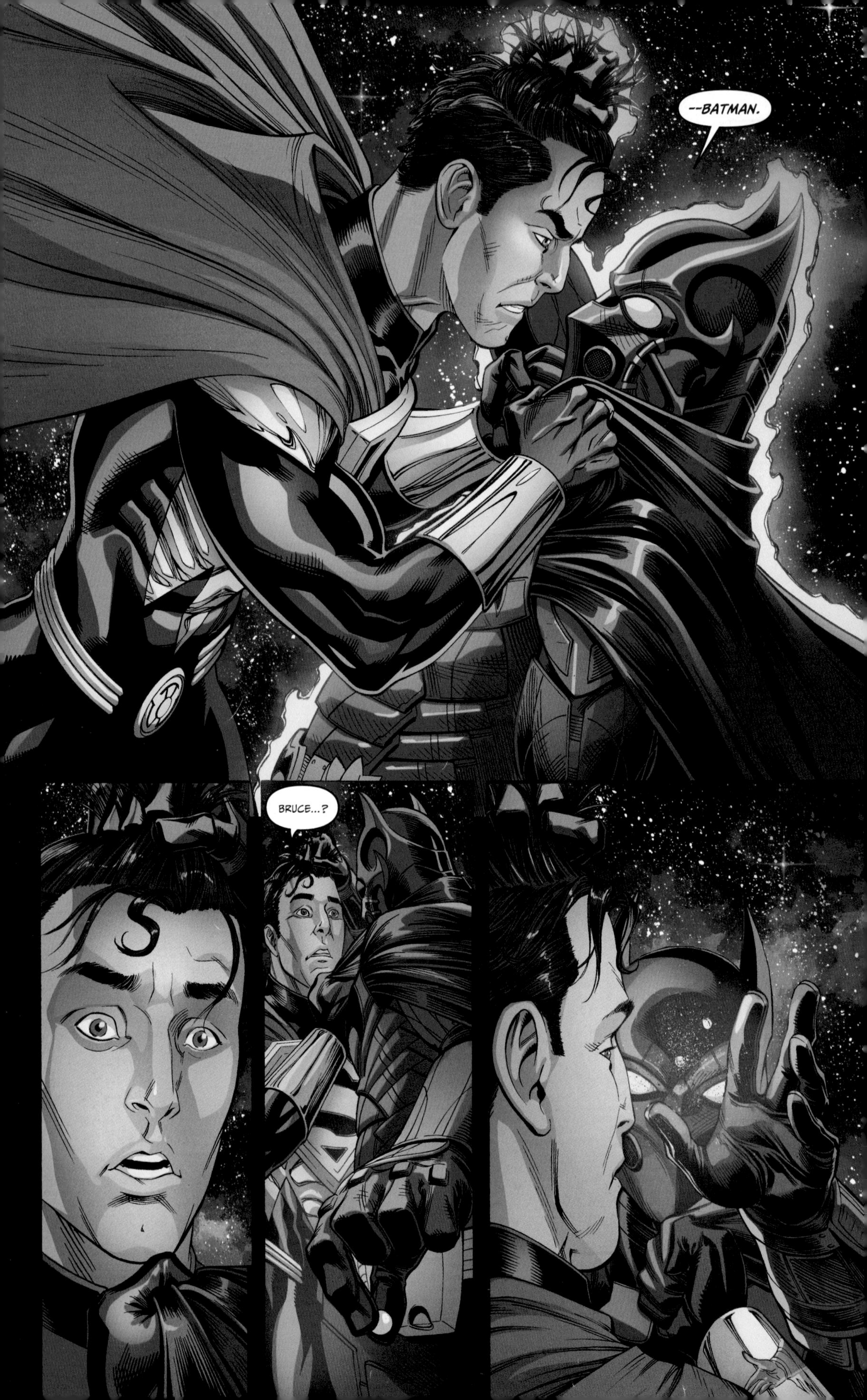
--BATMAN.
BRUCE...?

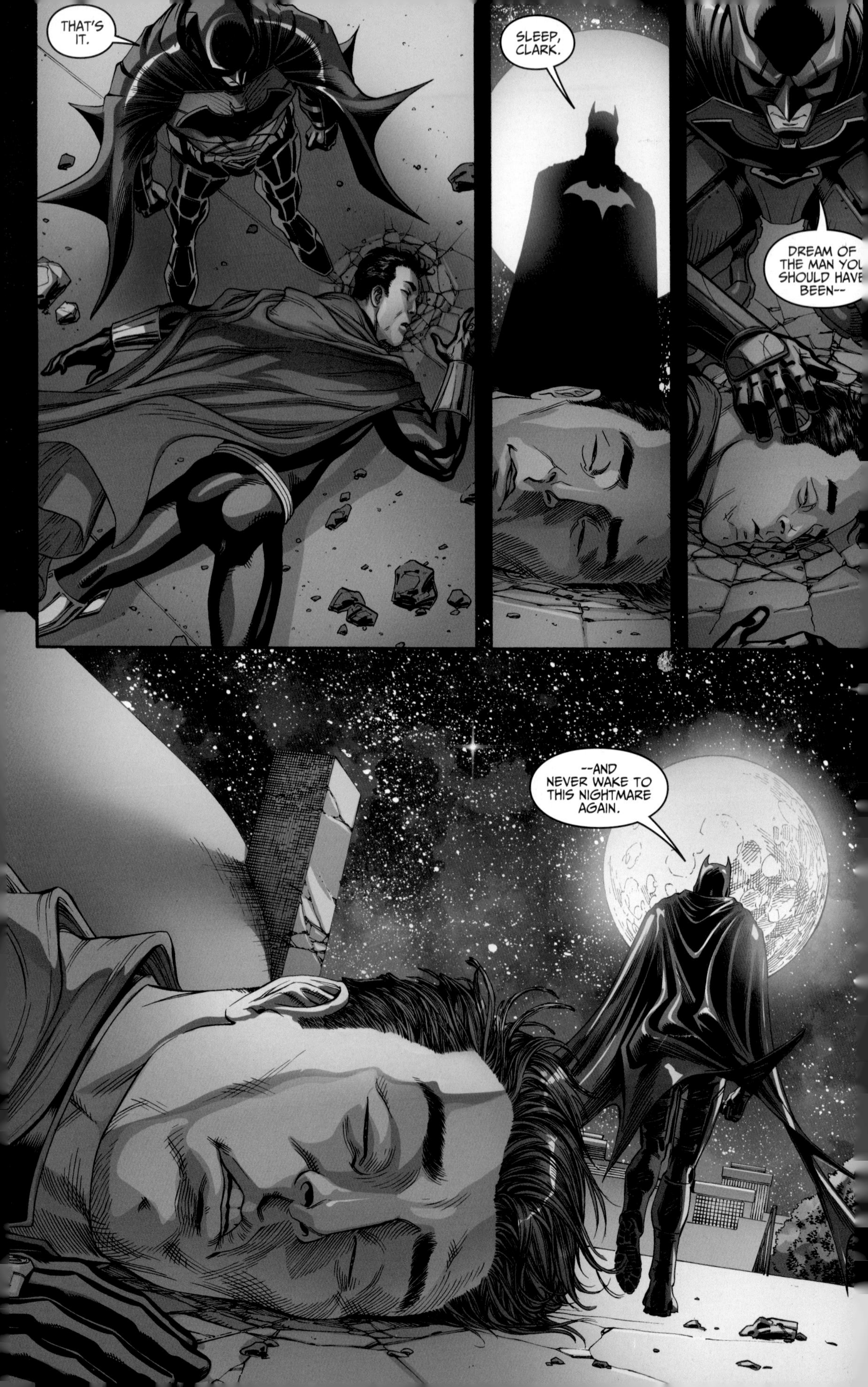
THAT'S IT.
SLEEP, CLARK.
DREAM OF THE MAN YOU SHOULD HAVE BEEN--
--AND NEVER WAKE TO THIS NIGHTMARE AGAIN.

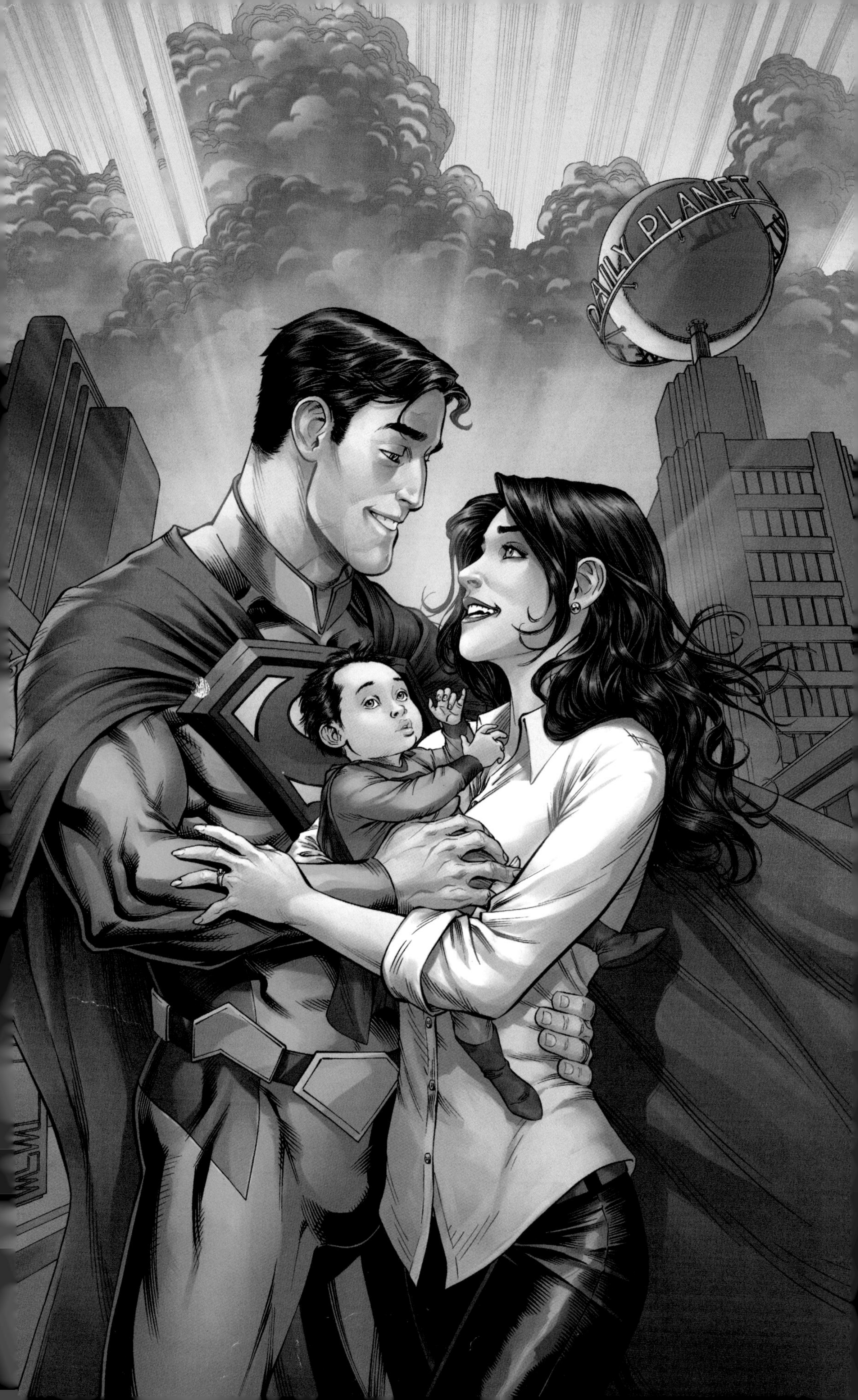
DAILY PLANET

"For the Man Who's Lost Everything" **Bruno Redondo, Xermanico, & Juan Albarran** Artists
Rex Lokus Colorist Cover Art by **Mike S. Miller & J. Nanjan**

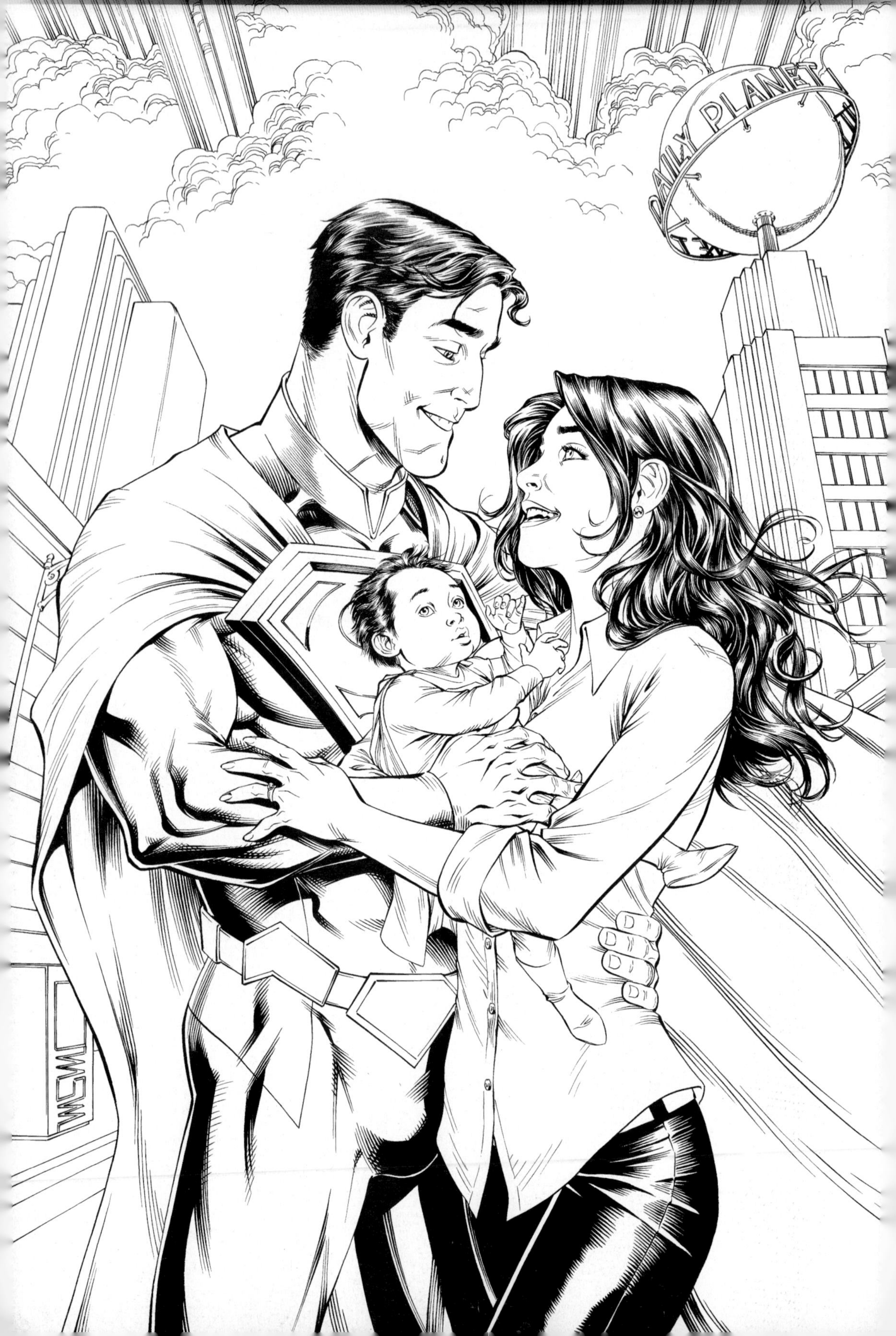
PLANET

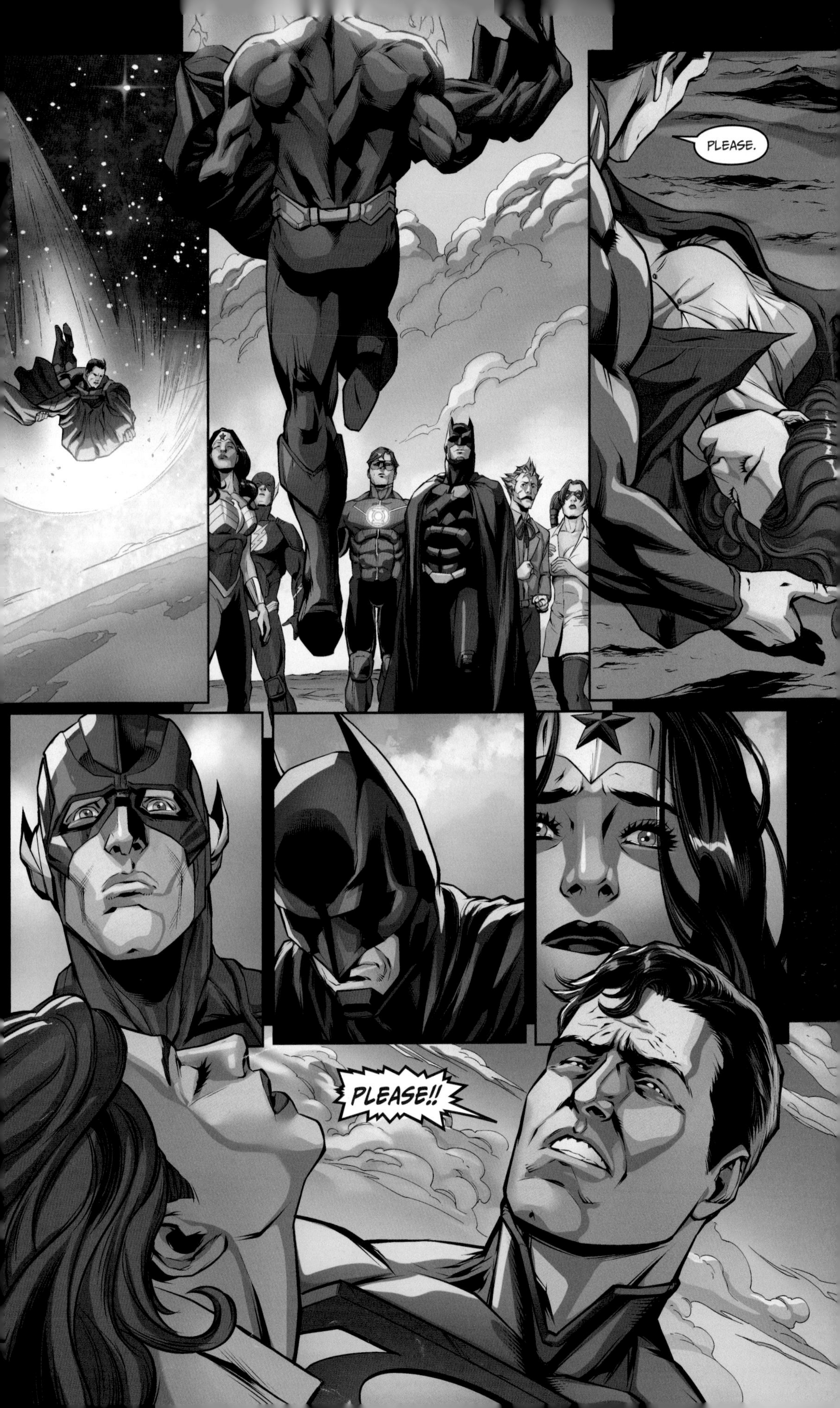
PLEASE.
PLEASE!!

FOR THE MAN WHO'S LOST EVERYTHING

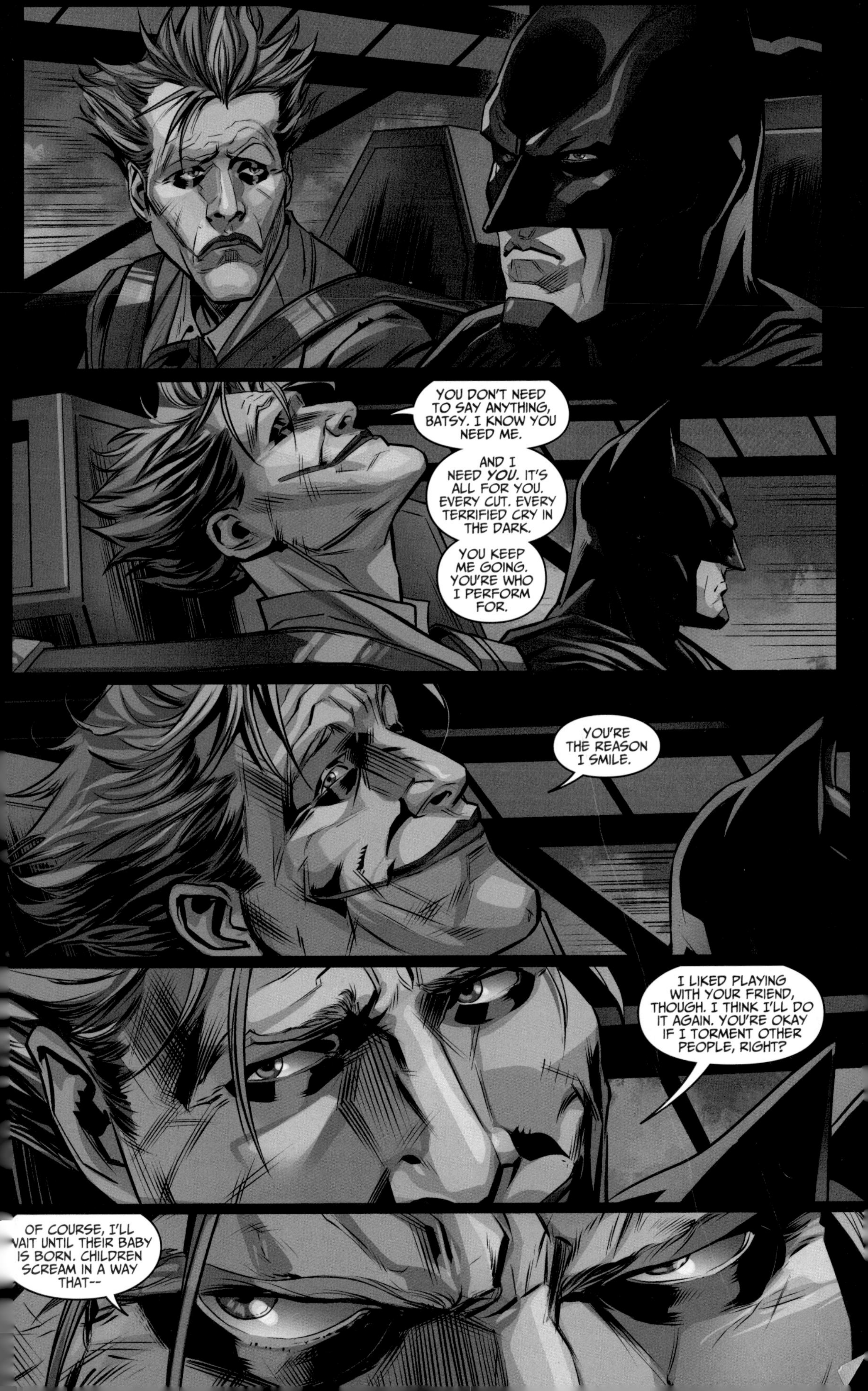
YOU DON'T NEED TO SAY ANYTHING, BATSY. I KNOW YOU NEED ME.
AND I NEED *YOU*. IT'S ALL FOR YOU. EVERY CUT. EVERY TERRIFIED CRY IN THE DARK.
YOU KEEP ME GOING. YOU'RE WHO I PERFORM FOR.
YOU'RE THE REASON I SMILE.
I LIKED PLAYING WITH YOUR FRIEND, THOUGH. I THINK I'LL DO IT AGAIN. YOU'RE OKAY IF I TORMENT OTHER PEOPLE, RIGHT?
OF COURSE, I'LL VAIT UNTIL THEIR BABY IS BORN. CHILDREN SCREAM IN A WAY THAT--

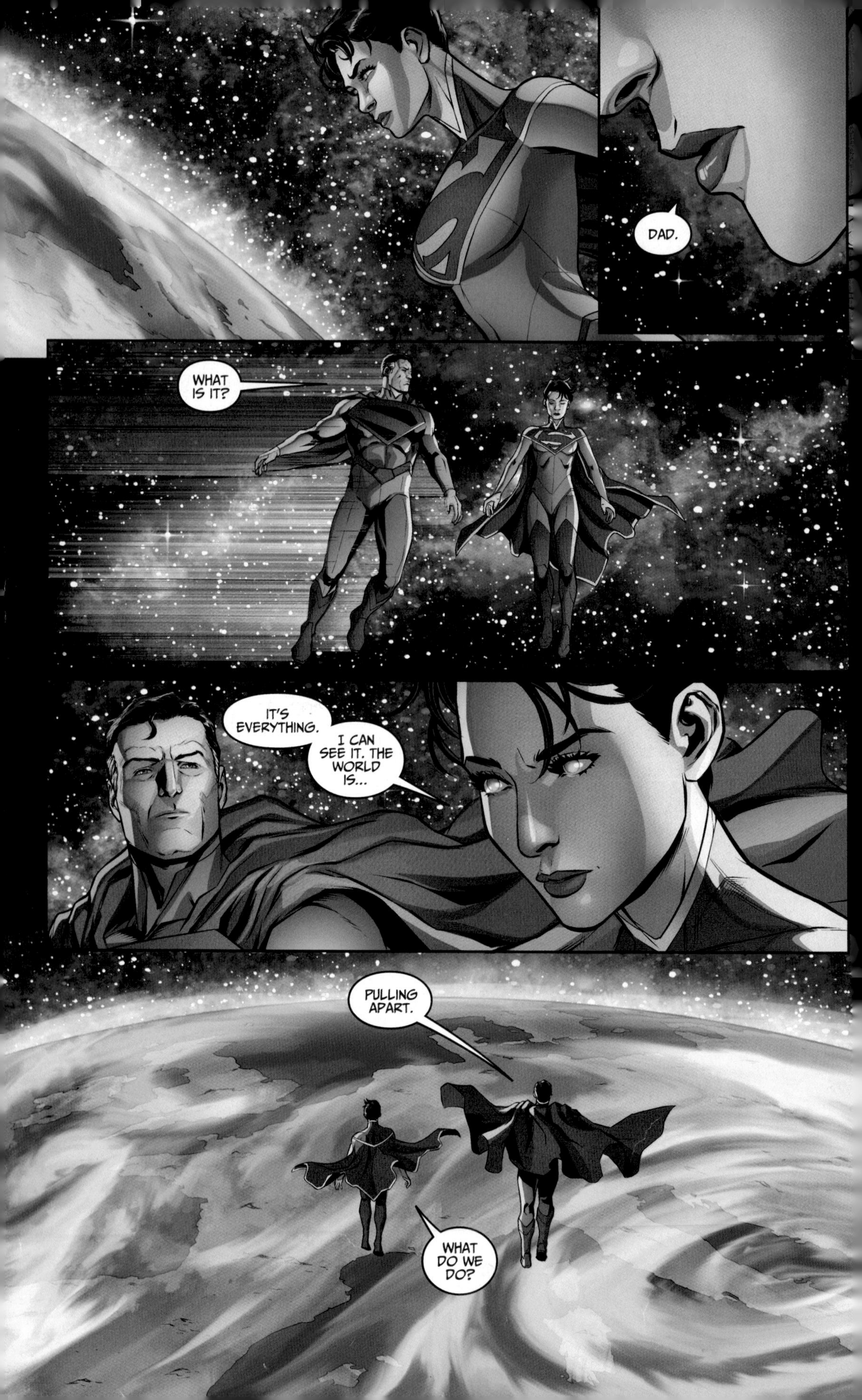
DAD.
WHAT IS IT?
IT'S EVERYTHING.
I CAN SEE IT. THE WORLD IS...
PULLING APART.
WHAT DO WE DO?